THE
Leadership
BRAIN

Leadership and learning are indispensable to each other.

— John F. Kennedy

THE
Leadership
BRAIN

HOW TO
Lead Today's
Schools
More
Effectively

David A. Sousa

CORWIN PRESS, INC.
A Sage Publications Company
Thousand Oaks, California

For information:

Corwin Press, Inc.
A Sage Publications Company
2455 Teller Road
Thousand Oaks, California 91320
www.corwinpress.com

Sage Publications Ltd.
6 Bonhill Street
London EC2A 4PU
United Kingdom

Sage Publications India Pvt. Ltd.
B-42, Panchsheel Enclave
New Delhi 110 017 India

Printed in the United States of America

Library of Congress Cataloging-in-Publication Data

Sousa, David A.
The leadership brain: How to lead today's schools more effectively /
David A. Sousa.
     p. cm.
Includes bibliographical references (p. 293) and index.
ISBN 0-7619-3909-1 (cloth : alk. paper) — ISBN 0-7619-3910-5 (paper : alk. paper)
   1. Educational leadership—United States. 2. School principals—United States.
3. Teacher-principal relationships—United States. I. Title.
LB2831.92.S68 2003
371.2′012—dc21

                               2003046051

This book is printed on acid-free paper.

        06 10 9 8 7 6 5 4 3

Acquisitions Editor:	Robert D. Clouse
Associate Editor:	Kristen L. Gibson
Editorial Assistant:	Jingle Vea
Production Editor:	Diane S. Foster
Proofreader:	Scott Oney
Cover Designer:	Tracy E. Miller

Contents

Tips for Leaders

About the Author

David A. Sousa, Ed.D., is an international educational consultant. He has made presentations at national conventions of educational organizations and has conducted workshops on brain research and science education in hundreds of school districts and at several colleges and universities across the United States, Canada, Europe, and Asia.

Dr. Sousa has a bachelor of science degree in chemistry from Massachusetts State College at Bridgewater, a master of arts in teaching degree in science from Harvard University, and a doctorate from Rutgers University. His teaching experience covers all levels. He has taught junior and senior high school science, served as a K–12 director of science, and was Supervisor of Instruction for the West Orange, New Jersey, schools. He then became superintendent of the New Providence, New Jersey, public schools. He has been an adjunct professor of education at Seton Hall University, and a visiting lecturer at Rutgers University. He was president of the National Staff Development Council in 1992.

Dr. Sousa has edited science books and published numerous articles in leading educational journals on staff development, science education, and brain research. He has received awards from professional associations, school districts, and Bridgewater State College (Distinguished Alumni Award) for his commitment and contributions to research, staff development, and science education.

He has been interviewed on the NBC Today show and on National Public Radio about his work with schools using brain research. He makes his home in Florida.

Introduction

CHANGING AMERICA'S SCHOOLS

In 1983, then-Secretary of Education Terrel Bell wrote a book, *A Nation at Risk,* that called for dramatic reform in American public education to stem the "rising tide of mediocrity" that he thought was pervasive in our schools. Many parents, politicians, and educators believed that his book would signal the beginning of major reforms in the structure, bureaucracy, and organization of school districts. Hope was high, and for the first time in decades, educators truly believed the nation was prepared to commit the resources necessary to transform all aspects of public education and prepare our schools and students for the challenges of a rapidly changing society. Something went wrong. The book was a hit, the follow-up, a dud.

Have Schools Really Changed? No and Yes!

The bad news is that in the two decades since the book was written, public school systems have barely changed. Some components have changed, but the system still relies heavily on an industrial model, an agrarian calendar, and instructional approaches from the mid-20th century. Irritated at the dramatically rising cost of public education, taxpayers demanded accountability. State legislators, responding to their taxpayers, enacted patchwork legislation establishing charter schools, voucher systems, and high-stakes testing. Rather than helping, these actions have, in many instances, served only to further politicize the scene and fragment attempts at a coordinated approach to school reform.

Concerns continue over how to close the widening achievement gap between white students and students of color. School violence is down but nearly 40 percent of students still report the presence of gangs in their schools. Debates still rage over the need for private charter schools and voucher programs, both of which divert taxpayer funds from public schools.

Dissatisfaction with public education in recent years is evidenced by the increased number of children schooled at home, now estimated by the National Center for Education Statistics to be more than 850,000 (NCES, 2002). According to the U.S. Census Bureau, only one-third of the parents school their children at home for religious reasons. A larger percentage believe they can give their children a better education at home and that a poor learning environment exists in their public schools (USCB, 2001).

Out of frustration with the lack of progress in school reform, Congress extensively revised the Elementary and Secondary Education Act (ESEA) of 2001, more familiarly called the "No Child Left Behind" Act. The 1,100-page act mandates that states create safe schools, adopt tough new academic standards, ensure that students are tested on those standards, and improve teacher quality. No one can argue that the act has a major goal of improving student achievement. What remains to be seen, however, is whether a federally monitored program that includes high-stakes testing will be able to ensure academic excellence while avoiding political manipulation. Parents, students, and educators may have a long wait for major top-down reform to occur because there are just too many political barriers to overcome.

The good news, though, is that productive change is occurring slowly and quietly at the school level. Across North America, there is significant change happening in schools where faculty members have decided to keep abreast of what science is revealing about how the brain learns and to use that information to guide their practice. The key is a principal who is a true leader and who gives the faculty the leeway to take appropriate curricular and instructional risks. When enough schools in a district adopt this approach, that district shines like a pearl in Bell's "sea of mediocrity."

In the real world, it turns out that the *instrument* of meaningful change is the classroom teacher and that the *unit* of change is the individual school. This reality places building principals in an extremely important position. By their actions, they can be the true catalysts or obstacles to change.

ABOUT THIS BOOK

Researchers, politicians, educators, and observers have written many books in recent years about why we need school reform; some have suggested how to accomplish it. Few books, though, have sought to include newer research into teaching and learning as the justification for the reform actions that educational leaders should consider. Dickmann and Stanford-Blair (2002) broke important ground with their book, which presented elegant and thoughtful arguments for aligning leadership with the growing body of research on intelligence.

Leaders need resources to expand their knowledge and develop their skills. Leadership means taking the members of an organization to new levels of accomplishment and fulfillment. It does not mean doing more of what we are already doing. Schools today are complex and complicated organizations. Society is becoming increasingly heterogeneous, more non-English-speaking students are arriving in our schools, students come to school with different views on learning, and stress is now a constant for both students and staff.

Despite these challenges, science may be the key to helping leaders lead. Cognitive neuroscientists are gaining greater insights into the workings of the human brain, including how the brain survives, interacts, and learns from its environment. Many of these insights can help educational leaders in their attempts to convince themselves and others of the importance of changing what we do in schools to help all students reach their full potential. Science can provide leaders with a deeper understanding of their own thinking processes so that their decisions are mindful and ethical. If leadership is the key to true educational reform, then thoughtful leadership is the key to thoughtful reform. To that end, I have written this book with the hope of providing educational leaders some insights into how research in cognitive neuroscience and other related areas can inform their practice.

Questions This Book Will Answer

This book will help answer questions such as these:

- ▸ What are the attributes of a successful leader?
- ▸ What are some basic facts that educational leaders should know about parts of the brain and their functions?
- ▸ How can a leader encourage and develop creativity in a school?
- ▸ How are the learning preferences of students different from those in the past, and what are the implications of these differences for curriculum and instruction?
- ▸ What are other ways of evaluating teacher effectiveness besides classroom visits?
- ▸ What are some strategies for resolving ethical dilemmas?

> ► How can we discuss spirituality in schools without violating religious beliefs or the U.S. Constitution?
> ► What are some effective ways of transforming the culture of a school?
> ► What can be done to develop aspiring and current educational leaders while retaining those we already have?

What Do We Mean by Brain-Compatible?

Wherever possible, I have used findings from cognitive neuroscience to help expand the concept of leadership, especially in the areas of how leaders need to think and act to resolve dilemmas, handle conflict, and promote desired change. At the same time, leaders themselves need to know what researchers are learning about cognition, so that the decisions educators make in schools are consistent with brain-compatible curricula and instruction.

Brain-compatible curriculum and brain-compatible instruction are *not* programs neatly packaged in kits that can be distributed conveniently throughout the school. **Rather, they represent a frame of mind whereby the educator recognizes that new information is being revealed periodically about how the brain learns, and that this knowledge may translate into new initiatives and teaching strategies that can help students reach higher levels of achievement.** Educational leaders must explain to teachers that the brain-compatible approach is not a program. Because of their experiences, some veteran teachers see any new initiative as a packaged program with a limited shelf life. I remember one war-torn teacher telling me: "I have survived learning styles, cooperative learning, and writing across the curriculum. Now, you want me to teach to the brain?" I did ask what body part he had been teaching to until now, but that only added to the awkwardness of the moment.

To some degree, I can understand this cynicism. Some staff development programs of the past offered sessions that were far too short to be meaningful experiences, so teachers went right back to doing what they always did. The big advantage to the brain-compatible approach is that it shifts focus from the teacher to the learner. It aims to uncover for teachers as much as possible about how the brain learns. And the more teachers know about how the brain learns, the more likely they are to develop and select strategies that will result in successful learning. We all use care in selecting our physicians because we want our bodily ailments treated by the most up-to-date professionals. Taxpayers, then, should also be able to send the minds of their children to the most up-to-date professionals in their schools.

Chapter Content

Chapter 1 discusses the attributes of leaders from the perspective that leaders are made, not born. It reviews various leadership styles, their advantages and disadvantages, and ways for leaders to assess their own style. Also mentioned here are some of the discoveries in brain research that have application to what leaders are trying to accomplish in school reform.

Chapter 2 presents some basic information about the major structures of the human brain and their functions. It discusses such topics as the difference between learning and retention, left and right hemispheric preferences, higher-order thinking, and the nature of creativity. True reform often requires creative solutions. Consequently, how leaders can be more creative and how they can honor and encourage creativity in school organizations is an important part of this chapter.

Chapter 3 proposes what should be included in a curriculum that is more compatible with the brain of students today. It discusses the influence that modern society has on student learning and why students come to school with a different set of expectations about learning than those students of a decade ago. Using recent discoveries from neuroscience, some suggestions are made about the nature and content of the 21st century curriculum with a view toward being more successful at meeting the needs of a rapidly changing society and student body. A brain-compatible curriculum framework is introduced and explained, with special emphasis on reading and language acquisition.

Chapter 4 offers a picture of what brain-compatible instruction and assessment should look like. The importance of classroom climate, novelty, retention strategies, closure, and imagery are discussed and supported with practical suggestions for classroom implementation. Practice, for example, can be a friend or foe, depending on how and when the student uses it. Suggestions for differentiated instruction and assessment are also presented to ensure that the needs of students of different ability levels are fully met.

Chapter 5 deals with teacher evaluation, one of the most sensitive areas of leadership. As we begin to recognize the extraordinary complexity of teaching, we need to revise our ways of evaluating its effectiveness. Part of that evaluation suggests that leaders encourage teachers to gain new knowledge about how the brain learns and to devise strategies that incorporate that knowledge into their practice. The chapter also discusses ways of expanding evaluation methods to include multiple data sources, such as portfolios, student test results, action research, and parent and student surveys. Evaluation methods should also be aligned with national professional standards and school reform.

Chapter 6 tackles a subject seldom discussed in educational circles, the need for ethical and spiritual leadership. Schools are ethical institutions and the leaders and staff should model ethical behavior. The chapter describes instances of unethical behavior by some leaders and suggests strategies to help leaders resolve ethical dilemmas. Also included are suggestions of how to discuss and model spirituality in schools without violating religious beliefs or the U.S. Constitution.

Chapter 7 deals with the nature and power of school culture and suggests ways to assess and transform the present condition of that culture. It addresses such basic ideas as school start times as well as year-round and extended academic calendars. Ways of ridding school culture of misconceptions about learning-disabled, gifted, and minority students are also advanced. The chapter discusses the importance of establishing and working with teams, as well as recommendations for building an articulated staff development program that supports a positive school culture.

Chapter 8 ties the previous chapters together by offering a model for a whole-brained approach to educational leadership. It describes the habits of mind that influence how we think and act, especially in situations involving problem solving and conflict resolution. Also included is how to apply this knowledge to build a community of learners within the school organization. Finally, the chapter discusses ways to develop current and aspiring educational leaders and offers some suggestions for how to tackle the difficult problem of retaining experienced leaders in the profession.

At the end of most chapters is a section called **Tips for Leaders.** These pages include suggestions, surveys, strategies, and self-assessments for translating research and concepts into school and classroom practice.

To implement meaningful and lasting reform, educational leaders must have a thorough understanding of how schools operate and what can be done realistically to improve them. This requires a thorough knowledge of the change process and the steps needed to successfully implement change. School leaders cannot do it alone; they need the help of all members of the school community. But leaders are vital instigators, and my hope is that this book will give them some of the information they will need to convince others to follow them.

Understanding Leadership

1

SCHOOLS NEED TRUE LEADERS

Public education in the United States today can best be described by the opening lines in *A Tale of Two Cities* by Charles Dickens: "It was the best of times, it was the worst of times." It is the best of times because never have we known so much about how the human brain develops, grows, and learns, so that we have the potential to be more successful with more students. We have better knowledge of the causes and treatments for learning difficulties, and new therapies are evolving for helping children with psychological problems and physical disabilities.

It is the worst of times in that never before have the public schools been asked to do so much for society. Schools not only teach children. They raise them. Teachers not only present their curriculum, but they are also asked to counsel on drugs, sex, family problems, and personal relationships. Child-rearing tasks, such as ensuring adequate sleep and a healthy breakfast, once left to the family, now occur in school by default. Important discussions and learning opportunities for children that once occurred during the family dinner hour barely exist these days as a result of absent parents or overscheduling.

Consequently, fewer adults have fewer opportunities to teach their children respect for the property and opinions of others and the rules of acceptable behavior. Schools, then, whether they like it or not, are left with the unenviable and daunting task of raising children as well as teaching them. The notion that teachers act *in loco parentis* has never been more accurate. In this best-of-times/worst-of-times scenario, educational leaders become the key to helping school staffs balance their responsibilities and priorities successfully. Managing cannot do it alone.

ATTRIBUTES OF A LEADER

Defining leadership has not been an easy task for social psychologists or anyone else for that matter. Nonetheless, most of us have some idea in our head of what constitutes leadership. Rather than define leadership, we tend to describe it using characteristics that are common among effective leaders. Many books have been written about the attributes of leadership, often using case studies to show examples of effective leaders in business, politics, and the military. Research literature abounds with references to leadership styles, leadership models, and leadership behaviors. After sifting through much of the research, seven attributes of leaders consistently emerge. Great leaders

- ▶ Are made, not born
- ▶ Know their stuff
- ▶ Have a clear vision of their mission
- ▶ Respect and care for their followers
- ▶ Have high expectations
- ▶ Demonstrate absolute integrity
- ▶ Are excellent role models

This list is by no means complete. But it is a good starting point, and it is worth exploring these attributes to see how they apply to educational organizations.

Leaders Are Made, Not Born

Some personality traits common to successful leaders, such as assertiveness and gregariousness, have been found to be moderately inheritable, but few studies have been done of the genetic basis of leadership. One study of 247 adult twin pairs found that about one-half of the personality traits associated with leaders could have a genetic basis (Johnson, Vernon, McCarthy, Molson, Harris, and Jang, 1998).

Leadership, however, is more than just personality traits. More often it is the result of developing characteristics that inspire people to work for the goals of an organization. These include understanding people, exercising power and authority judiciously, empowering colleagues, and being decisive. Leaders know their strengths and weaknesses. They use their strengths wisely, compensate for their weaknesses, and draw on the talents of other members of the organization. Schools are seldom ideal places to develop leadership skills because policies and regulations often place strict limits on the discretionary power of a school leader.

Leaders Know Their Stuff

No one expects leaders to know everything, but they should be well versed in the competencies needed to be successful in the organization. They should also know the rules that govern their position and control the exercise of their authority. In schools, this means that leaders need to know those regulations and policies that relate to the decisions they regularly make. What is more important, because school leaders often supervise and evaluate their staff, they need to possess the knowledge base to explain, and the skills to demonstrate, effective instructional strategies to those teachers requiring such support. Although playing politics may result in a promotion, it will not earn the principal the respect of the staff.

Leaders Have a Clear Vision of Their Mission

Leaders need to determine where they want the organization to go and how they will get it there. To know where they are headed, leaders must analyze, assess, plan, implement, and evaluate. A clear vision is particularly crucial when human and financial resources become tight or when competing factions are demanding services that could change the mission of the organization. Now the leader must decide which allocations of dwindling resources or which set of demands is less likely to prevent the organization from achieving its goals. In schools, the most common vision statement is that all children can learn. We know that students have their strengths and weaknesses and that some learn faster than others. Yet, school s treat most students as if they all learn the same way. We still

- ▶ Insist that students spend the same time at each grade level
- ▶ Follow an agrarian calender
- ▶ Use language competency as the main indicator of their intelligence
- ▶ Subject students to too much teacher talk at the secondary level

These structures run counter to the idea that all students can learn. Rather, they decrease the ability of the staff to individualize instructional services for students.

Leaders Respect and Care for Their Followers

Effective leadership is a partnership with others rather than a one-person operation. Mutual respect between leaders and followers is essential for developing a sense that all members of the organization care about and contribute to each other's success. Schools are usually tightly knit organizations. Consequently, the level of respect and interest that school leaders exhibit in their professional relationships with the staff is often the deciding factor in how much the staff will respond when the leader asks for assistance in solving difficult problems.

Leaders Have High Expectations

With few exceptions, job performance tends to rise or fall to the level of expectation set by the leader. High expectations yield high performance, generally followed by monetary and in-kind rewards for both leaders and followers. When setting high expectations in schools, educational leaders will find that some teachers will consistently meet and exceed those expectations. Others, however, may be more reluctant to rise to the expected level because of the absence of financial or other incentives that reward superior performance. Recent recognition of this human trait prompted some states and districts to offer bonuses to teachers in schools whose student performance indicators exceed preset goals.

Leaders Demonstrate Absolute Integrity

Trust is the cornerstone of the leader-follower relationship. Followers must feel confident that the leader speaks truthfully, keeps confidences, and avoids playing one member of the organization against another. School principals serve as leaders, coaches, and teachers, and must also be available to serve as counselors and to give praise and reprimand with objectivity. In schools with strong collective bargaining agreements, lack of mutual trust can easily engender or intensify an " us against them" mentality between the leaders and the staff.

Leaders Are Excellent Role Models

Successful leaders lead by example, demonstrating with their behavior the very attributes that they honor and reward in their followers. In schools, principals should model good instructional strategies when conducting their faculty meetings. If they believe in sharing power, then they must give decision-making authority to individuals and committees within the building and accept their decisions willingly.

Other Attributes of Leaders

For leaders to effectively demonstrate the seven attributes listed above, they must be able to be and do the following:

- Understand people
- Be decisive
- Communicate and listen well
- Be flexible
- Know when to delegate
- Be innovative
- Set priorities
- Be a visionary
- Know when to be intense and when to relax
- Be positive
- Have a sense of humor that avoids sarcasm
- Be willing to take risks
- Be introspective
- Develop good problem-solving and decision-making skills
- Know how to assess and coach the skills of others
- Be predictable
- Be there

ORGANIZATIONAL EXPECTATIONS

Organizations have expectations of their leaders. Some of the expectations cited by DePree (1992) for organizations in general can be modified to reflect what the staff members and students expect from their administrators. The principal

- Is responsible for the equitable assignment of teachers and other resources in the school.
- Provides the staff and students with a clear vision of the school's mission.
- Defines and expresses in writing and through behavior the beliefs and values of the school.
- Ensures that priorities are set, communicated to the staff and students, and adhered to in practice.
- Focuses on the climate and health of the school organization more than on his or her image as a leader.

- ▸ Is responsible for the continued renewal of the school through professional development and other similar activities.
- ▸ Applies policies to students and staff in a manner consistent with the vision, beliefs, values, and mission of the school.
- ▸ Never embarrasses members of the school.
- ▸ Ensures that planning receives direction and approval.

Leaders who are continually aware of these organizational expectations and who strive to fulfill them are very likely to be successful in winning the loyalty of the staff when proposing change and in times of crisis.

LEADERSHIP STYLES

Researchers since the late 1800s have examined how leaders lead within the context of their respective organizations. Consequently, theories about leadership have evolved as the contexts in which they were explored changed throughout the last century. Here is a summary of some of the more prominent theories of leadership style and the degree to which they affected school organizations.

Autocratic/Bureaucratic

From the late 1800s to the 1950s, autocratic style was prevalent in the early industrial organizations. The leadership style was dogmatic. Commands were issued and compliance was expected. The leader used power to give or withhold rewards and punishment. The growth of government during the depression era gave rise to a variation of autocratic style, called *bureaucratic* style, which valued rules, regulations, and rank. This style is obsolete in the private sector of modern industrialized societies but still prevails in government agencies and in the military.

Both autocratic and bureaucratic styles were prominent in schools during the first half of the 20th century. These styles, however, gave way to more democratic approaches through collective bargaining agreements when teachers unions began to gain strength in the late 1960s.

Democratic/Participative

The turbulent 1960s gave rise to demands for democratic and participative leadership that was characterized by consultation with members of the organization on significant actions and decisions. The leader encouraged and rewarded involvement in the process and made decisions with the approval of the members. The major weakness of this approach was the vulnerability of the organization to the will of the majority, that is, what is good for the majority is not always good for the organization.

Democratic leadership style in individual schools was severely limited by the myriad of local school board policies and state rules and regulations that put significant restraints on the ability of schools to establish their own procedures. Even today, the degree to which the organization and direction of individual schools can vary is limited by local, state, and federal regulations.

Situational

Situational leadership came to light in the early 1970s and was based on the idea that leadership should shift among members of the organization according to the needs of a particular group at a specific point in time. The leader and members of the decision-making group are selected depending on the particular situation and time frame in which the decision must be made. One weakness of this approach is that it is very difficult to predict in advance which type of leadership skills would be most effective in a particular situation. Consequently, situational leadership can be time-consuming because several groups may have to be formed with new leaders before a satisfactory decision is reached.

School districts have used situational leadership in limited ways for many years. One common example is the establishment of a district-wide committee to rewrite a specific curriculum. The committee leader and members are usually chosen because of their expertise in the content of that particular subject area.

Transactional and Transformational

As organizations grew more complex, transformational leadership gained favor during the1980s. This approach recognizes that, within an organization, there can be many leaders who share the same goals and who can be empowered to make certain decisions. Transactional leadership develops from the exchange process between leaders and subordinates wherein the leader provides rewards in exchange for the performance of subordinates. In this arrangement, the leader clearly specifies what he or she wants, determines what the employee wants, and brokers the contractual exchange of the two. The contractual relationship is based on agreed-upon goals, minimally acceptable performance levels, and a reward for satisfactory performance or a penalty for unsatisfactory performance. Some researchers believe that transactional leadership promotes mediocrity in that the focus is on minimum performance of assigned tasks. Transactional leadership is distinguished by negotiation, exchange, and contractual dimensions between manager and employee (Bass, 1985).

Transformational leadership goes beyond transactional leadership by motivating followers through charisma to emotionally identify with the vision of the leader and to sacrifice their self-interest for that of the organization. Followers are encouraged to question their own ways of doing things and their assignments provide them with new learning opportunities. According to Bass (1985), charisma, attention to individualized professional development, and the ability and willingness to provide intellectual stimulation are critical to leaders who want to transform organizations faced with demands for renewal and change.

Using transactional and transformational leadership is not easy in schools still laden with heavy bureaucracy and imbued with a top-down leadership ethic. But there are ways that it can be done. Transactional leadership, sometimes called bartering, is based on an exchange of services for various types of rewards that the leader controls. This approach works well only when both leaders and followers understand and are in agreement about which tasks are important. To be successful in schools, transformational leaders need to pursue the following three goals:

▶ Help staff develop and maintain a collaborative and professional school culture that reduces teacher isolation, shares leadership, delegates power, communicates norms and beliefs, and uses the bureaucracy to support cultural changes.
▶ Encourage the staff to internalize goals for professional growth.
▶ Help teachers work smarter, not harder, by recognizing that teachers as a group can develop better solutions than the principal can working alone.

Transformational leadership is no panacea, but it can be a part of a balanced approach to creating high student and teacher performance in schools.

Systemic

This leadership style emerged in the late 1980s and 1990s and becomes necessary when it is apparent that piecemeal efforts are not working and that true reform can come only by fundamentally changing an organization's hierarchy and basic systems. Societal forces (such as alternative family structures and a decrease in civic responsibility), economic forces (such as workers experiencing multiple career changes), and the impact of technology are placing new expectations on educators. In turn, educational leaders need to determine whether the current mission and offerings of their schools can meet these expectations. If not, then these leaders will need to use reflection, rethinking, and restructuring to make the systemic changes necessary so that the schools can effectively serve their communities.

For systemic change to succeed in schools, educational leaders need to consider the following:

- ▸ Demonstrate true support for change through personal vision, realistic goals, willingness to take risks, and by building community support.
- ▸ Establish a clear vision and mission for the educational institution.
- ▸ Ensure a strong role for building principals because they are in touch with all members of the school community and are more aware of the complex relationships in schools, thereby enabling them to help others in the school understand their unique role in systemic change.
- ▸ Encourage school board members to promote change and to concern themselves with strategic planning and educational outcomes rather than managerial responsibilities.

WHAT STYLE OF LEADER AM I?

Researchers in leadership and management today agree that no one leadership style will successfully manage the issues emerging from a rapidly changing and technologically complex world. In fact, some researchers warn that for educational leaders to successfully implement major school reforms, they must fully understand their own strengths and weaknesses so that they can find solutions within the school organization rather than be dependent on externally initiated changes.

Managing Oneself

Successful leaders know themselves. They know their strengths, their values, and how they perform best. Drucker (1999) maintains that leaders have to learn to manage themselves before they can lead others. He suggests that leaders examine at least six aspects to determine how well they manage themselves.

▶ *Determining Strengths.* A person performs best on strength, not weakness.

▶ *Assessing Performance.* How one performs is unique and dependent mainly on personality.

▶ *Examining the Value System.* Personal value systems often determine how leaders behave in an organization, especially when the values of the leader conflict with those of the organization.

▶ *Determining Job Position.* Leaders need to determine which leadership positions are compatible with their strengths, performance, and value system.

▶ *Deciding on Contributions.* Leaders are more likely to succeed if they have select contributions that are realistic and achievable.

▶ *Understanding Relationships.* Leaders get greater and more lasting results when they build relationships and work with others rather than alone.

> **LEADER'S QUESTION: What strategies can I use to manage myself as an effective leader? SEE TIP #1.1**

Leading From Within the Organization

Educational leaders, especially school principals, are often placed in the position of implementing changes that were externally initiated, such as state standards, curriculum reform, and standardized testing. Determining how long these changes will last is guesswork because many are the result of political rather than educational decisions. The demands of parents and the community, business interests, and government policy makers have placed a heavy burden on principals who feel overworked and underappreciated. How can they be true leaders when they spend so much time responding to daily crises and outside demands? This overload tempts principals to seek out, and become dependent on, packaged external solutions for internal problems.

Researchers in leadership suggest that the public school environment is so complex that principals must realize there is no one answer for how to carry out school reform. Hargreaves and Fullan (1998) propose that reform-minded leaders develop their own theories of change and test them against new situations. They offer the following four guidelines to help leaders overcome their dependency on outside solutions:

▶ *Respect those you want to silence.* People who are resistant to a reform initiative can often provide insight into how to deal with a complex problem. Leadership involves mobilizing people to tackle tough problems and to learn from dissonance.

▸ *Move toward the danger in forming new alliances.* Healthy school-community relations can help implement reform initiatives. Rather than withdrawing inside the school, principals should reach out to the public and see them as a positive component to reform, not as the enemy.

▸ *Manage emotionally as well as rationally.* Principals need to create a supportive environment by placing a high priority on reculturing, which involves changing the values, norms, and relationships in the school to develop new ways of working together (see Chapter 7). This process requires a strong emotional involvement from the leader and others in the organization. Reculturing gives people the stamina to face the challenges and anxieties that emerge during meaningful school reform.

▸ *Fight for lost causes.* Leaders who have hope are more likely to be successful because they can place their problems in a loftier perspective that helps them stay calm when the going gets rough. Principals should have and display hope because teachers need to be reminded that they, too, are working toward a greater purpose. Hope is not a promise, but an optimistic view that makes the school a healthier place for all.

Knowing that there is no clear solution to the complex problems facing our schools, educational leaders can shed their dependency on outside solutions and look for answers nearer at hand. By working closely with the staff, parents, and school community, principals can put their in-house solutions to the test and move closer to true and lasting reform.

A Leader or a Manager?

Teachers sometimes complain that their building and district administrators are managers and not leaders. By this they imply that the principal and central office personnel are bureaucrats who maintain the status quo and avoid adopting the changes necessary for districts to address the problems currently facing our schools.

Leaders are those who possess the attributes and skills discussed earlier in this chapter. They are proactive, committed, and decisive individuals who are willing to take risks while looking for creative ways to solve problems. Managers, on the other hand, tend to be reactive. They avoid risks and make decisions within the confines of rules and history. **Modern schools need leaders; there are already too many managers.**

IMPACT OF BRAIN RESEARCH ON LEADERSHIP

During the last two decades, research in the neurosciences has revealed new understandings about how the brain grows, develops, and learns. This information has important implications for what educators do in schools and classrooms. Educational leaders need to be aware of the new research as it applies to their practice. The most significant characteristic of a profession is that its members continue to add to their knowledge base those discoveries and insights that can allow them to be more effective with the clients they serve.

In the ensuing chapters, we will examine how some of the new revelations from neuroscience can help educational leaders become even more effective in bringing about those changes that will make our schools the most powerful teaching and learning organizations they can be. And why is this now so very important? Mainly because futurists and management researchers, such as Peter Drucker, seem convinced that the success of a society and its culture in the 21st century will be determined largely by their supply and productivity of knowledge workers (Drucker, Dyson, Handy, Saffo, and Senge, 1997).

The birthrate in most developed countries is declining, largely because the younger population is concerned about their ability to support a growing number of nonworking older people. Thus, the continual and systematic production of knowledge and knowledge workers is crucial to counterbalance the declining birth rate in the developed world. This evolving trend has implications for schools and their leaders. First and foremost is the realization that knowledge is a fragile commodity with a short shelf life. Knowledge workers must know how and what new skills and information they need to learn to remain competent and successful. Schools, therefore, need to focus more on helping students learn how to learn and how to recognize when it is time to learn something new in their job. Educational leaders become the key to ensuring that schools are not focused solely on dispensing knowledge, but more on developing individuals who will know what knowledge and skills are important for their continued success in the complex world of the 21st century.

How can leaders accomplish this critical task? Let us start this journey in the next chapter with an overview of brain structures and their functions, learning, and links between neuroscience and our understanding of leadership.

MAJOR POINTS IN CHAPTER 1

❏ Educational leaders are made and not born. They can learn and develop the knowledge and skills they need to be successful leaders.

❏ Organizations have expectations of their leaders. When school leaders meet these expectations, they are more likely to get the loyalty of the staff and students in times of crisis.

❏ Leadership style describes the general approach that leaders use to carry out their responsibilities. Some common styles are autocratic/bureaucratic, democratic/participative, situational, transactional and transformational, and systemic. In practice, school leaders may intuitively vary their style depending on the situation.

❏ No one leadership style will successfully manage the issues emerging from a rapidly changing and technologically complex world. To successfully implement school reforms, educational leaders must understand their own strengths and weaknesses so that they can find solutions within the school organization rather than be dependent on externally initiated changes.

❏ Managers tend to do things right while leaders do the right thing. Schools today need more leaders.

❏ Research in the neurosciences has revealed new understandings about how the brain grows, develops, and learns. This information has important implications for what educators do in schools and classrooms.

❏ Educational leaders need to ensure that schools are not focused solely on dispensing knowledge, but more on developing individuals who will know what knowledge and skills are important for their continued success in the complex world of the 21st century.

TIPS FOR LEADERS #1.1

Strategies for Managing Oneself

Successful leaders learn to manage themselves by developing their strengths and by placing themselves where they can make the greatest contribution to their profession (Drucker, 1999).

- *Building Strengths*. Discover your strengths through feedback analysis. Whenever you make a key decision, write down what you expect to happen. Later, compare the actual results with your expectations. You may be surprised at the insights you get about where your strengths lie. This method shows you what you are doing or failing to do to make full use of your strengths. It also reveals areas where you lack competence. Work to improve your strengths and acquire the knowledge and skills you need to fully realize your strengths.

- *Remedying Any Bad Habits*. Work, too, to remedy any bad habits that are revealed in the feedback analysis. For example, some leaders have great plans that never get realized because they fail to follow through. They must find the people who will carry out the plan and follow through when the plan is completed. Don't forget to say "please" and "thank you" and the simple rules of courtesy that make people in an organization feel valued.

- *Avoiding the Impossible*. All of us have areas in which we have little talent or skill, and almost no chance of getting good at them. Avoid getting involved in areas where you have little competence. Seek out those projects where your strengths will allow for accomplishment. Avoid spending too much time trying to change incompetent staff members into mediocre performers. It is better to make a competent person into a high performer.

- *Improving Performance*. Performance is often the product of personality traits, including learning style. Are you a reader or a listener? How do you learn best? How do you perform best? Do you work well with other people or alone? Are you a better performer as the superordinate, subordinate, or a team member? Do you work better under pressure or in a highly structured and predictable environment? Do you work better in a large or small organization? Are you more comfortable as a decision maker or an adviser? Answering these questions about yourself will help guide you to a leadership position where you can perform successfully.

- *Matching Values.* Leaders are more likely to be effective in organizations whose values match their own. Some school districts, for example, judge their worth largely on the results of standardized tests or on how many students in the graduating class get into college. Leaders whose value systems are focused on serving all students or on expanding offerings in the arts may be at odds with the values of the organization. The value systems do not have to be identical, but they must be close enough to coexist.

- *Deciding Where to Belong.* When you have a clear picture of your strengths, performance, and value system, you can better decide in which type of leadership position you belong and which type you should avoid. For example, if you are a better performer as an adviser, then avoid decision-making assignments. Assistant principals and assistant superintendents were often put in their positions by strong leaders who needed trusted advisers. Although highly successful in the advisory posts, they sometimes fail when placed in the top position and have the responsibility for making decisions.

- *Deciding What to Contribute.* Managers try to maintain the status quo; leaders contribute to the organization so that it can be even more successful in achieving its mission. Deciding on which contributions to make will depend on (1) what the situation requires, (2) your strengths, performance, and value system, and (3) what results have to be achieved to make a difference. Keep your timeline short but realistic. For example: What can you achieve that will make a difference in the next year? What you set out to do needs to be meaningful, visible, and, if possible, measurable.

- *Taking Responsibility for Relationships.* To accomplish their goals, leaders usually need to work with other people. Thus, building relationships is a vital task for a leader. Also, it is important to know the strengths, performance modes, and value systems of individuals before giving them specific assignments. Working relationships are based as much on the people as on the nature of the work. Principals, for instance, who were promoted from within the school often detect a strain in their relationships with their former faculty colleagues. Maintaining these relationships, however, is important to furthering the work of the school.

- *Taking Care of Yourself.* School leaders are under enormous stress from both internal and external forces. They often have 60- to 80-hour work weeks, leaving them little time to spend with their families or to take care of their physical and mental health. Find a stress-relieving hobby (for example, fishing, bicycle riding, or playing bridge). Devise an exercise plan and stick to it. Occasionally ask others to fill in for your evening responsibilities and have a quiet dinner together with the family or friends. If work-related stress continuously and seriously affects your relationships with loved ones, it is time to think of another position or career.

Linking Leadership to the Brain

Educational leaders are like teachers in one very important aspect: They try to change brains every day. Whether it is with a parent, student, teacher, or administrative colleague, educational leaders are usually arguing a point, explaining a rule, or defending a position in an effort to convince or teach the listener. Consequently, the more leaders know about how the brain works, the more likely they are to be successful at changing it.

To that end, here is some basic information about the human brain. The goal here is not to make neuroscientists out of leaders. Rather it is to give them enough knowledge and understanding about important brain structures and their functions so that leaders can be more effective in carrying out their many responsibilities.

BRAIN STRUCTURE AND FUNCTION

Exterior Structures

To understand some basic information about the structure of the brain, we need to look first at the major exterior parts of the brain (Figure 2.1). The wrinkles on the outside of the brain make it look like an oversized walnut. Although the minor wrinkles are unique in each brain, several major wrinkles and folds are common to all brains. These folds form a set of four lobes known as the *frontal, temporal, occipital,* and *parietal lobes*. Collectively they are called the *cerebrum* (Latin for brain). Each lobe specializes in performing certain functions.

The frontal lobe is the executive control center of the brain, monitoring higher-order thinking, directing problem solving, and regulating the excesses of the emotional system. Because emotions drive attention, the efficiency of this area is

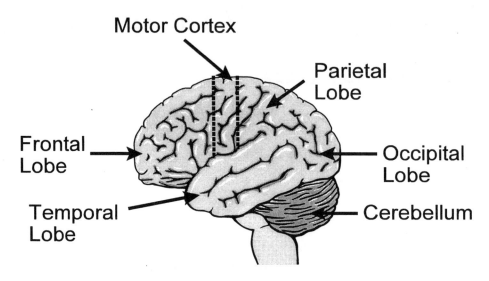

Figure 2.1 This diagram shows the four lobes of the brain (cerebrum) as well as the motor cortex and the cerebellum.

linked to the limbic centers. The frontal lobe also contains our self-will area, what some might call our personality. Trauma to the frontal lobe can cause dramatic, and sometimes permanent, behavior and personality changes. (Note: Educational leaders might discuss with parents the wisdom of allowing 10-year-olds to play football and soccer where the risk of trauma to the frontal lobe is so high.)

Because most of the working memory is located in the frontal lobe, it is the area where focus occurs. The frontal lobe matures slowly. MRI studies of postadolescents reveal that the frontal lobe continues to mature into early adulthood. Thus, the emotional regulation capability of the frontal lobe is not fully operational during adolescence, a major reason why adolescents often submit to their emotions and resort to high-risk behavior (Sowell, Thompson, Holmes, Jernigan, and Toga, 1999).

Voluntary body movements are controlled by the *motor cortex*, a narrow strip of neurons that runs from ear to ear along the top of the brain between the frontal and parietal lobes. Below the occipital lobe lies the cerebellum (Latin for little brain), which coordinates learned and involuntary movement. Table 2.1 lists the functions of the four lobes as well as of the motor cortex and the *cerebellum*.

Interior Structures

Next, let us take a look at some of the more important interior brain structures (Figure 2.2). At the base of the brain, just below the cerebellum, is the brain stem,

Table 2.1 Some Exterior Parts of the Brain

Structure		Function
Cerebrum	Frontal Lobe (often referred to as the *executive control center*)	Personality, curiosity, planning, problem solving, higher-order thinking, and emotional restraint
	Temporal Lobe	Interpretation of sound, speech (usually on the left side only), and some aspects of long-term memory
	Occipital Lobe	Visual processing
	Parietal Lobe	Orientation, calculation, sensory integration, and certain types of recognition
	Motor Cortex	Control of body movements
Cerebellum		The cerebellum coordinates every movement by monitoring impulses from nerve endings in the muscles. It is very important in the learning, performance, and timing of complex motor tasks, including speaking. The cerebellum may store the memory of rote movements, such as touch-typing and knitting. A person whose cerebellum is damaged cannot coordinate movement, has difficulty with speech, and may display the symptoms of autism.

which regulates critical body functions. At the top of the brain stem and deep within the central core of the brain lies the limbic area. This part of the brain regulates attention and emotional response. Of all the structures located in the limbic area, the thalamus, hippocampus, and amygdala are of great interest to educators. These structures play critical roles in the processing of incoming information, learning, and long-term storage.

For some still unexplained reason, the nerves from the left side of the body cross over to the right hemisphere, and those from the right side of the body cross over to the left hemisphere. The two hemispheres are connected by a thick cable, called the *corpus callosum*, composed of more than 250 million nerve fibers. The hemispheres use this bridge to communicate with each other and to coordinate activities (Table 2.2).

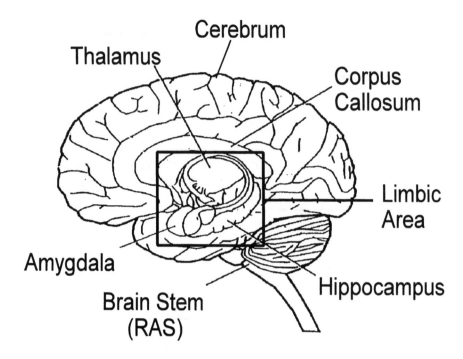

Figure 2.2 A cross section of the human brain showing the major parts of the limbic area, the cerebrum, and the brain stem.

Brain Cells

The control functions and other activities of the brain are carried out by signals traveling along brain cells. The brain is composed of a trillion cells of at least two known types: nerve cells and their support cells. Nerve cells are called *neurons* and represent about one-tenth of the total number of cells, roughly 100 billion. Most of the cells are support cells, called *glial* (Greek for glue) cells, that hold the neurons together and act as filters to keep harmful substances out of the neurons.

Neurons (Figure 2.3) comprise the functioning core of the brain and the entire nervous system. They come in different sizes, but it takes about 30,000 brain neurons to fit on the head of a pin. Unlike other cells, the neuron has tens of thousands of branches or *dendrites* (from the Greek word for tree) emerging from its center. The dendrites receive electrical impulses from other neurons and transmit them along a long fiber, called the axon (Greek for axis). Each neuron has only one axon. A layer called the *myelin sheath* (related to the Greek word for marrow) surrounds each axon. The sheath insulates the axon from the other cells and increases the speed of impulse transmission. The impulse travels along the neurons through an electrochemical process and can move the entire length of a 6-foot adult in two-tenths of a second.

Structure	Function
	**Table 2.2 Some Interior Parts of the Brain**
Structure	**Function**
Brain Stem	The oldest and deepest area of the brain, this is often referred to as the reptilian brain because it is similar to the entire brain of a reptile. Here is where vital body functions (such as respiration, body temperature, blood pressure, and digestion) are controlled and monitored. This area also houses the reticular activating system (RAS), responsible for the brain's alertness.
Limbic Area	Above the brain stem lies the limbic area, whose structures are duplicated in each hemisphere of the brain. Three parts of the limbic area are important to learning and memory: *Thalamus.* All incoming sensory information (except smell) goes first to the thalamus. From there it is directed to other parts of the brain for further processing. *Hippocampus.* Named for the Greek word for a sea monster resembling a seahorse, because of its shape, it plays a major role in consolidating learning and in converting information from working memory via electronic signals to the long-term storage regions, a process that may take from days to months. This brain area constantly checks information relayed to working memory and compares it with stored experiences. This process is essential for the creation of meaning. *Amygdala.* Attached to the end of the hippocampus, the amygdala (Greek for almond) plays an important role in emotions, especially fear. Because of its proximity to the hippocampus and its activity on PET scans, researchers believe that the amygdala encodes an emotional message, if one is present, whenever a memory is tagged for long-term storage.
Corpus Callosum	A bridge of nerve fibers that connects the left and right cerebral hemispheres and allows communication between them.

Neurons have no direct contact with each other. Between each dendrite and axon is a small gap of about a millionth of an inch called a *synapse* (from the Greek meaning to join together). A typical neuron collects signals from others through the dendrites. The neuron sends out spikes of electrical activity (impulses) through the

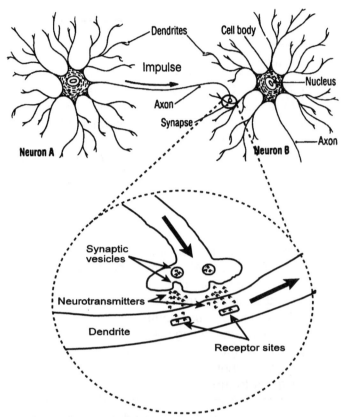

Figure 2.3 Neurons, or nerve cells, transmit impulses along an axon and across a synapse to the dendrite of a neighboring cell. The impulse is carried across the synapse to the receptor sites by chemicals called neurotransmitters that lie within the synaptic vesicles (Sousa, 2001a).

axon to the synapse where the activity releases chemicals stored in sacs (called *synaptic vesicles*) at the end of the axon. The chemicals, called *neurotransmitters*, either excite or inhibit the neighboring neuron. Nearly 100 different neurotransmitters have been discovered so far. Some of the common neurotransmitters are acetylcholine, epinephrine, serotonin, and dopamine.

LEARNING AND RETENTION

Learning occurs when the synapses make physical and chemical changes so that the influence of one neuron on another also changes. For instance, a set of neurons " learns" to fire together. Repeated firings make successive firings easier and, eventually, automatic under certain conditions. Thus, a memory is formed.

Learning is the process by which we *acquire* new knowledge and skills; memory is the process by which we *retain* knowledge and skills for the future.

Investigations into the neural mechanisms required for different types of learning are revealing more about the interactions between learning new information, memory, and changes in brain structure. Just as muscles improve with exercise, the brain seems to improve with use. Although learning does not increase the number of brain cells, it does increase their size, their branches, and their ability to form more complex networks.

LEADER'S QUESTION: Do I know enough about brain structure and function to have a meaningful conversation with another educator? SEE TIP #2.1

The brain goes through physical and chemical changes when it stores new information as the result of learning. Storing gives rise to new neural pathways and strengthens existing pathways. Hence, every time we learn something, our long-term storage areas undergo anatomical changes that, together with our unique genetic makeup, constitute the expression of our individuality (Beatty, 2001).

Learning and retention also occur in different ways. Learning involves the brain, the nervous system, and the environment, and the process by which their interplay acquires information and skills. Sometimes, we need information for just a short period of time, like the telephone number for a pizza delivery, and then the information decays after just a few seconds. **Thus, learning does not always involve long-term retention.** Retention occurs when individuals adopt certain knowledge or skill as their own by integrating it into established neural networks. To accomplish this, the individuals must recognize that the new knowledge or skill is relevant and suitable.

Implications for School Leaders

A good portion of the teaching done in schools centers on delivering facts and information to build concepts that explain a body of knowledge. Pressuring students to memorize large amounts of information puts a tremendous obstacle in the way of retention. To pacify their teachers, administrators, and parents, students may hold on to this information in working memory just long enough to take a test, after which the knowledge readily decays and is lost.

Retention, however, requires that the learner give not only conscious attention but also build conceptual frameworks that have sense and meaning for eventual consolidation into long-term storage networks. This is more apt to occur when students form a personal relationship with what they are learning, leading to interest and enthusiasm about the area of study. School leaders need to ensure that instruction focuses on making learning relevant to student needs. Instructional techniques for increasing retention are discussed in Chapter 4.

LEADERSHIP AND THE BRAIN

Neuroscience is revealing some fascinating information about the way the human brain processes and stores information and how it can synthesize old ideas into new ones. To understand how this remarkable process occurs, we need to examine the functions of the two cerebral hemispheres and the executive control system which, you will remember, resides in the frontal lobes.

The Cerebral Hemispheres

Since the work of Roger Sperry in the 1960s, neuroscientists have accepted the notion that the two cerebral hemispheres are not mirror images of each other (Sousa, 2001a). That is, they differ structurally, biochemically, and functionally. More evidence is accumulating that the brain has a much greater degree of specialization than was previously thought. Even so, because of advancements in neuroimaging, the earlier idea that the brain is a set of modular units carrying out specific tasks is giving way to a new model, which holds that moving across the cortical surface results in a gradual transition from one cognitive function to another. Goldberg (2001) refers to this as the "gradiental" view of brain organization. This view does not necessarily discard the notion that specific areas of the brain perform specific functions. Rather, it uses recent evidence from neurological studies to suggest a pattern of organization whereby the boundaries between the specific areas are fluid, not fixed. The ability of certain areas of the brain to perform unique functions is known as *lateralization* or *specialization* (Sousa, 2001a). Brain imaging studies reveal remarkable consistency in the way the two hemispheres store and process information (Figure 2.4).

Differences in Left and Right Hemisphere Processing

Left Hemisphere. The left brain is the *logical* hemisphere. It monitors the areas for speech, is analytical, and evaluates factual material in a rational way. It understands the literal interpretation of words and detects time and sequence. It also

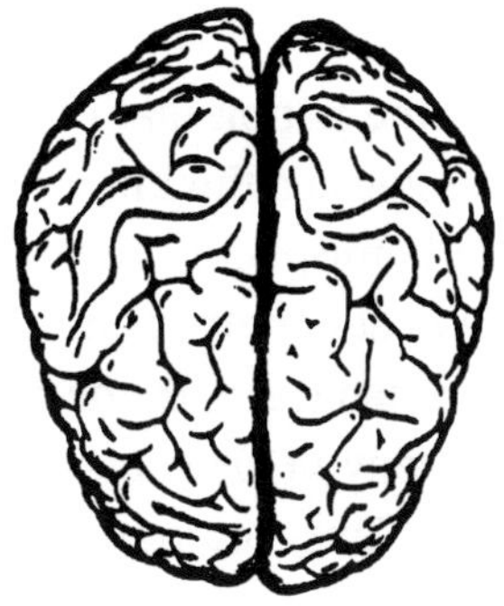

LEFT SIDE	RIGHT SIDE
Connected to right side of the body	Connected to left side of the body
Sequential	Holistic
Analytical	Abstract
Spoken language	Interprets language through gestures
Arithmetic operations	Relational operations
Reasoning	Insight
Routine operations	Novel operations

Figure 2.4 The left and right hemispheres of the human brain are specialized and process information differently.

recognizes words, letters, and numbers written as words.

Right Hemisphere. The right brain is the *intuitive* hemisphere. It gathers information more from images than from words and looks for patterns. It interprets language through context (that is, body language, emotional content, and tone of voice) rather than through literal meanings. It specializes in spatial perception and is capable of creativity. It also recognizes places, faces, and objects.

What Causes Specialization? No one knows why the brain is specialized although it does seem that such a capacity enables it to deal with a great amount of sensory data without going on overload. How it *becomes* specialized is another question. The key to answering this may lie in the structure and wiring of the brain. There is general agreement among neuroscientists now that the brain is hardwired for certain functions, such as spoken language, and that this hardwiring is localized.

Another factor may be that the left and right hemispheres are physically different. The hemispheres are made up of the cortex (the thin but tough surface) called *gray matter* and the support tissue below it called *white matter*. The left hemisphere has more gray matter, while the right has more white. The left hemisphere also has more tightly packed neurons that are better able to handle intense, detailed work. On the other hand, the white matter of the right hemisphere contains neurons with longer axons that can connect with modules farther away. These long-range connections help the right hemisphere to come up with broad but rather vague concepts. The information from each hemisphere is then pooled by sending signals across the corpus callosum (Carter, 1998).

Specialization Does Not Mean Exclusivity

The research data support the notion that each hemisphere has its own set of functions in information processing and thinking. These functions, however, are not always *exclusive* to only one hemisphere, and in even some simple tasks, it is possible for both hemispheres to be involved. In a normal individual, the results of the separate processing are exchanged with the opposite hemisphere through the corpus callosum. There is harmony in the goals of each, and they complement one another in almost all activities. Thus, the individual benefits from the integration of the processing done by both hemispheres and is afforded greater comprehension of whatever situation initiated the processing.

Implications of Hemispheric Preference

In recent years, new case studies and additional testing procedures have enabled researchers to understand more about the functions of each hemisphere. The research shows that most people have a preferred hemisphere, and that this preference affects personality, abilities, and learning style. The preference runs the gamut from neutral (no preference) to strongly left or right. Those who are left-hemisphere preferred tend to be more verbal, analytical, and able to solve sequential problems. Right-hemisphere-preferred individuals paint and draw well, are good at math, and deal with the world visually more easily than verbally. Hemispheric preference does not mean that we do not use both hemispheres. In doing a simple task, we use the hemisphere that will accomplish it more efficiently. When faced with a task that is more complex, our preferred hemisphere will take the lead, although the nonpreferred hemisphere will likely get involved as well (Weisman and Banich, 2000; Sousa, 2001a).

LEADER'S QUESTION: How can I determine my hemispheric preference? SEE TIP #2.2

To sum up, most of us have a hemispheric preference that influences the way we look at the world and how we interact with our environment, including leadership style. Thus, it is helpful for leaders to know their hemispheric preference so that they can get additional insight into how they will approach problem solving and decision making, and how they will interact with the colleagues.

The Prefrontal Cortex

Cognitive thought and related activities are located in the foremost part of the frontal lobes, called the *prefrontal cortex*. This area comprises about 29 percent of the total cortex and is interconnected to every distinct functional region (Figure 2.5). Often called the *executive control area*, the prefrontal cortex is embedded in a rich network of neural pathways so that it can coordinate and integrate the functions of all areas. Like the conductor of an orchestra, the prefrontal cortex blends individual inputs from various regions of the brain into a comprehensive and comprehendible whole. Its interpretations ultimately define personality, creativity, and motivation, and its decision-making abilities determine how successfully an individual copes with each day.

To accomplish this task, the prefrontal cortex must converge the inputs from within an individual with those from the outside world. The organization of the brain facilitates this process. Sensory signals from the outside environment pass along the sensory nerves to the thalamus and are routed to other areas toward the back of the brain (reception). These inputs are then directed to specific sites in the parietal and temporal lobes, as well as in the limbic areas, for further analysis (integration). Finally, the frontal lobes combine this input with information from long-term memory (interpretation) to determine what subsequent action, if any, should be taken.

The prefrontal cortex is strongly interested in task novelty. Several PET studies show that when processing new information, cerebral blood flow levels in the frontal lobes reached their highest levels. But when the subject became familiar with the task, frontal lobe involvement, as measured by blood flow, dropped

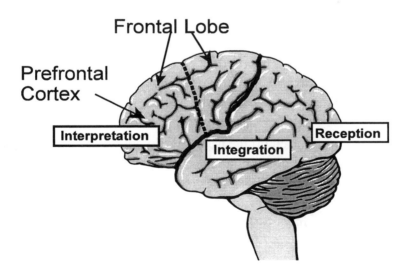

Figure 2.5 The entire area in front of the solid line is the frontal lobe. The area to the left of the dotted line is the general location of the prefrontal cortex. Incoming stimuli are routed first toward the back of the brain (Reception) and then toward the center for further analysis (Integration). The frontal lobes combine these data with past experiences (Interpretation) and determine a suitable course of action.

significantly (Goldberg, 2001). If a somewhat different task was introduced, frontal lobe activation picked up once again. We noted earlier that the right hemisphere was more associated with novelty than the left hemisphere. These findings suggest that the frontal lobes are more closely aligned with the right hemisphere when dealing with novel learning situations.

CREATIVITY

Creativity separates leaders from managers. Managers direct something that already exists; leaders create something new. Reforming schools is difficult because of all the policies, regulations, and collective bargaining agreements that often restrain rather than encourage change. Consequently, one of the most important attributes a leader can have is creativity. To be successful, leaders need to think outside the box by developing their own creative skills and cultivating creativity in others in order to find innovative ways to bring about change despite the dampening effect of regulatory restraints. Given the rapid pace of change in our society, educational leaders must garner the creativity of all members of the school community to build the change needed to serve the needs of our students now and for the future. **Furthermore, schools that do not use their collective creativity to solve problems internally are likely to fall prey to unimaginative solutions imposed externally.**

The Nature of Creativity

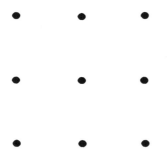

Look at Figure 2.6. Follow the directions and connect all nine dots with just four straight lines. Do not lift the pencil off the paper and do not retrace a line or go through a dot more than once. If you are having difficulty solving this puzzle, ask yourself what limitations you may be inadvertently setting up. The solution requires you to literally think outside the box.

Because the frontal lobe is the executive system of the brain, it is the most likely place where creative thought occurs. When people are creative by thinking outside the box, they usually get a feeling of enjoyment and pride in what they have accomplished. Accordingly, the emotional areas of the brain also contribute to fostering creative

Figure 2.6   Without lifting the pencil, connect all nine dots with just four straight lines. Do not retrace over a line or go through a dot more than once.

behaviors. The interaction of the emotional and rational systems can generate the intrinsic motivation that seems so important for creative people to continue to produce.

Most people tend to associate creativity with the arts but it can occur in any field. To be creative, an idea must also be appropriate, useful, and actionable. Somehow, it must influence the way something gets done, either by improving a product or by opening up a new way to approach a process.

Amabile (1998) proposes three main ingredients that lead to creativity in an individual: creative thinking skills, expertise, and motivation. Creative thinking skills refer to how people approach problems and solutions as well as their ability to put existing concepts together in nontraditional combinations. Expertise includes all that a person knows and can do in carrying out a task or job. It is difficult to be realistically creative if one does not possess all the information and skills needed to put ideas together in unexpected ways.

According to Amabile (1998), how a person uses expertise and creative thinking skills is often determined by motivation. There are two types of motivation, *extrinsic* and *intrinsic*. Extrinsic motivation comes from outside the person and usually involves rewards for completing a job and punishment for not. Although extrinsic motivation does not deter creativity, it rarely helps it either. True creativity is likely to come forth when the driving force is an internal desire to do something. This is intrinsic motivation. In this instance, the work itself is motivating, and the person engages in it for the challenge and the enjoyment.

Are Creativity and Leadership Separate Characteristics?

Creativity, of course, comes in many forms. For some, it is the ability to create an artistic product, such as an oil painting, a watercolor, or a symphony. For others, it is a way of looking at a problem and creating unexpected or nontraditional solutions. When this type of problem solver is the leader of an organization, the approach can be referred to as creative leadership.

Numerous research studies have investigated the nature of creativity and creative persons. Some have looked at successful leaders in schools and other organizations. But few studies have examined the relationship between creativity and leadership. In fact, the term *creative leadership* is seldom found in the research literature. Simonton (1984) maintained that the attributes of creativity and leadership had few distinctions because creativity is merely a variety of leadership. Subsequent researchers disagree, however, noting that creativity and leadership have separate components that may exist in varying degrees in one individual.

Norris (1990), suggests that educational leaders are creative when they have a broad knowledge base of educational theory, can analyze current situations in light of what they should be, and can conceptualize ways of bringing about change.

Developing Personal Creativity

What makes a person creative, and more important, what makes a person creative in the workplace? There are no simple answers to these questions. Researchers tend to explain creativity in the context of the workplace through a variety of perspectives, including attributes, conceptual skills, or the process of personal talents mixing with external influences. Here is a brief summary of each of these four perspectives (Gundry, Kickul, and Prather, 1994).

The Attribute Theory. This theory holds that people who possess certain attributes, such as openness, independence, autonomy, and spontaneity, are likely to be creative. The old notion, however, that people were born with these attributes has given way in recent years to the idea that most of them can be learned.

The Conceptual Skills Theory. Researchers who support this theory describe creativity as a set of skills that involve solving problems through unconventional means as well as visualizing models and modifying them. These individuals combine the factual, scientific information from their senses with a more intuitive, visual approach which enables them to see intangible patterns and relationships.

The Behavioral Theory. The behavioral theory of creativity focuses on the actions one takes to bring something new into being in response to a problem or situation. This view implies the need to reinforce desirable creative behaviors.

The Process Theory. Holding that creativity is a highly complex, multifaceted phenomenon, this view essentially combines some aspects of the other theories. Adherents suggest that creativity is the result of how individuals allow their talents, skills, and actions to interact with the task at hand and within the organizational context. This process will allow some new object or concept to be brought into existence to manage the situation.

These perspectives resulted mainly from research on leaders in industrial and business organizations. In an effort to find a link between the attributes of creativity and leadership in schools, Goertz (2000) conducted a study to determine if school principals who were perceived as effective leaders also displayed creativity. To measure creativity, she selected eight variables that emerged from an extensive review of relevant research studies, including the work of Amabile (1998). The variables and their definitions for the study were the following:

▶ *Passion for work,* the ability to mix personal and professional energy and enthusiasm

- *Independence,* the ability to initiate and sustain autonomous thought and action
- *Goal setting,* the ability to select a task and complete it
- *Originality,* the ability to develop novel approaches in problem solving
- *Flexibility,* the ability to adapt to new situations and ideas
- *Wide range of interests,* shows interest in a variety of subjects and participates in events
- *Intelligence,* beyond an IQ of 120
- *Motivation,* the need to achieve in all attempted activities and to self-evaluate

Goertz used a previously validated questionnaire and an in-depth interview to study four principals who had been deemed highly effective by their supervisors. Specifically, she wanted to see to what extent effective principals saw themselves as using the variables. The following is a summary of her findings.

Variable	Principals' Responses
Passion for Work	All participants felt they were hard workers and had a high degree of passion in what they did. They said they were persistent in looking for ways to solve problems and were strong champions for the mission of their school. They had positive attitudes about their work and thought of themselves as effective role models.
Independence	The principals exhibited independence of thought but were careful not to ignore the impact their decisions had on their staff. Principals valued having the authority to act independently through site-based management because it allowed them to take risks and find unusual ways to solve problems.
Goal Setting	The principals perceived themselves as having clear goals which they pursued relentlessly. For the most part, they completed what they started.
Originality	The principals frequently looked for unconventional ways to solve problems and to get things done. They also encouraged staff and students to propose solutions.
Flexibility	The principals demonstrated flexibility in problem solving

by generating a variety of ideas rather than quantity. They also were more adaptable to change.

Wide Range of Interests	They all had a wide range of interests which they felt allowed them to seek out alternative solutions to problems before a conventional one.
Intelligence	For these principals, intellectual play was as important as intellectual work. They exhibited intellectual curiosity by asking questions, taking risks, and listening and talking to people.
Motivation	These principals admitted that they had high levels of self-confidence and enthusiasm. They strongly expressed their opinions and pushed people to do more than they thought they could.

Variables of creativity were clearly a part of the leadership style displayed by the effective principals in this study. To fulfill their mission in today's rapidly changing world, schools need leaders who cannot only influence others to achieve goals, but who have the creativity to seek new ways to create and manage change—in short, the creative principal. Such a creative leader is flexible, enthusiastic, passionate, and purposeful. The creative administrator stands up for what is right, is willing to try new things, and is a motivator of people.

Making Schools Creative Organizations

LEADER'S QUESTION: Do I display traits associated with creativity? SEE TIP #2.3

For school leaders to be creative and think outside the box, they must share the values, behaviors, and norms that foster and reward creativity. Their behavior signals the school community whether creativity will be welcomed, ignored, or rebuffed. School leaders show that they embrace creative ideas and behaviors when they (1) encourage others to question standard practices that are not working, (2) build a school culture that welcomes constructive criticism and new ideas, and (3) organize opportunities for students and faculty to get together periodically to discuss innovative ways for furthering the school's mission.

The creative approach to problem solving is more likely to be effective when used on matters

- ▸ That are really important
- ▸ That are measurable and quantitative so progress can be measured
- ▸ Where all the stakeholders are committed to finding a solution
- ▸ Where there is no easy, obvious, or preconceived solution.

To be successful at developing a creative organization, all stakeholders in the school community need to have educational opportunities that build their creative thinking, problem-solving, and process skills. Then the stakeholders must apply these skills in realistic situations that recognize the outside limits of what can be done. All this must occur in an environment that welcomes creative approaches, implements them, and evaluates their success. When these three components come together, creativity is likely to flourish in the school organization (Figure 2.7).

Educating for Creativity

Remember that the human brain is programmed to be creative. Looking at patterns to solve problems is the brain's specialty. But it needs practice in examining new approaches to problem solving. Educating for creativity means instruction and training in the basics of creative thinking, along with the skills necessary to generate new, practical, and unexpected ideas.

Applying the Creative Process

Education about creative techniques is not enough. People must also learn to use these techniques to address an important problem or issue. This practice keeps the group focused and produces specific recommendations for action.

Dimensions of the Creative School's Environment

The climate in which staff and students carry out their work greatly influences the amount of creative thinking that flourishes in the school and district. Even in schools where significant resources are devoted to training students and staff in creativity, change is unlikely to occur unless the environment enables and supports the implementation of the ideas proposed by its members.

Gundry et al. (1994) suggest that the degree to which the environment of an organization supports creativity can be assessed along the following 10 dimensions:

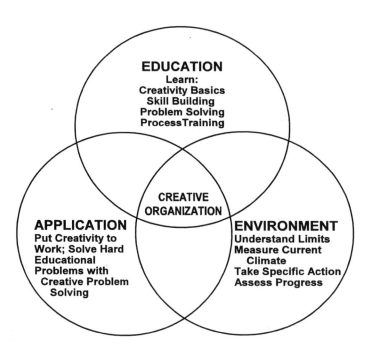

Figure 2.7 Creative organizations result when the members are trained in appropriate skills and use them to solve real problems, and do so in a climate that welcomes innovative approaches.

- *Freedom:* The degree to which individuals are given latitude in defining and carrying out their work.
- *Challenge:* The degree to which employees are "stretched" when doing their job.
- *Idea Support:* The way in which new ideas are received and treated by the administration.

  - *Dynamism:* The degree to which employees feel that the school is an active and exciting place to work.
  - *Risk Taking:* The degree to which employees feel comfortable making mistakes when trying out new ideas and a sense of how much ambiguity will be tolerated.
  - *Idea Time:* The amount of time employees use to develop new ideas and new possibilities.
  - *Trust and Openness:* The degree of emotional safety that employees feel in their working relationships with colleagues.

> **LEADER'S QUESTION:**
> How can I foster creativity in my school?
> SEE TIP #2.4

- *Conflicts:* The degree to which employees engage in personal conflicts.
- *Humor:* The degree to which spontaneity and humor exist, and employees are at ease in their working relationships.
- *Debates:* The degree to which employees feel free to actively debate issues, and the degree to which minority views are readily expressed and listened to with an open mind.

> **LEADER'S QUESTION: Is the climate in my school or district supportive of creative behaviors? SEE TIP #2.5**

Assessing the degree to which these dimensions exist in an organization can be very useful. Nevertheless, performing such an assessment but doing nothing to make improvements may further deteriorate the organizational climate. Therefore, the school or district should first make a commitment to undertake appropriate action based on the results of the assessment.

Pitfalls to Avoid When Developing a Creative Environment

Here are four common mistakes leaders make when attempting to get organizations to think and behave creatively (Gundry et al., 1994).

1. *Defining the Problem Incorrectly.* If the problem is not correctly defined, then staff members will end up addressing the wrong issues. For example, one high school examined ways to encourage more students to get to school on time in the morning. After much investigation it turned out that the real problem was an overtaxed school bus transportation schedule. Their efforts had to be refocused to address the correct problem.

2. *Judging Ideas Too Quickly.* Staff members will be reluctant to offer new ideas if they feel that their suggestions will be rejected by their colleagues or the administration without much thought. Creative ideas can be quickly squashed by killer phrases, such as "We have always done it this way," or "That proposal will cost too much," coupled with convergent thinking that implies there is only one way to accomplish something.

3. *Stopping With the First Good Idea.* Because of the pressure to solve problems quickly, people will often focus on the first good idea that emerges. The first idea is not necessarily the best, however, and the planning group should avoid stopping there. More brainstorming is likely to produce other ideas, some of which might be more practical and doable than the first.

4. *Failing to Get Support.* Few major changes can take place successfully in schools without the support of those affected by the change. Moreover, creative problem solvers must seek out those who are likely to oppose change and involve them early on in defining the problem, generating ideas, and planning a course of action.

Creativity and Empowerment

Creative people are not likely to remain creative if they feel powerless to implement their ideas. For meaningful change to occur in schools, staff members need to be empowered so that they can make choices, feel committed, take appropriate risks, be imaginative, and get involved. Of course, the choices that staff members make are limited to some extent by the federal, state, and local policies that govern and control educational organizations. Nonetheless, when workers are empowered to make choices, they are more likely to be creative.

> **LEADER'S QUESTION:** How can I develop a climate of creativity and empowerment in my school organization? SEE TIP #2.6

Creativity and empowerment are similar in many ways. They both result in individual expressions of independence, commitment, risk taking, and decision making. They flourish together in a climate that is receptive of change, and they are both in short supply in our schools.

Despite their similarities, creativity and empowerment have a few important differences. In simple terms, empowerment can be defined as the belief people have about their ability to exercise choice; creativity is the process that develops the choices. Some empowered people are not creative, and some creative people are not empowered. But when creative people *are* empowered, great things can happen.

Research studies conducted by Velthouse (1990) suggest that people who are both creative and empowered are characterized by self-confidence, self-control, self-efficacy, and self-awareness. They see their work environment as filled with alternatives and, therefore, tend to be visionary, imaginative, and optimistic about the future.

Here again, we see the importance of the environment which, in school organizations, is largely determined by the educational leaders. In most cases, these leaders also decide exactly whether and how much the staff members will be empowered. Those leaders intent on developing both creativity and empowerment need to consider using both cognitive and behavioral approaches.

The *cognitive approach* recognizes that the environment can influence thinking patterns and thus determine the extent that an individual can feel empowered to do creative things. Using this approach, leaders provide training to the staff, broaden their awareness of opportunities and options, and provide positive feedback on the staff's performance.

The *behavioral approach* recognizes that people can be creative and feel empowered when they are encouraged to carry out certain behaviors. For example, leaders can delegate authority, establish challenging goals for certain individuals, and even assign a devil's advocate.

The Downside of Creativity and Empowerment

It would be naive to ignore that both creativity and empowerment have negative aspects. Especially in schools, some creativity can be disruptive if it involves new interpretations of rules and regulations or affects time-sensitive events. Creative people may be dissatisfied with the status quo, impatient in their interactions with others, and estranged from their colleagues. Empowered people may not use their power wisely in some instances. They may ignore too much structure or discard too many rules and procedures.

These negative aspects can often deter leaders from encouraging creativity or empowering their staff. On the other hand, the many positive payoffs that emerge from a creative organization far outweigh these occasional irritations.

IMAGERY (VISUALIZATION)

Imagery (also called *visualization*) is the most basic cerebral language we have. Nearly everything we do in our mind is processed through images. This mental visualization of objects, events, and arrays represents a major way of storing information in the brain. Recall of those images can be provoked by tastes, smells, sounds, or a combination of sensory stimuli.

For most people, the left hemisphere specializes in coding information verbally, whereas the right hemisphere codes information visually. Imagery can take place in two ways: *imaging* is the visualization in the mind of something that the person has actually experienced; *imagining* depicts something the person has not yet experienced and, therefore, has no limits.

A mental image is a pictorial representation of something physical or of an experience. The more information an image contains, the richer it is. Some people are more capable of forming rich images than others, but the research evidence is clear: Individuals can be taught to search their minds for images and be guided through the process to select appropriate images that, through hemispheric integration, enhance learning and increase retention. When the brain creates images, the same parts of the visual cortex are activated as when the eyes process real-world input. Thus, the powerful visual processing system is available even when the brain is creating internal pictures in the mind's eye (Sousa, 2001a).

Implications of Imagery for Leaders

Imagery is such a powerful mental language that it influences our behavior and even our health. For example, the most common type of imagery is worry, and people in leadership positions tend to have plenty of opportunities to worry over matters within their area of responsibility. Continuing concern over job-related events, such as an impending parent meeting, developing a budget, a potential promotion, an upcoming speech, or a supervisory conference with a recalcitrant teacher, can affect the personality of a leader as well as induce stress, headaches, and a variety of other ailments. Learning to control and direct mental images can lead to better mental and physical health and help the leader combat the stress, tension, and anxiety that come with positions of responsibility.

Athletes use imagery all the time. Numerous research studies with athletes and other performers have shown that forming mental images can dramatically enhance performance. Imagery can also enhance mental processes, such as decision making and problem solving. Covey (1989) suggested that deliberate and positive mental images (he called them affirmations) can help us get through situations that might otherwise raise our anger. To be effective, the images had to be personal, positive, emotional, visual, and stated in the present tense. A possible affirmation before that supervisory conference with the obstinate teacher, for example, might be the following: "I will be very satisfied (emotional) if I (personal) respond (present tense) to the obstinate teacher with self-control and with useful suggestions for change" (positive). The mental statement should be followed by visualizations of possible verbal patterns and conference scenarios that can offer positive suggestions for changing the teacher's behavior.

LEADER'S QUESTION: What are the basic steps I should know to use imagery successfully? SEE TIP #2.7

Imagery is a valuable asset for leaders, allowing them to visualize every detail meticulously in their minds before carrying out the plan. When they do, it is likely to be done flawlessly because most of the problems have been solved during the visualization phase. Two recent studies on imagery may provide a partial explanation of why this is so. In one study, Ishai and Sagi (1997) used video displays to determine if imagery had a great effect on short-term or long-term memory. They found that imagery seemed to be particularly helpful in stimulating working (short-term) memory, rather than recalling a stored one, particularly if the participant was learning a new task.

Using PET scans, Mellet and his colleagues discovered that mental imagery stimulated not only the visual processing areas of the brain (occipital lobe) but also activated regions in the parietal and frontal lobes where higher-order thinking is carried out. They also found that the frontal lobe stimulation increased even more when the participant heard a verbal description of the mental image (Mellet, Tzourio-Mazoyer, Bricogne, Mazoyer, Kosslyn, and Denis, 2000). This finding implies that talking aloud about the mental image might provoke increased higher-order processing in the frontal lobes than just the image itself.

Educational leaders can use imagery in all areas of their lives: before a school board meeting, a faculty meeting, or a difficult confrontation with a colleague or family member. By previewing the situation mentally, and seeing it clearly, vividly, and repeatedly with all its possibilities, the individual creates an internal comfort zone so that the situation is no longer foreign or worrisome.

This chapter has focused on describing some basic brain structures and their functions as well as linking higher-level brain processing to the attributes of leadership and creativity. Several self-assessment instruments are included to provide leaders with greater insight into their own strengths, weaknesses, and preferences. These insights will help leaders determine how they can best initiate meaningful change in their educational organizations. The first change may be in what we teach. The next chapter suggests come considerations for designing a general curriculum that is likely to be compatible with today's students.

MAJOR POINTS IN CHAPTER 2

❏ Educational leaders need to have a working knowledge of how research in the neurosciences is expanding our understanding of how the brain learns.

❏ Learning is the process by which we *acquire* new knowledge and skills; memory is the process by which we *retain* knowledge and skills for the future. Learning does not always involve long-term retention.

❏ The left and right hemispheres of the brain are specialized for certain functions. This specialization can lead to lateral preferences that influence our personality, abilities, and learning style.

❏ The frontal lobe is the executive system of the brain, responsible for problem solving and higher-order thinking. Its interpretations determine personality, creativity, and motivation.

❏ Researchers tend to explain creativity in the context of the workplace through a variety of perspectives, including attributes, conceptual skills, or the process of personal talents mixing with external influences. Some attributes of creative leadership are passion for work, independence, originality, flexibility, wide range of interests, intelligence, and motivation.

❏ The 10 dimensions that help assess the openness of an organization to creativity are freedom, challenge, idea support, dynamism, risk taking, idea time, trust and openness, conflicts, humor, and debates.

❏ Four common mistakes that are made when trying to get members of an organization to behave creatively are the following: defining the problem incorrectly, judging ideas too quickly, stopping with the first good idea, and failing to obtain adequate support for change.

❏ Creative people need to be empowered to implement change. Educational leaders can use cognitive and behavioral approaches to establish a work environment that both cultivates creativity and promotes empowerment.

❏ Imagery enables leaders to be more successful in dealing with the stressful situations they encounter in their jobs. Some people visualize more easily than others, but most can become adept at imagery through consistent practice.

TIPS FOR LEADERS #2.1

Self-Assessment on Brain Structures and Their Functions

1. List at least one function of each of the brain's four lobes:
   Frontal lobe:_____
   Temporal: _____
   Occipital: _____
   Parietal: _____

2. What does the motor cortex control?_____

3. What functions are controlled by the cerebellum?_____
   _____

4. What does each of the following structures in the limbic area control?
   Thalamus: _____
   Hippocampus: _____
   Amygdala: _____

5. What is the main function of the corpus callosum? _____
   _____

6. Briefly describe the following:
   Neuron: _____
   Axon: _____
   Dendrite: _____
   Neurotransmitter: _____

7. The major difference between learning and retention is _____
   _____

TIPS FOR LEADERS #2.2

Testing Your Hemispheric Preference

Several instruments exist to help individuals assess their hemispheric preference. The one below takes just a few minutes. The results are only an indication of your preference and are not conclusive. You should use additional instruments to collect more data before reaching any firm conclusion about your hemispheric preference (Sousa, 2001a).

Directions: From each pair below, circle A or B corresponding to the sentence that best describes you. Answer all questions. There are no right or wrong answers.

1.   A.   I prefer to find my own way of doing a new task.
      B.   I prefer to be told the best way to do a new task.

2.   A.   I have to make my own plans.
      B.   I can follow anyone's plans.

3.   A.   I am a very flexible and occasionally unpredictable person.
      B.   I am a very stable and consistent person.

4.   A.   I keep everything in a particular place.
      B.   Where I keep things depends on what I am doing.

5.   A.   I spread my work evenly over the time I have.
      B.   I prefer to do my work at the last minute.

6.   A.   I know I am right because I have good reasons.
      B.   I know when I am right, even without reasons.

7.   A.   I need a lot of variety and change in my life.
      B.   I need a well-planned and orderly life.

8.   A.   I sometimes have too many ideas in a new situation.
      B.   I sometimes have no ideas in a new situation.

9.   A.   I do easy things first and the important things last.
      B.   I do the important things first and the easy things last.

10.   A.   I choose what I know is right when making a hard decision.
      B.   I choose what I feel is right when making a hard decision.

11. A. I plan my time for doing my work.
    B. I don't think about the time when I work.

12. A. I usually have good self-discipline.
    B. I usually act on my feelings.

13. A. Other people don't understand how I organize things.
    B. Other people think I organize things well.

14. A. I agree with new ideas before other people do.
    B. I question new ideas more than other people do.

15. A. I tend to think more in pictures.
    B. I tend to think more in words.

16. A. I try to find the one best way to solve a problem.
    B. I try to find different ways to solve a problem.

17. A. I can usually analyze what is going to happen next.
    B. I can usually sense what is going to happen next.

18. A. I am not very imaginative in my work.
    B. I use my imagination in nearly everything I do.

19. A. I begin many jobs that I never finish.
    B. I finish a job before starting a new one.

20. A. I look for new ways to do old jobs.
    B. When one way works well, I don't change it.

21. A. It is fun to take risks.
    B. I have fun without taking risks.

Scoring the Instrument:

Count the number of "A" responses to questions
1, 3, 7, 8, 9, 13, 14, 15, 19, 20, and 21. Place that
number on the line to the right.   A._____

Count the number of "B" responses to the remaining
questions. Place that number on the line to the right.   B._____

Total the "A" and "B" responses you counted.   Total _____

The total indicates your hemispheric preference according to the following scale:

0–5	Strong left hemisphere preference
6–8	Moderate left hemisphere preference
9–12	Bilateral hemisphere balance (little or no preference)
13–15	Moderate right hemisphere preference
16–21	Strong right hemisphere preference

Were you surprised by your score? Why or why not?

_____

_____

What implications does your score have for your approach to leadership?

_____

_____

TIPS FOR LEADERS #2.3

Assessing Your Creative Traits

Directions: Using the scale as a guide, circle the number that best represents the extent to which each statement reflects your behavior. When done, read the section on **Interpreting the Results.** There are no right or wrong answers.

Scale: Never	Infrequently	Sometimes	Frequently	Always
1 ---------------	2 ---------------	3 ---------------	4 --------------	5

1. I enjoy going to work each day.　　　　1 ----- 2 ----- 3 ----- 4 ----- 5

2. I have a clear vision of my goals for this organization.　　　　1 ----- 2 ----- 3 ----- 4 ----- 5

3. I am willing to listen to unusual solutions offered by others.　　　　1 ----- 2 ----- 3 ----- 4 ----- 5

4. I am curious about a lot of different things that can affect this organization.　　　　1 ----- 2 ----- 3 ----- 4 ----- 5

5. I am enthusiastic about my own ideas.　　　　1 ----- 2 ----- 3 ----- 4 ----- 5

6. I communicate my goals for this organization to the staff.　　　　1 ----- 2 ----- 3 ----- 4 ----- 5

7. I look for creative ways to solve problems.　　　　1 ----- 2 ----- 3 ----- 4 ----- 5

8. I analyze potential solutions for their advantages and disadvantages.　　　　1 ----- 2 ----- 3 ----- 4 ----- 5

9. I am enthusiastic about my work.　　　　1 ----- 2 ----- 3 ----- 4 ----- 5

10. I prefer to work alone.　　　　1 ----- 2 ----- 3 ----- 4 ----- 5

11. When looking for solutions to problems, I prefer variety to quantity.　　　　1 ----- 2 ----- 3 ----- 4 ----- 5

Scale: Never	Infrequently	Sometimes	Frequently	Always
1 -------------	2 -------------	3 -------------	4 -------------	5

12. I am innovative in my approach to problem solving and decision making.
1 ----- 2 ----- 3 ----- 4 ----- 5

13. I display intellectual curiosity.
1 ----- 2 ----- 3 ----- 4 ----- 5

14. I have self-confidence.
1 ----- 2 ----- 3 ----- 4 ----- 5

15. Intellectual play is as important as intellectual work.
1 ----- 2 ----- 3 ----- 4 ----- 5

16. I am not comfortable with arbitrary rules.
1 ----- 2 ----- 3 ----- 4 ----- 5

17. I commit myself to those principles I believe in.
1 ----- 2 ----- 3 ----- 4 ----- 5

18. The goals of our school organization are achievable within a reasonable time frame.
1 ----- 2 ----- 3 ----- 4 ----- 5

19. I take chances.
1 ----- 2 ----- 3 ----- 4 ----- 5

20. I adapt to change.
1 ----- 2 ----- 3 ----- 4 ----- 5

21. I have a wide range of interests outside of my job.
1 ----- 2 ----- 3 ----- 4 ----- 5

22. I encourage staff to explore new ways to solve old problems.
1 ----- 2 ----- 3 ----- 4 ----- 5

23. I encourage others to understand my views.
1 ----- 2 ----- 3 ----- 4 ----- 5

24. I enjoy pursuing the "what if" types of questions.
1 ----- 2 ----- 3 ----- 4 ----- 5

25. I have a clear vision of this organization's mission.
1 ----- 2 ----- 3 ----- 4 ----- 5

26. I lose track of the number of hours I spend on my job.
1 ----- 2 ----- 3 ----- 4 ----- 5

27. I enjoy deviating from routine.
1 ----- 2 ----- 3 ----- 4 ----- 5

Scale: Never	Infrequently	Sometimes	Frequently	Always
1 ---------------	2 ---------------	3 ---------------	4 -------------	5

28. I try to give the staff as much time as needed to generate a variety of ideas for solving problems.　　1 ----- 2 ----- 3 ----- 4 -----5

29. Listening to others is one of the most important parts of my job.　　1 ----- 2 ----- 3 ----- 4 ----- 5

30. I can draw on my experiences outside my job to solve job-related problems.　　1 ----- 2 ----- 3 ----- 4 ----- 5

31. I present my ideas to others enthusiastically.　　1 ----- 2 ----- 3 ----- 4 ----- 5

32. I look at my work as play.　　1 ----- 2 ----- 3 ----- 4 ----- 5

33. Site-based management makes a lot of sense to me.　　1 ----- 2 ----- 3 ----- 4 ----- 5

34. I consider myself to be an effective role model.　　1 ----- 2 ----- 3 ----- 4 ----- 5

35. Major initiatives must be consistent with the goals I have set for this organization.　　1 ----- 2 ----- 3 ----- 4 ----- 5

36. I recognize that the solutions to some problems may have to wait until the next school year.　　1 ----- 2 ----- 3 ----- 4 ----- 5

37. I tend to get input from lots of sources when solving a problem.　　1 ----- 2 ----- 3 ----- 4 ----- 5

38. I encourage people to do more than they think they can.　　1 ----- 2 ----- 3 ----- 4 ----- 5

39. I enjoy taking risks in my job.　　1 ----- 2 ----- 3 ----- 4 ----- 5

40. I support and give credit to others who have creative ideas.　　1 ----- 2 ----- 3 ----- 4 ----- 5

41. I am persistent when it comes to solving problems.　　1 ----- 2 ----- 3 ----- 4 ----- 5

Scale: Never	Infrequently	Sometimes	Frequently	Always
1 ---------------	2 ---------------	3 ---------------	4 --------------	5

42. I am able to complete the work that is directed toward my goals.

1 ----- 2 ----- 3 ----- 4 ----- 5

43. I do not feel like I have to make the same decisions that my fellow administrators do.

1 ----- 2 ----- 3 ----- 4 ----- 5

44. When forming a committee, I want to have a wide variety of views represented.

1 ----- 2 ----- 3 ----- 4 ----- 5

45. I am willing to implement solutions offered by others.

1 ----- 2 ----- 3 ----- 4 ----- 5

46. When I have to solve a problem, I ask questions.

1 ----- 2 ----- 3 ----- 4 ----- 5

47. By setting a good example, I move people to do good things.

1 ----- 2 ----- 3 ----- 4 ----- 5

48. I seek out conventional solutions to problems as a last resort.

1 ----- 2 ----- 3 ----- 4 ----- 5

Source: Adapted and revised by D. Sousa from Goertz (2000)

Interpreting the Results

The 48 questions are designed to elicit responses related to the eight categories of creative traits suggested by Amabile (1998) and Goertz (2000). To get a profile of how you perceived yourself in each of the eight areas, you will need to enter your responses in the following chart.

Directions: On the line to the right of each question, enter the number you circled as your response. When done, add the six numbers across the row and put the total on the line in the **Total Across Row** column. (Note: The total for each row cannot exceed 30.)

						Total Across Row	Trait
1.__	9.__	17.__	26.__	34.__	41.__	_____	Passion for Work
10.__	16.__	24.__	33.__	39.__	43.__	_____	Independence
2.__	6.__	18.__	25.__	35.__	42.__	_____	Goal Setting
7.__	12.__	22.__	27.__	37.__	44.__	_____	Originality
3.__	11.__	20.__	28.__	36.__	45.__	_____	Flexibility
4.__	15.__	21.__	30.__	40.__	48.__	_____	Wide Range of Interests
8.__	13.__	19.__	29.__	32.__	46.__	_____	Intelligence
5.__	14.__	23.__	31.__	38.__	47.__	_____	Motivation

You can judge the weight of your score as follows:

6-9:   You perceive yourself as exhibiting this trait **almost never.**
10-14: You perceive yourself as exhibiting this trait **seldom.**
15-20: You perceive yourself as exhibiting this trait **regularly.**
21-25: You perceive yourself as exhibiting this trait **frequently.**
26-30: You perceive yourself as exhibiting this trait **almost always.**

Were you surprised by your results? Why or why not?

_____

_____

_____

TIPS FOR LEADERS #2.4

Steps for Fostering Creativity
in School Organizations

- Encourage others to question what they are doing and how they are doing it with the view of finding better working methods.

- Provide professional development opportunities that offer staff unconventional ways of solving problems related to their practice.

- Discuss with faculty members both individually and as a group ways in which they can all improve their services to students.

- Do things that bring a sense of identity and belonging to a special culture, such as giving out pencils, tee shirts, and other items imprinted with the school's (or district's) name and logo. Make it a point to serve food at meetings.

- Look for ways for the staff and students to get together in informal settings to share ideas about creative ways to solve problems or deal with unexpected situations.

- Provide workshops and other training opportunities for students and staff to develop their creative thinking and problem-solving skills.

TIPS FOR LEADERS #2.5

Assessing the School's or District's Climate for Supporting Creativity

Directions: Using the scale as a guide, circle the number that best represents the current climate in your school organization. When done, read the section on **Interpreting the Results.** Note that by substituting "students" for "staff" where appropriate, this survey can also indicate the organization's receptivity to creative behaviors in students.

Scale: Never	Infrequently	Sometimes	Frequently	Always
1 -------------	2 -------------	3 -------------	4 -------------	5

1. Staff members are encouraged to improve their content knowledge and instructional skills.

   1 ----- 2 ----- 3 ----- 4 ----- 5

2. Staff members participate in decisions involving topics of importance to them.

   1 ----- 2 ----- 3 ----- 4 ----- 5

3. Staff members are given latitude in deciding how to define their jobs.

   1 ----- 2 ----- 3 ----- 4 ----- 5

4. Staff members are given latitude in deciding how to carry out their jobs.

   1 ----- 2 ----- 3 ----- 4 ----- 5

5. Staff members describe this school/ district as an exciting place to work.

   1 ----- 2 ----- 3 ----- 4 ----- 5

6. Staff members trust each other.

   1 ----- 2 ----- 3 ----- 4 ----- 5

7. Staff members trust the administration.

   1 ----- 2 ----- 3 ----- 4 ----- 5

8. The administration trusts staff members.

   1 ----- 2 ----- 3 ----- 4 ----- 5

9. Staff members are given time during their workday to discuss new ideas and possibilities.

   1 ----- 2 ----- 3 ----- 4 ----- 5

Scale: Never	Infrequently	Sometimes	Frequently	Always
1 -------------	2 -------------	3 -------------	4 -------------	5

10. Staff members feel at ease in faculty meetings.

1 ----- 2 ----- 3 ----- 4 ----- 5

11. Humor (not sarcasm) is part of our meetings.

1 ----- 2 ----- 3 ----- 4 ----- 5

12. Staff members get along with each other.

1 ----- 2 ----- 3 ----- 4 ----- 5

13. The administration gets along with staff members.

1 ----- 2 ----- 3 ----- 4 ----- 5

14. The administration conveys to the staff that it welcomes new ideas.

1 ----- 2 ----- 3 ----- 4 ----- 5

15. The administration treats new ideas from staff members with respect.

1 ----- 2 ----- 3 ----- 4 ----- 5

16. The administration conveys to the staff that it welcomes debate over important issues.

1 ----- 2 ----- 3 ----- 4 ----- 5

17. The administration listens to minority views with an open mind.

1 ----- 2 ----- 3 ----- 4 ----- 5

18. The administration is supportive of staff members who take appropriate risks to try out new ideas.

1 ----- 2 ----- 3 ----- 4 ----- 5

Number of circles in each column:
(Total across should add to 18)

1___ 2___ 3___ 4___ 5___

Interpreting the Results:

Profile: After completing the survey connect the circles with straight lines to get a graphic profile of the extent to which the organizational climate supports creative behaviors in its staff. Lots of left to right sways of the profile line indicate multiple inconsistencies in the organizational climate for creative behaviors. A smoother line (e.g., a line running mostly through the number 3) indicates consistency in the climate of the organization within that scale range (in this example,"Sometimes").

Column Totals: Total the number of circles in each range and insert them in the spaces at the bottom of the survey. These totals reveal the frequency of each of the scale choices and should add up to 18 (the number of responses). Look at how the totals are distributed along the scale. If, for example, there are nine or more circles (i.e., 50 percent or more) in the *Never* and *Infrequently* columns, then the school or district organization is not providing a consistently open climate for creative behaviors. On the other hand, a total of nine or more responses in the *Frequently* and *Always* columns indicates a climate where creativity is valued.

Were you surprised by the survey results? Why or why not?

_____

_____

If any areas got low scores, what can you or the staff do to improve those areas?

_____

_____

_____

TIPS FOR LEADERS #2.6

Developing a Climate for Creativity and Empowerment in a School Organization

Educational leaders can use both cognitive and behavioral approaches to develop creativity and empowerment together (Velthouse, 1990).

Cognitive Approaches

- Explain which alternative scenarios are possible and encourage creative thinking. If things go wrong, avoid blaming, identify the contributing factors, and focus on alternatives for the next time.

- Provide opportunities for staff to improve their creative skills as they relate to organizational goals.

- Ensure that all staff members, including janitors, cafeteria workers, bus drivers, and aides, are included in this training so that they recognize how their job performance contributes to the success of the total organization.

- Focus on the goals of the school organization and let the staff exercise choice and be creative in their approaches so that they can determine new ways to serve. Avoid criticizing new approaches that do not work.

- When giving feedback at supervisory sessions, emphasize the capabilities, skills, and competence of the staff members. Act as a coach to improve performance while expressing confidence in their abilities.

- Provide opportunities for staff members to observe each other in the workplace and to share ideas. In high school, encourage teachers to observe colleagues in different departments to get a fresh slant on teaching techniques.

- Discourage responses that are commonplace or are given just in hopes of winning administrative approval. Practice brainstorming in staff meetings to encourage and expand on new ideas.

- Relax rules that are there just to maintain bureaucracy. The extent of creativity and empowerment is inversely related to the number of rules and procedures used by the organization. Where possible, develop a set of organizational values (e.g., intellectual honesty, quality, and commitment) to guide behavior rather than step-by-step procedures.

Behavioral Approaches

- When possible, give staff members stimulating assignments outside their routine and focus on the stimulating aspect of the job. Assignments to curriculum writing committees or accreditation review committees can be seen as deadly unless school leaders indicate that the assignment has real potential for changing what is taught or can permanently alter other aspects of the school's operation.

- Delegate authority when possible. Making individuals responsible for new tasks tends to make them act responsibly.

- Assign a staff member the role of asking the "what if" questions. It is a stimulating experience for the staff member and keeps all others alert to new possibilities and problems. Rotate the role periodically.

TIPS FOR LEADERS #2.7

Some Basic Steps for Using Imagery Successfully

Just about everyone can use imagery successfully with patience and persistence. Like learning any other skill, practice and discipline are important.

- Start by practicing your imagery for 15 to 20 minutes a day. As you become more skilled and comfortable with the technique, you will be able to do it for just a few minutes for each occasion that you want it.

- Imagery works best when you are relaxed. Find a quiet area, take off your shoes, and sit comfortably in a chair. Dim the lights if possible, take a few deep breaths, and close your eyes. Picture yourself descending an imaginary staircase until you feel completely relaxed.

- Next, imagine the scene that will soon take place (a supervisory conference, for example) and place yourself in it. When you feel comfortable in the image, direct your mind toward what you would like to see happen during the conference. If several possibilities come to mind, choose one and stick with it for that imagery session. Visualize the steps you want to take during the real conference. If possible, say them aloud so that the auditory input strengthens the image and the decision-making process.

- When finished, picture yourself climbing back up the imaginary staircase and gradually become aware of your surroundings. Open your eyes, stretch your limbs, and go on with your day.

Brain-Compatible Curriculum

Designing curriculum for students of the 21st century is no easy feat for several reasons. First, students come to school today with a different set of expectations about learning than did students of just 15 years ago. Second, schools are being asked to provide more of the services that used to be provided in the home by the family. Third, students who have learned how to learn are likely to be more successful in life than those who just amassed information.

For these three reasons alone, educational leaders need to continually review what is being taught in schools. They need to determine the extent that current curriculum can prepare students to be successful in a world where change is a constant, where technology will play an increasingly larger role, and where they will likely have seven different careers during their life span. To make sound judgments about an appropriate curriculum, we have to examine the set of expectations that students have about learning.

STUDENTS' EXPECTATIONS ABOUT LEARNING

Educators often remark that students today are very different in the way they learn from students of just a decade ago. They seem to have shorter attention spans and become bored more easily than ever before. Why is that? Is something happening in the environment of learners that alters the way they approach the learning process? Does this mean that more students will have learning problems? What should schools do to address this situation?

Students *are* different today and so are their brains. They have grown up in an environment different from their parents'. Beginning at birth (some say earlier), the brain is collecting information and learning from its environment. Here are some ways in which the brain of today is learning in an environment quite different from that of a few years ago.

- *The Home Is More Technologically Advanced Than the School.* The home environment of a child several decades ago was usually quiet—some might say even boring—compared with today. Parents and children did a lot of talking and reading, often together. The occasional radio program was an exciting event. For these children, school was an interesting place because it had films, field trips, and guest speakers—experiences not usually found at home. With few cultural distractions, school was an important influence in the life of a child and the primary source of new information. Today, many children have technology at home far exceeding that at school. Thus, the temptation is very great to stay home and play with video games and contact the World Wide Web.

- *The Impact of Novelty.* Family life, media, and other environmental stimuli moved slower decades ago. Today, children have become accustomed to rapid sensory and emotional changes in their environment and respond by engaging in all types of activities of short duration at home and in the malls. By acclimating itself to these changes, the brain is attracted more than ever to the unique and different—what neuroscientists call *novelty*. This attraction to novelty is not the result of any changes in the physical structures of the brain, but the result of neural associations and networks responding to the multiplicity of today's input.

- *Different Toys.* Compare the toys of this new millennium with the toys of the 1960s and 1970s. The major difference is advancing technology. Schoolchildren who were playing an inexpensive yet mentally challenging electronic game on the school bus may balk when met with a paper-and-pencil, fill-in-the-blank worksheet in the classroom.

- *Other Distractions Beside School.* Back a few years, school was essentially the most important and time-consuming factor for a child. Today, school is but one of *many* factors influencing our children. Even the younger students are wrestling with the need to be unique while under pressure to conform. As preteens enter puberty, they have to develop and deal with relationships, identify peer groups, and respond to religious influences without adequate maturity. They are often overscheduled, running from school to dance classes to soccer and softball games with barely enough time to eat a decent meal. Add to this mix the changes in family patterns and lifestyles, as well as the sometimes drastic effects of modern diets, drugs, and sleep deprivation, and one can realize how very different the environment of today's child is from that of just a decade ago.

Changing Sensory Preferences of Students

Dramatic changes in the environment have also had an impact on the sensory preferences of students. Our five senses collect enormous amounts of information from the environment. This information is filtered by the brain so that important data (e.g., a favorite television show) is processed while unimportant stimuli (e.g., background noise) is ignored. For most of us, the five primary senses do not all contribute equally to our learning. We have preferences. Just as most of us are either left-handed or right-handed, most of us also have sensory preferences, that is, we tend to favor one or two senses over the others when gathering information to deal with a complex learning situation. The preferences tend to be among the senses of sight, hearing, and kinesthetic-tactile (the expanded concept of touch).

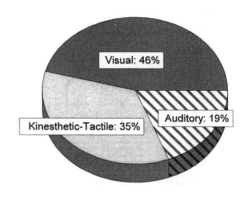

Figure 3.1 The sensory preferences of the U.S. student population in grades 3-12 for the mid-1990s. (Swanson, 1995; Sousa, 1997)

Although no one knows *exactly* what causes sensory preferences, the current explanation is that it is a mix of both mild genetic and strong environmental influences, especially in an individual's early years. Preferences, of course, are just that: *preferences*. They do not mean that the individual is not able to process with other senses. Just as a right-handed person can use the left hand with competence, a visually preferred person is able to use all the other senses when needed. But when faced with a complex task, most of us will rely more on our preferences to accomplish that task.

Studies of sensory preferences in schoolchildren throughout the past 40 years have shown shifts among the percentage of students with particular preferences. Figure 3.1 shows the best estimates for the sensory preferences of the student population in grades 3 to 12 in the mid-1990s (Sousa, 1997). Other studies have found similar results (Swanson, 1995). Note that nearly one-half of this population has a visual preference and just under one-fifth has an auditory preference. Yet, in too many secondary school classrooms, talk is the main mode of instruction, often accompanied by a minimal display of overheads or charts. More than one-third of students have a kinesthetic-tactile preference, indicating that movement helps their learning. But think of how much kids in secondary schools just sit at their desks, moving only to change classrooms.

To sum it up, students come to school today anticipating multisensory presentations of short duration that include technology. They expect emotional connections to their learning by becoming active participants, and they even expect to have some say in what they learn and how they are evaluated.

How Have Schools Changed?

Schools and teaching really haven't changed that much. A few teachers are holding their ground, hoping that the good old days will return. But the reality is that many students remark that school is a dull, nonengaging environment that is much less interesting than what is available outside of school. The computers used in many schools provide few of the options that students get with their more powerful computers at home. In high schools, lecturing continues to be the main method of instruction, and the overhead projector is sometimes the most advanced technology used. They have a difficult time focusing for extended periods and are easily distracted. Because they see little novelty and relevancy in what they are learning, they keep asking the relentless question, "Why do we need to know this?" Some teachers interpret this attitude as alienation from school while other teachers see it as a sign of a learning disability. In both instances, they are likely to refer the student for counseling and diagnosis. Consequently, it is possible that more children are being referred for special education evaluation not because they have true learning difficulties but because an inflexible (though well-meaning) school environment has not adapted to their changing brains.

> **LEADER'S QUESTION: What can I do to ensure that our schools accommodate the brain of today's student? SEE TIP #3.1**

It is extremely important that the characteristics we see in the brains of today's students are not viewed as good or bad, but just different. Some educators think they can change these brains back to those of the students they remember years ago. These teachers will insist, "We have to teach them to sit still and be quiet, because that's how I learned." This approach is not only frustrating, but futile. The environmental influences that helped design the cerebral networks and preferences have done their work in the early years of brain development. Rather than bemoan this new brain, why not adapt our curriculum and instruction to be of meaningful service to our students?

Educational leaders are in the unique position of making the appropriate adjustments to schools and classrooms that can accommodate these changing brains. As we gain a more scientifically based understanding about today's novel brain and how it learns, we must rethink what and how we teach. Maybe then more students will find schools to be exciting and dynamic places to learn about their talents and their world.

DECIDING WHAT SHOULD BE LEARNED

Structure of the 21st Century Curriculum

The organizational features of the curriculum needed to prepare students for the new millennium are considerably different from what schools have traditionally offered. As changes in all areas of society continue at a rapid pace, schools, too, must change their menu of offerings and their instructional techniques if they are to provide students with the knowledge and skills they will need to be successful adults.

The new curriculum should differ from the traditional curriculum in the following ways (Glatthorn and Jailall, 2000):

- *Skills and Knowledge.* The new curriculum will use both skills and knowledge to solve real-world, contextual problems, unlike the traditional curriculum, which puts an overemphasis on using just knowledge to solve contrived and isolated problems.
- *Depth of Coverage.* The new curriculum will place more emphasis on covering fewer topics in depth so that students can develop a real understanding and build conceptual frameworks about what they are learning, unlike the current "an inch thick and a mile wide" traditional curriculum.
- *Horizontal and Vertical Coordination.* The new curriculum will be highly coordinated in three ways: (1) by related subjects (e.g., mathematics coordinated with science), (2) across grade levels so that 6th grade mathematics builds on the 5th grade content, and (3) the sequence of units in a given subject should make sense. The traditional curriculum is replete with fragmentation.
- *Addressing Individual Differences.* The new curriculum will provide for a wide variety of abilities in the same classroom, using the techniques of differentiated curriculum and instruction. The traditional curriculum tries to teach students as through they all learn the same way.
- *Focus on Results.* The new curriculum has clearly delineated objectives written in a teacher-friendly format that focus on results and give less attention to mindless activities that are too often found in the traditional curriculum.
- *Common Core for All Students.* The new curriculum offers a common core that draws students and the school together rather than the traditional approach which sends students off in different directions through fragmentation.

- *Emphasis on Personal Relevance.* The new curriculum pays greater attention to learning that is personally relevant to students. It encourages students use their cognitive processes and a technological approach to solve problems.

Content of the 21st Century Curriculum

Selecting the specific topics and units to be included in a K–12 curriculum is not the purpose of this book. The intent here is to discuss some of the fundamental concepts about what should be learned as well as current approaches to curriculum and other designs that are more likely to be compatible with today's student.

If the purpose of schooling is to prepare today's students to be productive citizens in a changing society, then the content of the curriculum should center on the needs of our youth and the needs of society.

Needs of Our Youth

A child's brain is developing in a society where family structures are changing, human values are being questioned, widely different cultures are mixing and clashing, and few adults are taking responsibility for their actions. For this brain to feel secure in a learning environment and successful for its lifetime, Glatthorn and Jailall (2000) suggest that the new curriculum should

- ▶ Stress character development, including honesty and respect for others
- ▶ Be meaningful by helping students find purpose in what they are doing and make sense of their lives
- ▶ Make connections with the students' past and with their place as members of a future global community
- ▶ Reflect human values that transcend sectarian and ethnic differences and politics
- ▶ Stress the unity of the democratic traditions that bind us together while celebrating the diversity that is our strength
- ▶ Emphasize responsibility, recognizing that what we do to gratify our individual needs may have adverse effects on others

Needs of Society

Significant challenges face our nation in the near future. Out students will have to face, for example:

▶ *Aging*. The graying of our nation and the world will present all kinds of problems, including affordable home and medical care.

▶ *Technology*. The advent of new technologies that will extend and enrich the learning process.

▶ *Nationalism and Globalism*. The continued pressure for separatism across the globe and the impact of regional and global alliances.

▶ *Conflict*. Battles between ethnic groups, cultures, and nations.

▶ *Equity*. The fight for fairness in the distribution of the world's resources.

▶ *Alienation*. The loss of commitment to religious institutions, political parties, and moral and ethical codes.

▶ *Continuing Change*. An unstable world where changes occur frequently in all aspects of our culture, including family, leisure, work, and technology.

No pre-established curriculum can expect to anticipate the learning needs and preferences of all children and of society. Nevertheless, today's curriculum must, at the very least, center on three things: (1) what children ought to learn to survive as fully functional individuals, (2) what they desire to learn, and (3) what will inspire them to be kind, responsible, and ethical members of an unstable and rapidly changing world. Before we can design a curriculum that meets these three criteria, we need to look at the approaches that now dominate the K–12 curriculum.

Prevailing Curriculum Approaches

Curriculum initiatives throughout the last decade or so have revolved around three major approaches: the back-to-basics movement, the push for higher standards, and constructivism. Ediger (1999) suggests that educational leaders should examine and question each approach carefully before taking the lead in guiding staff to develop a brain-compatible curriculum.

Back to Basics

This approach arises from the long-standing belief that there is a traditional core body of knowledge that all students should achieve. Major attention is given to language arts, science, social studies, and mathematics. Academic specialists in each area chose the basic topics that are deemed to be essential.

Recent disenchantment with the success of public schools has convinced some state legislatures to push for a back-to-basics curriculum. The question, though, is: Back to whose basics? **If we return to the basics that the legislators experienced in school, we end up educating students for** *our past* **rather than for** *their future!*

If we expect to engage the brain of today's student, educational leaders must pose several questions before they entertain this approach.

▶ How relevant can this curriculum be for students if the content is selected externally by those removed from the classroom setting?
▶ To what extent should students be involved in choosing the content?
▶ Is it really possible in this day of information explosion to agree upon what topics represent the basics of the new millennium?

This movement is fraught with problems because the basics that those in power have in mind (essentially, a major emphasis on reading, writing, and mathematics at the expense of other areas) are generally not the basics needed for students to be successful workers in the 21st century. Furthermore, the technology-acclimated brain would not see this approach as compatible with its learning preferences.

Higher Standards

The standards movement resulted from continuing complaints from the media and legislators that American students were lagging behind students in the rest of the industrialized world. The curriculum was too lax and our country would not remain competitive unless students achieved more challenging and complex learning objectives. This approach proposed that content experts set high standards for students to achieve so that they can be ready for the workplace in a highly complex world. Despite the well-intentioned purpose of higher standards, educational leaders need to ask the following questions:

▶ How can outside experts know how difficult it is for students to achieve the new standards?
▶ Does achieving higher academic standards equate with being more successful in the future workplace?
▶ Does setting higher standards result in improved teaching and learning?
▶ Does the high-stakes testing program associated with the standards divert too much time and resources to teaching for the test at the expense of other worthwhile curricular activities?

It is difficult to argue against higher standards for learning and achievement. On the other hand, the questions listed above need to be addressed to ensure that imposing higher standards achieves the intended goal. The risk is that teachers may feel the pressure to "drill and kill" on just those concepts they believe will be tested. Consequently, instruction could revert to the didactic, lecture-centered approach that is hardly brain compatible for most students.

Constructivism

Constructivism is based on the concept that the brain constructs its own meaning during the learning process and that these constructs are more likely to occur when the learner is actively involved in choosing the content, context, and sequence of the learning opportunities. Students and teachers agree on the course content and the teacher acts more like a guide than a deliverer of information. Assessment is also a cooperative venture, using portfolios of student products more than testing to evaluate progress. This approach is radically different from the traditional classroom where the teacher is always in charge of setting the pace, delivering content, and following a scope and sequence originally determined by outsiders.

At first blush, it seems that constructivism is a much more brain-compatible approach than the traditional instructional model. But constructivism has its detractors, who ask:

> ▸ Should teachers and students have the responsibility for deciding what should be taught, rather than external groups such as state departments of education and professional organizations?

> ▸ How should portfolios be evaluated when the evaluation methods used to determine student achievement differ greatly from standardized testing?

> ▸ Can students learn basic subject matter in a student-centered curriculum?

These questions also deserve to be answered, especially if this approach holds promise for being more brain compatible than others.

Solution: A Sensible Mix

Rather than being forced to select one of these approaches over the others, why not take the best of each and combine them into an integrated program. This program accepts that there are basic tenets that all students must learn, that students should be pushed to achieve the highest level of achievement possible, and that students can select from among many pathways toward achieving the same learning objective.

An integrated program like the one just described meets the fundamental intent of each original approach while, at the same time, addressing the major questions posed by each (Figure 3.2). Outside experts can make recommendations of what constitute the basics, but students, teachers, and educational leaders work together to make the final determinations. Evaluating standards achievement can be a mix of the usual paper tests combined with portfolio assessment through rubrics.

In reality, some schools have arrived inadvertently at this integrated approach by making ad hoc adjustments to their curriculum, allowing for greater teacher and

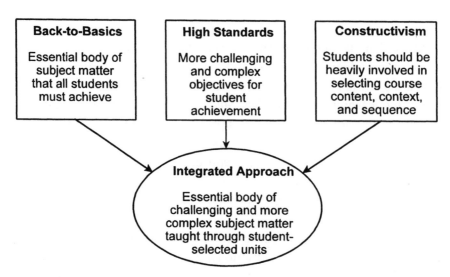

Figure 3.2 An integrated approach would take the best of Back-to-Basics, High Standards, and Constructivism.

student choice. But a carefully organized, purposeful plan for integration is likely to lead to more stable and consistent results than the ad hoc method.

REVISING CURRICULUM

As the needs and preferences of students change, educational leaders should make appropriate adjustments to curriculum within a reasonable time frame. Regrettably, opportunities to revise established curriculums are rare. This is largely because such revisions almost always result in the adoption of a new textbook or basal series, which can be very expensive. Consequently, it may make more sense to center the new curriculum around student- and teacher-developed units, which are far less costly and which can be revised periodically when necessary.

Three Steps for Curriculum Revision

There are lots of ways to revise curriculum and I have been involved in all of them during my educational career. But in recent years, I have focused on one method that has been particularly effective in designing curriculum for meeting the needs and learning preferences of 21st century children. The method is based on the following three strategies that are firmly established in cognitive neuroscience:

- Eliminate unnecessary and redundant topics
- Chunk related elements
- Identify the critical attributes of each concept

I strongly suggest that educational leaders get actively involved in curriculum revision and that they encourage the use of these strategies so that the final product is more likely to be brain compatible.

Eliminating Unnecessary and Redundant Topics

Have you ever noticed that the K–12 curriculum is a patchwork quilt? Every curriculum seems to acquire units of study and pet topics from those educators who last revised it. They may have even retained pet projects from previous revisions. Another temptation is to include topics covered in earlier courses or grades on the premise that students never seem to remember them, so let's do it again. Sometimes, topics are included only because they appear in the basal text and not because students need to learn them.

As a result, the curriculum grows and grows while the amount of time to teach it remains the same (essentially, 180 days). Using the metaphor of a car traveling on a highway, the only way to cover more distance in the same amount of time is to travel faster. Consequently, as each school year draws to a close, teachers are talking faster to cover the required material within the rapidly diminishing time. High school classrooms during this period often sound like tobacco auctions—lots of fast and occasionally unintelligible teacher talk. Higher-level questioning, cooperative learning activities, and other student-centered strategies are abandoned as too time-consuming. Students have no time to process the information for sense or meaning. As a result, the student's brain retains little or nothing.

> **LEADER'S QUESTION:** What are some ways of deciding which topics to eliminate during curriculum revision? SEE TIP #3.2

Having experienced this myself, I empathize with teachers caught in this frustrating situation. It is a predicament, however, that is largely of our own making. For some unknown reason, we abide by an unwritten law in our profession that prohibits the abandonment of any curriculum topic for a period of at least 25 years! The first step in meaningful curriculum revision, therefore, is to get rid of those unnecessary and redundant topics.

Chunking Related Topics

The conscious processing of new information occurs in a temporary memory called *working memory*. This is a place of limited capacity where we can build, take apart, or rework ideas for eventual storage somewhere else. When something is in working memory, it captures our focus and demands our attention. Scanning experiments show that most of working memory's activity occurs in the frontal lobes, although other parts of the brain are often called into action (Sousa, 2001a).

Working memory can handle only a few items at once. This functional capacity changes with age. Preschool infants can deal with about two items of information at once. Preadolescents can handle three to seven items, with an average of five. Through adolescence, further cognitive development occurs and the capacity increases to a range of five to nine, with an average of seven. For most people, that number remains constant throughout life.

This limited capacity explains why we have to memorize a song or a poem in stages. We start with the first group of lines by repeating them frequently (a process called *rehearsal*). Then we memorize the next lines and repeat them with the first group, and so on. In effect, we are increasing the number of items within the functional capacity of working memory through a process called *chunking*.

LEADER'S QUESTION: What are some ways of chunking curriculum? SEE TIP #3.3

Chunking occurs when working memory perceives a set of data as a single item, much as we perceive *information* as one word (and, therefore, one item) even though it is composed of 11 separate letters. Chunking allows us to deal with a few large blocks of information rather than many small fragments. Problem solving involves the ability to access large amounts of relevant knowledge from long-term memory for use in working memory. The key to that skill is chunking. The more a person is able to chunk in a particular area, the more expert the person becomes. These experts have the ability to use their experiences to group or chunk all kinds of information into discernable patterns.

Chunking is a very effective way of enlarging the capacity of working memory. It can be used to memorize a long string of numbers or words. Most of us learned the alphabet in chunks—for some it may have been *abcdefg*, *hijklmnop*, *qrs*, *tuv*, *wxyz*. Chunking reduced the 26 letters to a smaller number of items that working memory could handle. Even people can be chunked, such as couples (e.g., Romeo and Juliet, Bonnie and Clyde, Lewis and Clark), in which recalling the name of one immediately suggests the name of the other. Although working memory has a functional capacity limit as to the number of chunks it can process at one time, **there appears to be no limit to the number of items that can be combined into a chunk.** Teaching students (and yourself) how to chunk can greatly increase learning and remembering. In this second step of curriculum revision, look for ways to chunk topics so that students are able to deal with more information at one time and make the necessary connections that will result in retention of learning.

Identifying Critical Attributes

We design curriculum with the hope that students will eventually store what they have learned into their brains' long-term storage sites. But in order for the brain to locate that learning in the future, a retrieval cue must be associated with it. The more specific the cue that working memory attaches to a new learning, the easier it is for long-term memory to identify the item being sought. This process leads to an interesting phenomenon regarding long-term storage and retrieval: **We store by similarity, but we retrieve by difference.** That is, long-term memory most often stores new learnings into a network that contains learnings with similar characteristics or associations, as perceived by the learner. This network identification is one of the connections made in working memory during rehearsal. To retrieve an item, however, long-term memory identifies how it is *different* from all the other items in that network (Figure 3.3).

Here is a simple example. How would you recognize your best friend in a crowd? It is not because he has two arms, two legs, a head, and a torso. These characteristics make him *similar* to all other humans. Rather, it is his more subtle *differences,* such as facial features, walk, and voice, that allow you to distinguish him from everyone else. His unique characteristics are called his *critical attributes.*

Critical attributes, characteristics that make one idea unique from all others, are the cues of *difference* that learners can use as part of their storage process. Statements like *Amphibians live both on land and in water, Homonyms are words*

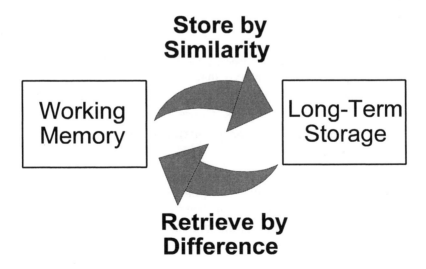

Figure 3.3 We tend to store information in networks by similarity but retrieve it back into working memory by difference (Sousa, 2001a).

that sound alike but have different spellings and meanings, and *To produce sound, something must vibrate* are examples of identifying critical attributes.

Identifying the critical attributes of a concept is not an easy task. We live in a culture driven by a quest for equality for all. This culture places a higher value on similarities than on differences. Thus, our cerebral networks are organized around similarity from an early age, and teachers frequently use similarity in the classroom to introduce new ideas. But, more often, successful retrieval from mental storage areas is accomplished by identifying differences among concepts. Consequently, teachers can help learners process new learnings accurately by having them identify the unique characteristics that make one concept different from all others. For example, what are the critical attributes of an explorer? Will these attributes help to separate Vasco da Gama from Napoleon Bonaparte? Students can use critical attributes to sort concepts so that they are stored in logical networks with appropriate cues. This will facilitate long-term memory's searches and increase the probability that it will accurately identify and retrieve the concept being sought (Sousa, 2001a).

> **LEADER'S QUESTION:** What are the steps for identifying the critical attributes of a concept? SEE TIP #3.4

During curriculum revision, the critical attributes of all concepts should be identified. Teachers should ensure that the critical attributes are an integral part of the lessons where each concept is introduced.

A Brain-Compatible Curriculum Framework

Educational leaders should recognize that a brain-compatible curriculum framework needs to include methods that are based on the way today's students learn best. It should offer variety, challenge, choices for students, and alternative ways of assessing academic progress. Consequently, the framework should have opportunities for teachers to present curriculum through any and all of the following ways (Figure 3.4):

- *Authentic Problems.* This method puts students in the position of solving a multifaceted problem of significant complexity. The problem resembles a real-life situation in that the students lack some information needed to solve the problem or are not clear on the steps they must take. The students critically analyze the problem from different points of view, look for alternative solutions, select a solution, and develop a plan of action for its implementation. In this format, the teacher is more of a guide than a provider of information. The open-ended nature of problem-based learning

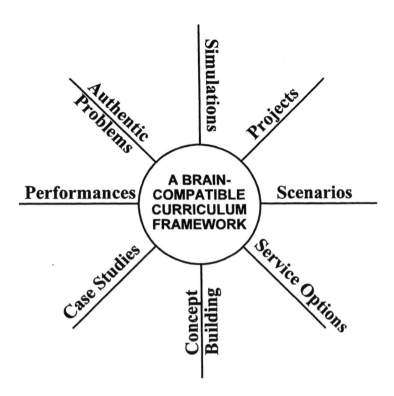

Figure 3.4 The diagram shows the different methods that should be part of a brain-compatible curriculum framework.

allows for differentiation of curriculum and instruction. An example: Should high schools have a later morning start time? Why or why not?

- *Simulations.* This creative method organizes students into small groups so that they can role-play actual or fictional persons in history or demonstrate political, economic, and social situations of the past or present. Simulations allow students to develop empathy for the roles they portray, to get a greater understanding of the conditions that prevailed during a certain period in history, and to see a situation from multiple perspectives. Furthermore, simulations develop personal communication and collaboration skills. An example: simulating the Continental Congress' deliberations when writing the U.S. Constitution.

- *Projects.* Projects are a means of promoting student involvement in their own learning. With this method, students recognize that seemingly abstract ideas and principles can be applied to real-life situations. The project can be as simple as writing a play to as complex as building a house. By working together toward completing a common goal, they learn collaboration, communication, and how to build consensus.

- *Scenarios.* Scenarios allow students to explore the "what if" aspects of their learning. Here they have a chance to investigate different futures based on their understanding of specific issues in the present. Through brainstorming, analysis, and communication, students can examine options without becoming anxious over the lack of information regarding our future. An example: What scenarios describe life on this planet in the next 50 years if global warming continues or even accelerates?

- *Service Options.* This method can tie the curriculum into the larger context of the community. It involves having students perform some type of volunteer service in their community, such as helping out in a home for senior citizens or in a soup kitchen for the homeless. Such experiences increase students' awareness of their surroundings as well as helping them to become more tolerant, respectful, and empathetic of the plight of others.

- *Concept Building.* The more connections students can make between new learning and their past experiences, the more likely they are to become interested in that learning and to remember it. Concept building provides students the opportunity to go beyond the basic facts of the concept and to explore applications to their own interests. For example, in a unit on ecology, students might interview the local director of water management to find out how the water table, reservoirs, and aquifers are managed and protected. Newspaper articles and information from appropriate Web sites could also be included.

- *Case Studies.* Case studies are often used in the study of law and medicine to help students analyze facts, draw conclusions, and look for possible causes and solutions. The case studies that are chosen should include issues that are directly relevant to students. For example, when dealing with issues such as teenage drinking and drug use, students often have to confront their own value system as they seek out viable solutions.

- *Performances.* Performance is learning by doing the actual task. Whether in the science laboratory, in the computer room, or on the theater stage, the student demonstrates understanding and application through the performance itself. The teacher is the mentor and coach, but the student is the performer. Assessment of the student's work is done usually through a rubric.

A curriculum framework that includes these methods offers challenging, complex, and interesting ways for students to learn concepts as well as opportunities to have choices and a variety of assessments. This approach is about as brain compatible as a curriculum can get.

What About Differentiated Curriculum?

Differentiated curriculum is actually an instructional approach based on the idea that students learn in different ways. Thus, teachers engage students in learning by using different sensory modalities, by varying the rate of instruction, by raising or lowering the level of complexity as needed, and by appealing to a variety of interests. Students are held to high standards, but they compete more against themselves than against each other.

If a curriculum framework contains most or all of the methods discussed above—from authentic problems to performances—then it already includes the essential components necessary for teachers to differentiate curriculum. For more on differentiated curriculum, see Chapter 4 and Tomlinson (1999).

What About a Multiple Intelligences Curriculum?

Some elementary and middle schools have formally adopted curriculums based on the theory of multiple intelligences (MI). This theory is the work of Harvard researcher Howard Gardner (1983, 1993), who suggested that intelligence is not a unitary concept, that humans possess at least seven intelligences (recently, he added an eighth), and that an individual is predisposed to developing each of the intelligences to different levels of competence. The eight intelligences are

- ▸ *Bodily/Kinesthetic:* The capacity to use one's body to solve a problem, make something, or put on a production.
- ▸ *Naturalist:* The ability to discriminate among living things and sensitivity to other features of the natural world.
- ▸ *Logical/Mathematical:* The ability to understand logical systems and to manipulate numbers and quantities.
- ▸ *Musical/Rhythmic:* The capacity to think in music and to hear, remember, recognize, and manipulate patterns.
- ▸ *Verbal/Linguistic:* The capacity to use one's language (and other languages) to express oneself and understand others.
- ▸ *Visual/Spatial:* The ability to represent the spatial world internally in one's mind.
- ▸ *Interpersonal:* The ability to understand other people.
- ▸ *Intrapersonal:* The capacity to understand one's self.

For Gardner, the intelligences represent ways of processing information and of thinking and are not the same as thinking style, which tends to remain consistent and independent of the type of information being processed. Rather, individuals at any given time use those intelligences that will allow them to solve specific problems, generate new problems, or create products or services of value to their particular culture. As the information and tasks change, other intelligences are called into action.

MI theory has obvious implications for curriculum and instruction. Gardner has not endorsed any particular approach but has encouraged schools to implement MI theory in the classroom in a way that best fits each school's unique situation.

Incorporating an MI approach into curriculum has occurred mainly in elementary schools and in a few middle schools. In high schools, the MI approach is rarely incorporated formally into the curriculum. Rather, it is more apt to occur informally in those classrooms where teachers have studied MI theory and feel comfortable using the related strategies.

Elementary schools that have restructured their curriculum around MI report mostly favorable results (Mettetal, Jordan, and Harper, 1997). Educational leaders should bring this research to the professional staff at all grade levels and encourage them to use instructional strategies based on MI. MI offers another method for differentiating instruction and for using some of the previously described methods that make for a brain-compatible curriculum.

What Is a Brain-Compatible Reading Curriculum?

Although I mentioned earlier that this chapter would not focus on specific content areas, I am making an exception. Most school districts spend more money and put more human resources into their reading program than any other curriculum component. For that reason alone, it should be addressed here. But my real reason for including reading is that, at this point in time, it is one of only two curriculum areas (language acquisition is the other) where discoveries in neuroscience have made their greatest impact. Reading is an excellent example of why educational leaders should keep current on those aspects of brain research that can assist them in making important decisions about educational practices. Allow me to explain by presenting a summary of the current beliefs on how the brain learns to read and what this means for selecting a reading program.

Learning to Read

Reading does not come naturally. The brain's ability to acquire spoken language with amazing speed and accuracy is the result of genetic hard-wiring and specialized cerebral areas that focus on this task. But there are no areas of the brain that specialize in reading. In fact, reading is probably the most difficult task we ask the young brain to undertake. Reading is a relatively new phenomenon in the development of humans. As far as we know, the genes have not incorporated

How the Brain Reads

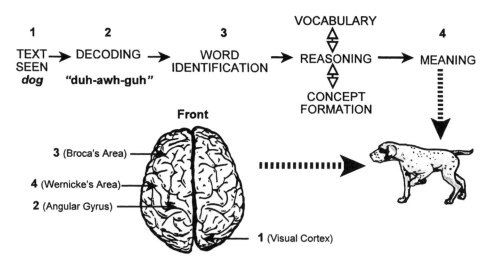

Figure 3.5 In reading the word dog, it is first seen (1), then decoded into its phonological elements (2), and identified (3). The higher-level functions of reasoning and concept formation provide the meaning (4) and produce the thought of a furry animal that barks (Sousa, 2001a).

reading into their coded structure, probably because reading—unlike spoken language—has not emerged over time as a skill necessary for human survival.

To read correctly, the brain must learn to connect the abstract symbols of the alphabet to sound bits it already knows. In English, the brain must first learn the alphabet and then connect those 26 letters to the 44 or so sounds of spoken English (phonemes) that the child has been using successfully for years. Thus, reading involves a recognition that speech can be broken into small sounds (phonemes) and that these segmented sounds can be represented in print (phonics).

Unfortunately, the human brain is not born with the insight to make these sound-to-symbol connections, nor does it develop naturally for most children without direct instruction. Children of literate homes may encounter this instruction before coming to school. Others, however, do not have this opportunity. For them, classroom instruction needs to focus on making the phoneme-phonics connections before reading can be successful. If children cannot hear the "-at" sound in *bat* and *hat* and perceive that the difference lies in the first sound, then they will have difficulty decoding and sounding out words quickly and correctly.

Using brain imaging techniques, researchers are getting a clearer picture of the cerebral processes involved in reading: The word (for example, *dog*) is first recorded in the visual cortex (Figure 3.5), then decoded by a structure on the left side of the brain called the angular gyrus, which separates it into its basic sounds, or phonemes (e.g., the letters *d-o-g* are pronounced "duh, awh, guh"). This process activates Broca's area so that the word can be identified. The brain's vocabulary store and reasoning and concept formation abilities, along with activity in Wernicke's area, combine to provide meaning, producing the thought of a furry animal that barks (Shaywitz, 1996). All this occurs in a fraction of a second.

Although the process outlined in Figure 3.5 appears linear and singular, it is really bidirectional and parallel, with many phonemes being processed at the same time. That the brain learns to read at all attests to its remarkable ability to sift through seemingly confusing input and establish patterns and systems. For a few children, this process comes naturally; most have to be taught (Sousa, 2001a).

Learning to read, therefore, starts with phoneme awareness, a recognition that written spellings represent sounds (called the *alphabetic principle*), and that this combination applies phonics to the reading and spelling of words. These skills are *necessary* but not *sufficient* to learn to read the English language with meaning. The reader must also become proficient in grasping larger units of print, such as syllable patterns, whole words, and phrases.

Phonological Awareness

What Is Phonological Awareness? This is the recognition that oral language can be divided into smaller components, such as sentences into words, words into syllables and, ultimately, individual phonemes. Being phonologically aware means having an understanding of all these levels. In children, phonological awareness usually starts with initial rhyming and a recognition that sentences can be segmented into words. Next comes segmenting words into syllables and blending syllables into words. The most complex level of phonological awareness is phonemic awareness—the understanding that words are made up of individual sounds and that these sounds can be manipulated to create new words.

How Does Phonological Awareness Help in Learning to Read? New readers must recognize the alphabetic principle and that words can be separated into individual phonemes, which can be reordered and blended into words. This enables learners to associate the letters with sounds in order to read and build words. Thus, phonological awareness in kindergarten is a strong predictor of reading success that persists throughout school. Early instruction in reading, especially in letter-sound association, strengthens phonological awareness and helps in the development of the more sophisticated phonemic awareness (Sousa, 2001b).

Phonics Versus Whole-Language Approaches to Reading

Throughout the history of teaching reading, a great debate has existed between whether it is better to start with word sounds (phonics) or to teach words as they derive their meaning from a larger context (whole language). Unfortunately, some schools that adopted the whole-language approach abandoned the teaching of phonics altogether. In fact, in any school that exclusively adopted one approach, there was always a block of students who still did not learn to read. Even those schools that purported to use a "blended" or "eclectic" approach often failed to include systematic instruction in phonological awareness, phonics, and their component skills.

Nonetheless, the research is clear: successful reading starts with phonemic awareness of sound-to-symbol correspondences and the blending of sound-spellings until almost any unknown word can be accurately decoded (Moats, 2000). Starting with the phonemic awareness approach is one of the few aspects of reading supported by a substantial and long-term body of research.

An *exclusively* whole-language approach minimizes or omits the systematic teaching of phoneme awareness, spelling patterns, and rules of grammar. Whole language appears to be primarily a system of intentions and beliefs from the late 1960s proposing that early reading instruction should focus on purpose and meaning and that word analysis skills should arise only incidently to contextual reading. Its philosophy, however, was derived from an analysis of how *adults* read and long before the development of brain imaging technologies. The whole language approach gained great popularity in the late 1970s, and by the early 1980s, school districts were replacing phonics-based programs with programs based on individual reading instruction with children's literature. Yet no solid body of research existed then or exists now to support the effectiveness of exclusively using the whole-language approach with all beginning readers (Sousa, 2001b).

Children bring a knowledge of spoken language when they encounter the printed page. They need to learn the written symbols that represent speech, and to use them accurately and fluently. Reading instruction should begin with phonemic awareness and then move to contextual and enriched reading as the student gains competency and confidence. Thus some of the principles of whole language can be incorporated later as part of reading development (Moats, 2000).

Learning World Languages

Acquiring spoken language is the other curriculum area where neuroscience has made a dramatic impact. Studies show that proficiency in learning a second language depends not on *how long* nonnatives have been speaking the language, but on *how early in life* they began learning it. The power of a young child's brain to learn spoken languages is so immense that it can learn several languages at one time. It seems, however, that the parts of the brain prewired for language acquisition lose their ability in the preteen years to discriminate sounds between its native language and nonnative languages. The implication here is that if we wish children to acquire a second language, it makes sense to start that acquisition during the early years when the brain is actively creating phonemic sound and syntactic networks.

Learning a second language later is possible but more difficult. Other areas of the brain must be programmed to recognize, distinguish, and respond to foreign phonemes. Furthermore, imaging studies show that second languages acquired in adulthood are spatially separated in the brain from native languages. However, when acquired in the preteen years, native and second languages are represented in the same frontal areas (Kim, Relkin, Lee, and Hirsch, 1997). Hence, younger and older brains react to second language learning very differently.

Although it seems that younger brains are more adept at language learning, this research should not be interpreted to discourage adolescents and adults from pursuing second language study. Nor should it be assumed that youngsters will become fluent solely by studying a second language a few hours a week in the primary grades. **What the research does imply, however, is that schools should begin teaching second language acquisition as early as possible.**

CURRICULUM FOR SPECIAL NEEDS STUDENTS

Continuing research on learning disabilities is revealing what neuroscientists have long suspected: Having a learning disability in one area seldom means that the child has learning problems in other areas. This finding, coupled with greater insights into brain functions thanks to neuroimaging, suggests that educators need to take another look at how we provide students with special needs access to the general curriculum.

Amendments to the Individuals With Disabilities Education Act (IDEA) place on educational leaders the obligation of ensuring that students with special needs have access to the general education curriculum. No longer is it enough for students to just be present in general curriculum classrooms. They must be provided with the necessary and intentional support systems that will ensure their *progress* in the curriculum. Under the IDEA revisions, educators of students with special needs can no longer claim that the curriculum is the student's Individual Education Plan (IEP). Instead, these educators must now find ways to focus on how the general education curriculum can enhance the student's learning.

The days of presenting watered-down or remedial curriculum to impoverished or special needs students have ended. Educational leaders now have the responsibility of ensuring that curriculum matters, and of facilitating a dialogue between the professionals in both regular and special education that focuses on the challenge of having special needs students succeed in the general curriculum areas.

Pugach and Warger (2001) propose that this dialogue focus on three important and complex issues.

1. *Lack of Appropriate Curriculum Materials.* Few curriculum materials are available that address the full range of student needs. Typically, schools set the level of difficulty in the curriculum for the midrange of abilities and then pull out students with special needs into separate classes that use specially designed materials that barely match the general curriculum. The IDEA revisions take a dim view of this common approach. The good news is that some special educators are working on curriculum materials that can accommodate a wide range of students and motivate them as well. Pisha and Coyne (2001) report on a curriculum approach developed at the nonprofit Center for Applied Special Technology (CAST) called the Universal Design for Learning (UDL), which creates digital textbooks that can support the educational needs of a wide range of students, including those with learning disabilities. This approach offers promise because it can specifically design the educational curricula, materials, methods, and environments that will help each student with special needs be successful.

The UDL design is firmly rooted in neuroscience in that it addresses the three major cerebral systems that imaging shows are activated when the brain performs mental tasks: the recognition system, the frontal lobe's executive system, and the emotional (limbic) system. When available, these materials will ease the burden of regular classroom teachers and free up special educators to deal with more complex curricular issues.

LEADER'S QUESTION: What is being done to develop curriculum materials for students with special needs? SEE TIP #3.5

2. *Lack of Basic Skills.* This issue centers on how teachers can help students with learning difficulties acquire a complex curriculum that requires deep understanding when they have limited abilities and lack many of the basic skills. In the past, this problem was addressed by offering diluted curriculum based on the assumption that these students could not handle activities that require any higher-order thinking. But now we are discovering that even students with learning disorders can do higher-order thinking in carefully structured situations. One study reports, for example, that students with special needs participated in a high-level and complex study of novels at the middle school level (Pugach and Warner, 2001).

3. *Deciding on the Appropriate Curriculum.* Not surprisingly, the third issue involves identifying exactly what counts as curriculum across the broad spectrum of students with disabilities. Although there is a consensus on the need to provide meaningful learning experiences to students with special needs, little formal action has occurred to develop such a curriculum. Ford, Davern, and Schnorr (2001) have suggested a curriculum approach that focuses on developing fundamental skills that

will help special needs students develop literacy, do problem solving, manage the tasks of living, and contribute to society. Dubbed the *foundation approach*, it incorporates a set of five principles that are applied in a very conscious and systematic way for students with special needs, especially those with significant learning disabilities. The five principles are as follows:

- *Every student should receive priority attention to the development of foundation skills.* These skills include interacting with people, problem solving, making useful contributions, and doing these things within an ethical framework.
- *Individualization is at the core of a good education.* In a truly individualized curriculum, students should not be forced into categories, especially since expanding technology is showing how much these students can learn when they have sophisticated tools.
- *Educational priorities should be pursued through schedules and locations that respect the student's membership in a learning community.* Most individual priorities can be addressed by good elementary and secondary teachers within the context of the rich and varied classroom environment.
- *Students should have an opportunity to experience a sense of mastery or accomplishment over the tasks that they undertake.* When there is a lack of clearly defined priorities for individual students, there are few opportunities for students to feel a sense of mastery or completion.
- *Being attentive to the quality of a student's immediate experience is as important as our concern for the future.* Although long-term curricular outcomes are important, they should not be pursued at the expense of the present moment. Equally important are the moment-to-moment interactions between adults and students as well as between students and students. Recognizing the importance of the immediate experience should not be confused with having low expectations.

Educational leaders should consider these principles as the basis for developing curriculum outcomes for students with disabilities of all types.

INTEGRATING TECHNOLOGY INTO THE CURRICULUM

Integrating technology into the curriculum is absolutely essential to prepare students for the 21st century. Some teachers, for a variety of reasons, are still skittish about technology and use little of it in their lessons. Yet, we know that most students today have not only grown up with technology in their environment but also expect to use technological tools as an integral part of their learning experiences. Educational leaders, therefore, must insist that technology be integrated into all areas of the curriculum and must provide teachers with the training and technical support necessary to make that happen.

The What, Why, and How of Technology Integration

For the more technologically shy staff members, educational leaders may have to explain what technology integration really is, why teachers should do it, and how it is done.

What Is Technology Integration? Technology integration is more than just putting computers in the classroom and telling students to do something with them. Rather, it is the purposeful, creative, and effective use of computers and other technology that allows students to use their skills for learning new materials and skills in meaningful ways. Integration means using technology so that it enhances student learning by ensuring that the curriculum drives technology usage rather than technology driving the curriculum.

Why Integrate Technology? Even in this technological age, some educators are still struggling with this question. Nevertheless, students need to be proficient at using technology to advance their learning and to provide a good quality of life in a rapidly changing world. Their brains are already primed and comfortable with technology. So, the following are just a few reasons for why schools should integrate technology into all areas of the curriculum:

> **LEADER'S QUESTION:** **What steps can help teachers use technology skills in their content area? SEE TIP #3.6**

- Students learn how to find what they need in a vast sea of information.
- Because students are accustomed to technology, they are more motivated to use it and thus increase their academic engagement time.
- Students develop computer skills by learning something else rather than in isolation.
- By careful design, students probe topics in greater depth.
- By getting more deeply involved in a topic, students move to higher levels of thinking and problem solving.

How to Integrate Technology. To be successful at integrating technology skills into the curriculum, the skills must relate directly to the content area and to the classroom assignments as well as being part of a logical stream of instruction.

THE PITFALLS OF CURRICULUM CHANGE

The landscape of educational reform is littered with the corpses of well-intentioned curriculum initiatives that didn't survive for very long. Although there may be many reasons to explain their demise, most attempts at curriculum change fail because (1) the administrative and organizational structure of the school district did not change sufficiently to support the initiative, (2) the teachers and other stakeholders did not have a significant role in discussing or selecting the initiative, (3) there was little or no meaningful staff development to assist teachers in implementing the initiative, and (4) monitoring and evaluation efforts were inadequate to sustain the initiative.

> **LEADER'S QUESTION: What steps can I take to facilitate curriculum change? SEE TIP #3.7**

All the good work that educational leaders can do to bring about change in the curriculum will be wasted if these four pitfalls are not avoided. Keep in mind that young teachers now entering the profession have been raised in that novelty-centered environment and thus possess many of the characteristics of the novel brain. They expect to participate in their own learning and want to have some control over what and how they teach.

Curriculum change is most likely to succeed and endure if it includes all the appropriate stakeholders in the planning process, provides for effective and continuing staff development, is fully supported by administrative and organizational structures, and is carefully monitored and evaluated. Educational leaders are in the unique position of ensuring that all this occurs.

MAJOR POINTS IN CHAPTER 3

❑ The brains of today's students are attracted more than ever to the unique and different—what is called *novelty*.

❑ Nearly one-half of the grades 3 to 12 student population has a visual preference and just under one-fifth has an auditory preference. More than one-third of students have a kinesthetic-tactile preference, indicating that movement helps their learning.

❑ An integrated approach to curriculum combines the best components of the Back-to-Basics, Higher Standards, and Constructivism movements resulting in an essential body of more challenging and complex knowledge taught through student-selected units.

❑ The effective revision of curriculum requires eliminating unnecessary and redundant concepts, chunking related topics, and identifying critical attributes.

❑ A brain-compatible curriculum framework must be based on the way today's students learn best. It should offer variety, challenge, choices for students, and alternative ways of assessing academic progress. Some of the curriculum methods are authentic problems, simulations, projects, scenarios, service options, concept building, case studies, and performance.

❑ Educational leaders are responsible for facilitating a dialogue between the professionals in both regular and special education that focuses on ensuring that special needs students succeed in the general curriculum areas.

❑ Educational leaders must insist that technology be integrated into all areas of the curriculum and must provide teachers with the training and technical support necessary to make that happen.

❑ Curriculum change is most likely to succeed and endure if it includes all the appropriate stakeholders in the planning process, provides for effective and continuing staff development, is fully supported by administrative and organizational structures, and is carefully monitored and evaluated.

TIPS FOR LEADERS #3.1

Accommodating the Brain of Today's Students

Here are just a few questions that educational leaders should consider when deciding if their schools are compatible with today's students:

- Have teachers learned of the recent discoveries in neuroscience about the brain and how it learns?
  Yes____ No ____ Comment_____

- Does the professional development program include regular reviews of new information on how the brain learns?
  Yes____ No ____ Comment_____

- Do teachers understand the difference between learning and retention, and do they know strategies that can increase retention?
  Yes____ No ____ Comment_____

- Are teachers using sufficient visuals in their lessons?
  Yes____ No ____ Comment_____

- Do students have regular opportunities to stand up, move, and talk about their learning during a lesson?
  Yes____ No ____ Comment_____

- Do teachers recognize the need for novelty in their lessons to maintain student interest?
  Yes____ No ____ Comment_____

- Are teachers using different types of technology in the classroom on a regular basis?
  Yes____ No ____ Comment_____

TIPS FOR LEADERS #3.2

Eliminating Topics From the Curriculum

Revising a curriculum offers a rare opportunity for the members of the revision committee to discard those topics that are no longer relevant to the modern student. Although there are several ways that this can be accomplished, the educational leader of the committee might consider the following method.

- First, make a list of all the topics that are to be covered in this curriculum for one course or grade level.

- Have each committee member, working alone, number every topic in order of importance, starting with number 1 as the most important, and so on. One standard for deciding on the priority of topics is to ask this question: "Is it really important for the student to know this information five years from now?"

- When this task is completed, the committee members get back together, discuss their rankings, and reach a consensus on a final ranking for all the topics on the list.

- The topics in the bottom 20 percent of the list are candidates for elimination. Retain only those in this group that the committee is convinced will be included in a state, local, or standardized testing program.

- If necessary, take a vote to decide which topics to keep and which to eliminate.

- Strongly resist the temptation to replace the eliminated topics with new ones unless they meet the five-year test or are very likely to be on a state or standardized assessment.

TIPS FOR LEADERS #3.3

Using Chunking to Increase Retention of Learning

One of the most valuable contributions that educational leaders can make is to insist that curriculum be chunked. Chunking is the process whereby the brain perceives several items of information as a single item. Words are common examples of chunks. *Hippopotamus* is composed of 12 letters, but the brain perceives them as one item of information and quickly forms a mental image. The more items we can put into a chunk, the more information we can process in working memory and remember at one time. Chunking is a learned skill and, thus, can also be taught. There are different types of chunking. During curriculum revision, topics that fit into any of the following types of chunking should be taught together regardless of where they appear in the basic text.

Pattern Chunking: This is most easily accomplished whenever we can find patterns in the material to be retained.

- Review the topics that are to be covered in the curriculum **before** determining the instructional sequence. Look for patterns between and among topics. For example, do some topics occur within a similar time frame or are they related geographically? Almost any pattern that the learner perceives can be the basis for chunking.

- Learning step-by-step procedures, such as tying a shoelace and copying a computer file from a floppy to a hard disk, are examples of pattern chunking. We group the items in a sequence and rehearse it mentally until it becomes one or a few chunks. Practicing the procedure further enhances the formation of chunks, and subsequent performance requires little conscious attention.

Categorical Chunking: A more sophisticated chunking process because the curriculum sequence is designed so that the learner establishes types of categories to help classify large amounts of information. The learner reviews the information, looking for criteria that will group complex material into simpler categories or arrays. The different types of categories can include the following:

- *Advantages and Disadvantages*. The information is categorized according to the pros and cons of the concept. Examples include energy use, abortion, and capital punishment.

- *Similarities and Differences*. The learner compares two or more concepts using attributes that make them similar and different. Examples are comparing the Articles of Confederation to the Bill of Rights, mitosis to meiosis, and the U.S. Civil War to the Vietnam War.

- *Structure and Function*. These categories are helpful with concepts that have parts with different functions, such as identifying the parts of an animal cell, a short story, or the human digestive system.

- *Taxonomies*. This system sorts information into hierarchical levels according to certain common characteristics. Examples are biological taxonomies (kingdom, phylum, class, etc.), taxonomies of learning (cognitive, affective, and psychomotor), and governmental bureaucracies.

- *Arrays*. These are less ordered than taxonomies in that the criteria for establishing the array are not always logical, but are more likely based on observable features. Human beings are classified, for example, by learning style and personality type. Dogs can be grouped by size, shape, or fur length. Clothing can be divided by material, season, and gender.

TIPS FOR LEADERS #3.4

Identifying the Critical Attributes of a Concept

Critical attributes are characteristics that make one concept *unique* among all others. During curriculum revision, educational leaders should insist that these attributes be clearly identified and teachers should make sure that they are included in the instructional process. All subject areas have major concepts whose critical attributes should be clearly identified. Here are a few simple examples:

Area	Concept	Critical Attribute
Social Studies	Law	Rule made by a government entity that is used for the control of behavior, is policed, and carries a penalty if broken.
	Culture	The common behavior of a large group of people who can be identified by specific foods, clothing, art, religion, and music.
Science	Mammal	An animal that has hair and mammary glands.
	Planet	A natural heavenly body that revolves around a star, rotates on its axis, and does not produce its own light.
Mathematics	Triangle	A two-dimensional figure that is closed and three-sided.
	Prime	An integer with a value greater than 1 whose only positive factors are itself and 1.
Language Arts	Sonnet	A poem of 14 lines, written in iambic pentameter with a specific rhyming pattern.
	Simile	A figure of speech that compares two unlike things.

In addition to identifying the critical attributes for each concept, the curriculum should also include the following:

- *Simple Examples*. Include simple examples for the teacher to give the students. Be sure that each example clearly illustrates the critical attributes.

- *Complex Examples*. Also include complex examples that may not be so obvious to students. For example, if the concept is mammals, then a complex example would be a porpoise or a whale, which, unlike most mammals, live in water. It is important here to show again how the critical attributes apply.

- *Limits of the Critical Attributes*. Include any exceptions to help students recognize that critical attributes may have limits and may not apply in every instance. For example, platypuses have the critical attributes of mammals but are in a separate classification because they also have attributes of birds and amphibians.

When the curriculum identifies critical attributes, students learn how one concept is different from all other similar concepts. This strategy leads to clearer understanding, concept attainment, the ability to relate the new concept properly to others, and the likelihood that it will be stored and recalled accurately.

TIPS FOR LEADERS #3.5

Developing Curriculum Materials for Students With Special Needs

To provide students with special needs full access to the general curriculum, educational leaders will need to keep abreast of upcoming initiatives that can fulfill this obligation. One promising initiative is an approach developed at the Center for Applied Special Technology (CAST) called the Universal Design for Learning (UDL). It stems from the Universal Design project in architecture which was needed to make all public buildings accessible to people with many different types of handicaps. Using that same premise, this program designs the curriculums, materials, methods, and environments needed to support and challenge the entire range of learners who could be in today's classrooms, including those with moderate to severe disabilities.

UDL is particularly effective because it is based on neuroimaging scans showing that the recognition, executive, and emotional systems are activated when the brain performs certain mental tasks.

- *Recognition System*. This function relies on long-term memory to help interpret and recognize sensory input. Students with learning difficulties may not be able to decode words from the traditional textbook. UDL uses technology to produce different digital textbooks and to provide multiple ways of presenting the material.
- *Executive System*. The executive system enables the learner to interpret information and to plan a course of action. The UDL approach facilitates this process by offering a manageable array of hints and models that the learner can use to devise strategies for action. In doing so, the student develops metacognition and self-regulation.
- *Emotional System*. The emotional (limbic) system regulates the amount of engagement an individual has toward the learning situation, usually determined by that person's likes, dislikes, and interests. Students, however, are often faced with curricular topics that they find uninteresting. This lack of interest can lead to failure. UDL can provide some latitude for learner choice and offer a range of instructional supports and approaches. This flexibility of support and challenge allows each student to succeed and build confidence as a learner.

The UDL approach encourages educators to see students with disabilities not as disabled or normal, but as representing a range of educational needs that can be met in a model classroom. Although students learn when they overcome obstacles, some of these obstacles have nothing to do with the learning at hand. For example, a vision problem may prevent a student from being successful in either learning or being tested in mathematics. The work at CAST, using the UDL approach, centers on eliminating these obstacles.

When this book went to press, the UDL materials were still being piloted. Because there is great interest in this approach, educational leaders should follow its progress on the CAST Website (see **Resources**).

TIPS FOR LEADERS #3.6

Steps for Tying Technology Skills to Content Areas

Educational leaders often find themselves having to prod technology-shy teachers to integrate computers and other technology into the curriculum. Integration is more than just letting the students do their thing on the computer. It requires purposeful and clever planning so that the technology becomes the lesson's tool rather than its goal. The following are suggestions that educational leaders can make to teachers so they can ease their way into technology integration:

- Select the content or core area (e.g., mathematics, science, reading) where the technology skills will be applied.

- Decide what technology skills can best be taught in this area or application.

- Start with a lesson or unit that can be taught or enhanced through the computer. Pick something easy and comfortable.

- Find a software program or other technological medium that focuses on the content of that lesson or unit.

- Try it out on yourself first. Make any revisions and give it to the students to use during the lesson.

- Evaluate what went right and what, if anything, went wrong. Make additional revisions as needed. Use it again if necessary or move on to the next unit.

By understanding the importance of integrating technology into the curriculum, educators are better able to prepare students for the complex challenges of a technologically advanced information age.

TIPS FOR LEADERS #3.7

Worksheet for Facilitating Curriculum Change

Use this part of the worksheet to help explain why a curriculum change is necessary.

Why the Change?

Educational leaders can facilitate curriculum change by first ensuring that the change will accomplish a clearly identified learning goal and that it does not merely represent change for change's sake. Thus, the following questions need to be addressed:

- What will teachers and other stakeholders need to know about the change in order to put it into practice?
  Answer:_____
  _____

- What kind of help will teachers need to put the change into practice in their own classrooms and who should provide that help?
  Answer:_____
  _____

- How will teachers and administrators be kept informed about the proposed change and plans for implementation?
  Answer:_____
  _____

Making It Happen

Check whether these steps have been taken to accomplish that change:

- The school district is fully committed to providing the administrative and organizational structures needed to support the curriculum change. (Because most proposed curriculum changes cannot subsist by themselves, it is important that the emotional, collegial, and budgetary support be present to sustain the change.)

Yes_____ No _____ If no, what needs to be done?_____

_____

- Teachers and other stakeholders must have a significant role in planning the change, communicating it to other stakeholders, such as students, and establishing timelines for its implementation. (Teacher involvement from the beginning will garner the critical support and commitment needed for the change to succeed.)
  Yes_____ No _____ If no, what needs to be done?_____

_____

- Appropriate staff development has been planned or carried out. The plan identifies the resources and materials needed for the curriculum change as well as the instructional approaches that the change represents for both teachers and students. Furthermore, the plan should identify potential problems and fears associated with the implementation of the change.
  Yes_____ No _____ If no, what needs to be done?_____

_____

- Ways of monitoring and evaluating the change are in place. (These are necessary to understand how the teachers and students are doing and how the implementation is working out. This process should identify strengths and weaknesses, address unanticipated consequences, gather and analyze data on student achievement, identify teacher concerns, help make decisions about ongoing staff development, and make suggestions for change.
  Yes_____ No _____ If no, what needs to be done?_____

_____

Brain-Compatible Instruction and Assessment

The title of this chapter may seem a bit strange. After all, schools have always taught to the brain. Right? Of course they have, but to which brain? The original brain-compatible model of instruction was devised about a hundred years ago when most information was passed from one person to another by word of mouth. As a result, most students probably learned best through the auditory modality. Schools, then, were brain compatible if students sat quietly and listened while the teacher did most of the talking.

In Chapter 2, we discussed how the environment has affected the contemporary student brain compared with that of just 20 years ago. Clearly, the sit-down-be-quiet-and-listen model is *not* compatible with the brains of many students who now cross the thresholds of our schools. Those teachers who design and use instructional strategies based on their deep understanding of how the brain of today learns are going to have the greatest impact on student achievement.

COMPONENTS OF BRAIN-COMPATIBLE INSTRUCTION

If educational leaders believe that classroom instruction should be based on what we know about how the brain learns best, the ensuing question has to be, "What does brain-compatible instruction look like?" There are, of course, certain instructional strategies that are more likely to attract the attention of students than others. We mentioned earlier that lessons composed largely of teacher talk are less likely to hold student interest than lessons involving technology and the active participation of the learner.

As part of their responsibilities, educational leaders usually visit classrooms and make judgments about the competence of teachers. That judgment should be

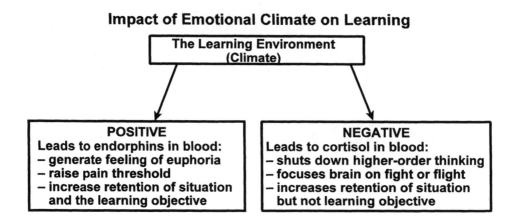

Figure 4.1 The biological effects on a student in a positive classroom climate are very different from those in a negative climate.

grounded on sound theory and evidence from cognitive psychology and neuroscience. What follows now are some of the components of brain-compatible classrooms that educational leaders should be looking for. This collection is by no means complete or magical, but it does include instructional strategies that are based on our current understanding of how the brain attends to, processes, and retains new learning.

Setting the Classroom Climate

Climate, in this context, refers to the emotional atmosphere that pervades the learning environment. Just as the principal sets the climate for the school, the teacher sets the climate in the classroom. Learning occurs best in climates that are free from threats and intimidation.

Human biology readily explains why this is the case (Figure 4.1). In a classroom where the climate is positive, students have respect for each another as well as their teacher. Humor (not sarcasm) abounds, and there is a feeling that the classroom is a place where the teacher and students are learning together. Assessment is seen more as helping students review what they have learned rather than as a "gotcha" exercise. In this low-threat atmosphere, chemicals called *endorphins* are freely flowing in the bloodstream. Endorphins are very similar to opiates in molecular structure and their presence (1) produces a feeling of euphoria, (2) raises the pain threshold, so that a sore muscle or headache is not as annoying, and (3) stimulates the brain's limbic area, thereby increasing the likelihood that both the class situation and learning objective will be remembered.

If, on the other hand, the teacher generates a classroom climate that is negative, students will develop anxiety about the situation and feel stress. The endorphins are now replaced by a steroid-like chemical called *cortisol*. Similar to adrenaline but not as potent, cortisol alerts the body that stress is present. The brain shuts down higher-level processing, shifts its attention to the cause of the stress, and determines whether further action is needed to protect its owner. Because the environmental information may be useful in the future, the brain remembers the situation but the curriculum learning objective is long gone.

Readers who are skeptical about the power of endorphins and cortisol may want to try this simple exercise. Think of one of the best teachers you ever had as a student. Chances are you will remember the teacher, other students in the class, and where the teaching occurred. Chances are high, too, that you will remember a lot of what you learned in that class. Now, clear your mind and think of the worst teacher you ever had as a student. Here, too, you are very likely to remember the teacher, other students, and the location. Remembering specific content, however, will be much more difficult. Though rarely generated intentionally, negative climates can result inadvertently. For example, how a teacher alerts the class to an upcoming test can easily set the stage for anxiety. "The unit test is on Friday" will generate a different level of stress from "The unit test on Friday will be very difficult, so be sure to study hard."

> **LEADER'S QUESTION:** What are some ways of developing a classroom climate conducive to learning? SEE TIP #4.1

How Much to Teach in a Lesson? Less Is More

Working Memory

Working memory is the temporary memory where conscious processing occurs. It is an area of limited capacity where we can build, take apart, or rework ideas for eventual storage somewhere else. When something is in working memory, it generally captures our focus and demands our attention. Scanning experiments show that most the activity of working memory occurs in the frontal lobes, although other parts of the brain are frequently called into action.

Capacity of Working Memory. In Chapter 3 we discussed that working memory can handle only a few items at one time. Preschool infants can deal with about two items of information at once; preadolescents can handle three to seven items, with an average of five; adolescents have a range of five to nine; the average is seven.

These functional limits mean that the elementary or middle school teacher who announces that the lesson will cover eight causes of the Revolutionary War is already in trouble. So, too, is the high school teacher who expects the class to master in one lesson the 10 rules for using a comma in punctuation. Retention is much more likely to occur if the teacher keeps the number of items to be learned within the limits of working memory. Unfortunately, the pressure to cover the curriculum often prompts teachers to cram as much information into a lesson as possible. **The moral here is that less is more, and that teachers should resort to chunking strategies to allow more information into working memory.**

Using Novelty Effectively

Novelty is an effective tool for maintaining student interest and engagement. Students quickly acclimate to the habits of their teachers and come to class every day with preconceived notions of how a lesson will go. When the presentation violates this preconception, however, novelty occurs. Student focus increases because the unexpected is happening. Younger teachers already appreciate the power of novelty but are sometimes hesitant to use it for fear that administrators will not approve. **Educational leaders must indicate that they not only approve of *appropriate* novelty, but also encourage all teachers to try novel approaches to their lessons.** The key word here, of course, is "appropriate," and inexperienced teachers may need guidance on what type of novel activities are suitable.

> **LEADER'S QUESTION: What are some ways of adding novelty to lessons? SEE TIP #4.2**

Novelty is particularly called for when veteran teachers are faced with those curriculum topics for which they hold less enthusiasm than others. Their decrease in interest will be readily apparent to the students unless they enliven the lesson with a new approach. Adding music, humor, field trips, technology, and guest speakers are all examples of novel components to lessons.

Timing in a Lesson: Shorter Is Better

The Primacy-Recency Effect

In a learning episode, we remember best that which comes first, and remember second best that which comes last. We remember least that which

comes just past the middle of the episode. This pattern in remembering is a common phenomenon known as the *primacy-recency effect*. The effect is not a new discovery. It was first reported in studies completed in the 1880s. Figure 4.2 shows how the primacy-recency effect influences retention during a 40-minute learning episode. The times are approximate and averages. The first high retention area is called *prime-time-1*, and the second or recency mode is called *prime-time-2*. Between these two modes is the time period in which retention during that lesson is least, known as the *down-time*.

The learning episode begins when the learner focuses on the teacher with intent to learn (indicated by "0" in the Figure 4.2 graph). New information or a new skill, therefore, should be taught first, during prime-time-1, because it is most likely to be remembered. The new material should then be followed by practice during the down-time. At this point, the information is no longer new and the practice gives the learner the time to organize it for further processing. Closure should take place during prime-time-2 because this is the second most powerful memory position and an important opportunity for the learner to determine sense and meaning (Sousa, 2001a).

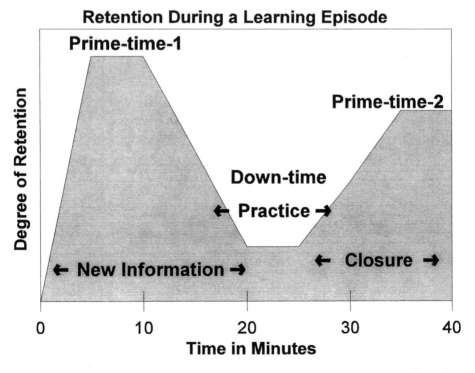

Figure 4.2 New information and closure are best presented during the prime-time periods. Practice is appropriate for the down-time segment.

Retention Varies With Length of Teaching Episode

Another fascinating characteristic of the primacy-recency effect is that the proportion of prime-times to down-time changes with the length of the teaching episode. Look at Figure 4.3 and note that during a 40-minute lesson, the two prime-times total about 30 minutes, or 75 percent of the teaching time. The down-time is about 10 minutes, or 25 percent of the lesson time. If we double the length of the learning episode to 80 minutes, the down-time increases to 30 minutes, or 38 percent of the total time. As the lesson time lengthens, the percentage of down-time increases faster than the prime-times. Information is entering working memory faster than it can be sorted, and it accumulates. This cluttering interferes with the sorting and chunking processes and reduces the ability of the learner to attach sense and meaning, thereby decreasing retention.

Figure 4.3 also shows what happens when we shorten the learning time to 20 minutes. The down-time is about 2 minutes, or 10 percent of the total lesson time. As we shorten the learning episode, the down-time decreases faster than the prime-

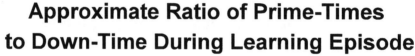

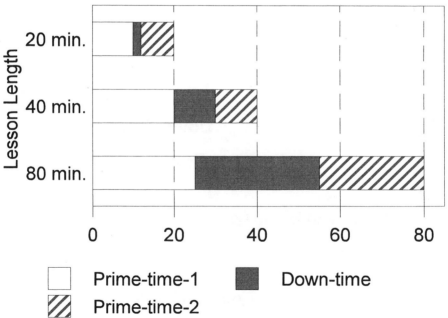

Figure 4.3 The proportion of down-time to prime-times for 20-, 40-, and 80-minute learning episodes, when taught as one lesson.

times. This finding indicates that there is a higher probability of effective learning taking place if we can keep the learning episodes short and, of course, meaningful.

Thus, teaching two 20-minute lessons provides 20 percent more prime-time (approximately 36 minutes) than one 40-minute lesson (approximately 30 minutes). Note, however, that a time period shorter than 20 minutes may not give the learner sufficient time to determine the pattern and organization of the new learning, and is thus of little benefit. Apparently, more retention occurs when lessons are shorter.

Impact on Block Scheduling

Many secondary schools have shifted to block scheduling for a variety of reasons. One advantage of the longer block is that it offers more time for students to process what they are learning. But because students are accustomed to novelty in their environment, many find it difficult to concentrate on the same topic for long periods of time. This is particularly true if the teacher is doing most of the work, such as lecturing. The primacy-recency effect has a particularly important

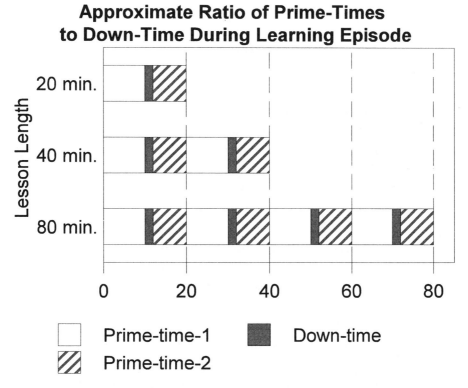

Figure 4.4 By dividing each learning episode into 20-minute segments, there is proportionately more prime-time to down-time.

LEADER'S QUESTION: What are some strategies that are particularly effective in block scheduling? SEE TIP #4.3

impact on block scheduling, in which an 80-minute period can be a blessing or a disaster, depending on how the instructional time is used. Figure 4.4 shows that a block containing four 20-minute segments will often be much more productive than one continuous lesson. This is because the primacy-recency cycle restarts after each segment, resulting in much higher proportion of prime-time to down-time. To maintain student interest and engagement, only one or two of the four block segments should be teacher directed.

Rest Between Block Lesson Segments. Most teachers believe that staying on-task throughout the learning period is best. But studies seem to support the idea that teachers are more likely to keep students focused *during* the lesson segments if they go off-task *between* the segments (e.g., telling a joke or story, playing music, or just taking a quiet rest break). The results are not surprising given the higher novelty-seeking behavior of modern-day students. Teachers in nonblock classes (that is, 40 to 45 minutes in length) who take an off-task break about halfway through the period have reported similar results (Buzan, 1989; Sousa, 2001a).

The Awesome Power of Closure

Unlike its meaning in common conversation, closure in this context does not mean to pack up and leave. Rather, it refers to a very important instructional strategy whereby the teacher allows students the opportunity and time to mentally process what has been learned. One thing is for sure: When that learning episode is over, the brain of the student must decide what to do with the information in working (temporary) memory. The two choices are either to tag it for long-term storage or delete it.

The goal of closure is to provide the time for mental rehearsal in the hope that the student will be successful in attaching sense and meaning to the new learning. Sense and meaning are two of the major criteria that the brain uses to determine whether new information (or skill) should be tagged for long-term storage. Closure is one of the most effective instructional tools to enhance retention of learning.

Closure is not review. In review, the teacher is usually doing the work, going over key points that were made during the lesson and perhaps asking related questions. Students may or may not be actively involved in this process. But in closure, the teacher asks the students to mentally rehearse what they have learned and then follows up with some form of overt activity (e.g., share with another student, write it down, or demonstrate) that holds the students accountable for what they silently processed. As mentioned earlier, prime-time-2 is usually the appropriate time for this deliberate activity to occur.

LEADER'S QUESTION: How can I help teachers use closure in their lessons? SEE TIP #4.4

Imagery (Visualization) as a Retention Strategy

In Chapter 2, we discussed the importance of imagery (also called visualization) as a powerful mental function that can enable leaders to be more successful in dealing with the situations they encounter in their job. This technique can also be used in the classroom. Training students in imagery encourages them to search long-term storage sites for appropriate images and to use them more like a movie than a photograph. Imagery is a survival skill that should become a regular part of classroom strategies as early as kindergarten. In the primary grades, the teacher should supply the images to ensure accuracy (Sousa, 2001a).

Imagery can be used in many classroom activities, including notetaking, cooperative learning groups, and alternative assessment options. Mindmapping is a specialized form of imagery that originated when the left-brain/right-brain research emerged in the 1970s. The process combines language with images to help show relationships between and among concepts, and how they connect to a key idea. Buzan (1989) and Hyerle (1996) illustrate different ways in which mind maps can be drawn.

Get Students to Stand and Deliver

Talk Is a Memory Device

Talk is a helpful memory tool because it adds another set of sensory data to the learning process. Thus, explaining what one is learning *while* learning is a powerful method of increasing retention. During the explanation, the brain of the learner is sorting out the new information and making connections to past experiences. This process helps the student attach sense and meaning to the learning, increasing the likelihood that it will be retained.

Whoever explains, learns. If the teacher is doing all the explaining, then the teacher is doing all the learning. No wonder we know our content so well! At some point in the lesson, though, the teacher should have a structured activity where the students are talking about their learning.

Movement and Learning

Figure 3.1 in Chapter 3 shows that more than one-third of students have a kinesthetic preference and thus find movement to be helpful during their learning. Yet, the mainstream educational community has often regarded thinking and movement as separate functions, assigning them different priorities. Activities involving movement, such as dance, theater, and occasionally sports, are often reduced or eliminated when school budgets get tight. But as brain studies probe deeper into the relationship between body and mind, the importance of movement to cognitive learning becomes very apparent. Recent research centered on the cerebellum shows that its nerve fibers communicate with other areas of the cerebrum as well. Movement is first detected by the sensory systems in the inner ear which sends impulses to the cerebellum, and from there to the rest of the brain, including the sensory areas and the visual cortex. The inner ear also stimulates the reticular activating system, which regulates incoming data and, thus, is critical for getting our attention. The interaction among these various brain areas helps us keep our balance and convert thought into action.

> **LEADER'S QUESTION:** How can I help teachers get students to move around and talk more during a lesson? SEE TIP # 4.5

Studies have found that signals from the cerebellum go to multiple areas in the cerebrum, arousing attention, memory, spatial perception, and the cognitive functions of the frontal lobe, the same areas that are stimulated during learning (Middleton and Strick, 1998). **It seems that the more we study the cerebellum, the more we realize that movement is inescapably linked to new learning.**

Movement also increases the amount of oxygen in the blood, which the brain needs for fuel. The concentration of oxygen affects the ability of the brain to carry out its tasks. A recent study confirmed that higher concentrations of oxygen in the blood significantly enhanced cognitive performance in healthy young adults. They were able to recall more words from a list and had faster reaction times. Moreover, their cognitive abilities varied directly with the amount of oxygen in the brain (Scholey, Moss, Neave, and Wesnes, 1999).

Incorporating movement activities into lessons is interesting and fun for the teacher and the students. Trading a few minutes of teacher talk for a movement activity can actually increase the amount of learning retained, making it a worthwhile investment of time. Combining movement and talking is an effective strategy because it is multisensory, increases student engagement, is emotionally stimulating, and encourages socialization. School leaders should encourage teachers to use movement activities in their lessons.

Practice Does Not Make Perfect

After introducing and explaining new information or a skill, teachers usually give the students an opportunity to practice what they have learned, either in the classroom or at home, or both. Does practice make perfect? No, practice makes *permanent*. Consequently, we want to ensure that students practice the new learning correctly from the beginning. This early practice (referred to as *guided practice*), is done in the presence of the teacher, who can offer corrective feedback to help students analyze and improve their practice. When the practice is correct, the teacher can then assign *independent practice,* in which the students can rehearse the skill on their own to enhance retention.

Occasionally, teachers run out of time during a lesson and instead of guided practice, they may suggest that students practice on their own until the next lesson. **Teachers should avoid giving students independent practice before guided practice.** Because practice makes permanent, allowing students to rehearse something for the first time while away from the teacher is very risky. If they unknowingly practice the skill incorrectly, then they learn the incorrect method well! This will present serious problems for both the teacher and learner later because it is very difficult to change a skill that has been practiced and remembered, even if it is not correct.

Worried About High-Stakes Testing?
Try Concept Mapping

The human brain is exceptionally competent at detecting patterns. This ability most likely emerged as a lifesaving skill during our earlier days as hunters and gatherers. To survive, for example, we had to pick out animals for food from among the patterns of the forest, and learn the patterns of the seasons and crop cycles. Test your brain on its ability to find patterns by looking at Figure 4.5. Although you see a white triangle in the diagram, it does not exist. Rather, the brain is inferring a white triangle in order to find a pattern that makes sense.

Ironically, the technology-rich environment that students grow up in today may be further enhancing the pattern-seeking abilities of the brain. Think of how the

Figure 4.5 The white triangle you may see does not exist. It is the result of the brain's attempt to find a pattern that makes sense.

toys and games that youngsters play with are based on finding patterns in order to win. In other words, students are getting even better at finding patterns in what they are observing and learning.

But this enhancement may be at the expense of something that most brains are not very good at: detail acquisition. To be blunt, the human brain sees little *survival* value in knowing what year Arizona became a state or the difference between a simile and an analogy. Yet, much of our in-school testing still centers on memorizing detail. We rarely ask questions about patterns. The main reason for this situation is that questions on details lend themselves more readily to response formats, such as true-false, multiple-choice, and fill-in-the-blank, that can be easily and quickly graded.

There are some important details and facts that all students should learn. Nonetheless, is it fair to continue to give students so many tests for detail when we know that their brains are getting worse at this aptitude and better at seeking patterns? Further, given the heavy emphasis on higher standards, I think we will be seeing those detail-centered tests for a long time to come. So, is there a way that we can take advantage of this pattern-seeking ability to help students learn more details and facts, and thus be more successful in high-stakes testing? The answer is yes, and one effective way to do this is through *concept mapping*.

Concept mapping consists of extracting details and ideas from curriculum content and plotting them visually to show relationships between and among them. Thus, to create concept maps (also called *graphic organizers*), students must be able to identify important facts and ideas, decide on the relationship these items have to one another, and then construct the appropriate map or organizer to accurately represent these relationships. The strategy requires student engagement, rehearsal, and most important, the association of factual information to a pattern. When recalling the pattern, the learner is also likely to recall the details.

Concept mapping is also an effective technique to use in an administrative meeting whose agenda is to design or revise curriculum or plan any other complex project.

LEADER'S QUESTION: What are some guidelines for helping teachers use concept mapping in their lessons? SEE TIP # 4.6

Pushing Thinking to Higher Levels

Every bit of evidence available in cognitive psychology suggests that the human brain is *designed* for thinking at many different levels of complexity. So if the brain is capable of higher-order thinking, why do we see so little of it in the normal course of student discussion and performance?

LEADER'S QUESTION: What are some guidelines for understanding and using Bloom's Taxonomy? SEE TIP #4.7

The reason our students are not thinking critically is that we have not exposed them consistently to models or situations in schools that require them to do so. Schooling, for the most part, demands little more than convergent thinking. Its practices and testing focus too much on content acquisition through rote rehearsal, rather than the processes of thinking for analysis and synthesis. Too often, merely repeating the answer is considered more important than the process used to get the answer. Consequently, students and teachers are accustomed to dealing with learning at the lowest levels of complexity. We are trying now to recognize these limitations, rewrite curriculum, retrain teachers, and encourage students to use their innate thinking abilities to process learning at higher levels of complexity.

What Thinking Skills Model to Choose?

What model should teachers use to promote higher-level thinking in the classroom? The answer depends on the model that the school and district have adopted and on the nature of the staff development program that familiarized the teachers with the model's components. My own preference is the model proposed by Benjamin Bloom (1956), which describes a taxonomy of six levels of increasing complexity of human thought: knowledge (rote), comprehension (understanding), application (using), analysis (separating), synthesis (creating), and evaluation (judging). I favor this model mainly because it is familiar, user-friendly, and simple, requires little retraining of staff, can be implemented immediately in every classroom, costs little to nothing, and remains consistent with the latest research on thinking functions.

This model also makes it easier to distinguish between two critically important concepts: *complexity* and *difficulty*. Complexity and difficulty describe completely different mental operations, but are often used synonymously. This error, resulting in the two factors being treated as one, limits the use of the taxonomy to enhance the thinking of all students. Complexity describes the *thought process* that the brain uses to deal with information. In this taxonomy, it can be described by any of the six words representing the six levels. The question "What is the capital of Rhode Island?" is at the knowledge level, while the question, "Can you tell me in your own words what is meant by a state capital?" is at the comprehension level. The second question is more *complex* than the first because it is at a higher level in the taxonomy.

Difficulty, on the other hand, refers to the *amount of effort* that the learner must expend *within* a level of complexity to accomplish a learning objective. It is possible for a learning activity to become increasingly difficult without becoming more complex. For example, the question " Can you name the states of the Union?" is at the knowledge level of complexity because it involves simple recall for most students. The question "Can you name the states of the Union and their capitals?" is also at the knowledge level but is more difficult than the prior question because it involves more effort to recall more information.

These are examples of how a student can exert great effort to achieve a learning task while processing at the lowest level of thinking. When seeking to challenge students, classroom teachers are more likely (perhaps unwittingly) to increase difficulty rather than complexity as the challenge mode. This may be because they do not recognize the difference between these concepts and they believe that difficulty is the method for achieving higher-order thinking (Sousa, 2001a).

Other models that promote higher-order thinking are certainly valuable and worth considering. In the triarchic approach proposed by Robert Sternberg, for example, teachers plan their lessons not only for memory but also for analytical, creative, and practical processing. Analytical thinking occurs then teachers ask students to judge, compare and contrast, evaluate, and critique. Creative thinking activities would have students suppose, invent, imagine, explore, and discover. Practical thinking is involved when students implement, use, apply, and contextualize. Classroom applications of the theory have shown positive results in terms of student achievement (Sternberg, 1985). Robert Marzano, who has worked for years on developing a thinking skills program, recently suggested a new taxonomy of educational objectives that reflect the needs of modern-day students (Marzano, 2001). **Regardless of the program that is chosen, educational leaders have a responsibility to ensure that classroom instruction pushes the human brain to high levels of thinking.**

Dealing With the Variety of Student Abilities

All children can learn, if we can find the way to teach them. Of the many challenges that teachers face, one of the most frustrating is trying to meet the needs of students of widely diverse abilities, from the learning disabled to the gifted, in the same classroom. This diversity is likely to increase as more students with special needs are mainstreamed into the regular classroom and as districts facing tighter budgets drop their pullout programs for gifted students.

Efforts to present the identical curriculum simultaneously to this diverse group are not generally successful. The slower learners feel lost and the faster learners are bored. One recent and promising approach to this growing problem is the concept of differentiating the curriculum and instruction to meet the needs of all learners. Although this may appear impossible at first glance, there are some strategies that have proved successful in providing differentiation for students without driving the teacher insane.

In the differentiated classroom

- ▸ Students are allowed to make learning choices based on their interests
- ▸ Differences among students become the basis for lesson planning
- ▸ Multiple materials, rather than a single text, are used
- ▸ Assignments give students options
- ▸ Instructional time is flexible according to the needs of the students
- ▸ Students are assessed in multiple ways
- ▸ Achievement is defined primarily by the growth of an individual from a pre-measured point
- ▸ Students work with the teacher to establish individual and whole-class learning objectives

By using strategies that will differentiate curriculum and instruction, teachers help more students of varying abilities become successful learners. Educational leaders can be key figures in making this approach happen by becoming knowledgeable about the aspects of differentiated curriculum and instruction and by providing teachers with the staff development sessions they need to feel comfortable with its implementation. For more information on differentiation, see the work of Tomlinson (1999) and Gregory and Chapman (2002).

ASSESSMENT

Although there has been much discussion in recent years about using assessment systems in addition to traditional written tests, progress in this area has been slow. Alternative assessments (sometimes called authentic assessments) include observation techniques, performance-based assessments, portfolios, and student self-assessment. These forms of assessment are said to be authentic indicators of student achievement because they closely resemble what students might be asked to do in class or in a real-world situation. When these options, especially performance assessments, are well designed and properly implemented, they align closely with curriculum and instruction that emphasize the construction of knowledge and problem solving in authentic contexts.

It seems, however, that the national pushes for high standards and powerful accountability systems based on norm-referenced test scores have been largely responsible for hesitancy among educational leaders to encourage broad-based assessment options. Consequently, teachers who might have been willing to consider alternative assessments may not implement them because of perceived time constraints or administrative pressure to teach to the test. For the foreseeable future, pressure for teacher, school, and district accountability based on large-scale assessment will most likely intensify and become a source of debate about its fairness and impact.

New Views of Learning Versus Political Realities

If educators accept the idea that students learn in different ways, then it also makes sense to accept the notion that students will use different ways to report what they have learned. Because of research in cognitive neuroscience, our understanding of how people learn has moved away from the behaviorist view (stimulus-response) and closer to a more constructivist approach. Learning is more than the receiving (and parroting back) of information. Rather, learning involves integrating knew knowledge with what one already knows and applying that new learning to construct additional knowledge. This view of learning requires assessment techniques that determine if students can organize information and use it to solve complex, context-based problems. These techniques need to include performance assessments.

Even though cognitive scientists and educators have accepted this newer view of how learning occurs, the general public and their political representatives have not. They believe that schools are not sufficiently challenging students, that they need to put more emphasis on the basics, and that accountability must be determined essentially through traditional norm-referenced written tests. By their very nature, high-stakes tests tend to *narrow* the curriculum and steer instruction toward demonstrating the knowledge or skills that the assessment asks for.

Meanwhile, the business community is calling for students to bring a lot more than just a knowledge of basic skills to the workplace. To be successful in the business environment of the future, students need to be able to make decisions, meet deadlines, get along with colleagues, solve contextual problems, and communicate effectively. These skills are better measured by performance assessment than by written tests. In some areas of the country, the strong voice of the business community has helped to balance and even offset the impact of groups that lobby for traditional curriculum and testing (Grissmer and Flanagan, 1998).

It is too early to predict how or when the old learning/written assessments versus new learning/multiple assessments battle is going to end. It seems clear, though, that if we tie school funding as well as teacher compensation and evaluation to high-stakes testing, then teachers will teach to the test. Testing, then, becomes both the beginning and end of instruction, and other important needs of the students may be forgotten. Furthermore, most of these high-stakes tests are summative in nature, occurring after the instruction on a unit of study has been completed. Although summative assessments are necessary, formative assessments that measure what happens during and in the middle of learning lead to greater student achievement.

Leadership for Assessment Reform

Educational leaders cannot sit back and be just observers in this battle. As we gain greater understanding into *how* the human brain learns and *what* it must learn to be successful in this new millennium, assessment reform becomes a high priority. This is no easy task for several reasons. First, leaders must still operate within the constraints set by policymakers. Second, the alternative assessment choices are varied and complex. Third, assessment choices often involve tradeoffs in quality and feasibility, which may sometimes conflict with each other, forcing difficult choices. Fourth, traditional teachers tend to favor standardized tests if there is little administrative support for alternative assessments (Schwager and Carlson, 1994). Nonetheless, if schools are to meet the challenge of preparing students to be successful adults, educational leaders must find ways to introduce and encourage alternative assessments while, at the same time, convincing policymakers that these options can provide the accountability they seek.

Assessment Quality

When selecting types of alternative assessments, leaders need to judge their quality. The basic psychometric concepts of reliability, validity, and fairness are used in research to determine the quality of an assessment instrument by addressing the following three questions (Rahn, Stecher, Goodman, and Alt, 1997):

How accurate is the information gathered? This component is known as *reliability* and measures the extent to which a similar score is likely to result if the same or similar test is given again. High reliability limits the possibility that chance factors will lead to inaccurate scores.

How confident are we about drawing conclusions from the scores about student performance? Referred to as *validity*, this component deals with how closely the test measures what it is intended to measure. Can accurate conclusions be drawn about the knowledge or skills being assessed?

Is the instrument fair to all the students who take it? Fairness measures the probability that all students of equivalent abilities will achieve similar scores. If factors such as ethnicity, socioeconomic status, or gender can affect the score, the test is considered to be low in fairness.

Reliability, validity, and fairness are important because they can be used to convince policymakers that these assessments are acceptable alternatives or supplements to written norm-referenced tests. It is possible, however, that assessments with these components may not be feasible for several reasons.

Feasibility

Even assessments of high quality may not be feasible to implement because of their cost and time for administration, complexity, and acceptability.

Cost and Time. Many of the decisions that school leaders make are based on these two scarce resources: cost and time. Assessments that are alternatives to multiple-choice tests are more costly and time-consuming to draft, pilot, administer, and score. Teachers may need specialized training in how to design these types of instruments.

Complexity. In addition to the high cost of development, assessments of performance tasks and portfolios are complex and demand a higher level of sophistication from those who administer them. Teachers may need training in the development of reliable scoring rubrics and in the use of equipment and materials needed for alternative testing.

Acceptability. The people who will use the results of these assessments, such as students, teachers, administrators, parents, and employers, must feel that the assessment options are credible. If these stakeholders lack familiarity with alternative methods, they may be resistant to their implementation. This resistance can often be overcome through training and by allowing the stakeholders to participate in decisions about assessment options.

The Value of Performance Assessment

Despite these potential problems, educational leaders may still be able to find ways to convince policymakers of the value of alternative assessments, especially performance assessments, which are a better measure than standardized tests of what students will need to accomplish in the real world. According to Clark and Clark (2000), performance assessment

- ▸ Guides rather than judges, giving educators the opportunity to discover if students can chose their own learning activities and create their own answers
- ▸ Documents what students have done and learned over a given time period
- ▸ Replicates the authentic tasks that students will face in the real world
- ▸ Serves the needs of students
- ▸ Assesses knowledge in terms of its usefulness to construct learning in the future
- ▸ Requires students to prove that they have mastered learning objectives by having them monitor their own progress, judge the quality of their work, and design remediation strategies
- ▸ Allows teachers to see students tackle and solve ambiguous problems, pose questions, collect evidence, and decide on what purposeful actions to take

Introducing performance assessment may present challenges to the existing school culture, especially if that culture is focused solely on raising test scores. Nevertheless, performance assessments respond to the needs of students. As such, teachers need to be involved in the design and implementation of performance assessments and support them with their classroom practices.

Do Teachers Support Assessment Reform?

Although many researchers and educational theorists propose the use of alternative assessments, their actual implementation will depend on the actions of teachers in the classroom. A few research studies have looked at the attitudes of teachers regarding alternative assessment. One study found that the attitudes of teachers toward assessment practices differed significantly, depending on whether the teachers were viewed as traditional or innovative and the extent to which the

LEADER'S QUESTION: What are some guidelines for establishing performance assessments? SEE TIP #4.8

school administration supported alternative assessments. Not surprisingly, innovative teachers valued alternative assessments more than traditional teachers, who tended to favor traditional testing, especially if the school administration showed little support for alternative assessments (Schwager and Carlson, 1994).

More recently, a major survey study of nearly 900 teachers in 34 schools examined the influence of experience, grade level, and subject area on the assessment practices of teachers. The researchers found that teachers used performance- and observation-based assessments much more frequently than portfolios and self-assessment. More experienced teachers (20 years or more) reported using alternative assessments more frequently than less experienced teachers (6 years or less) did. Elementary level teachers reported using alternative assessment strategies significantly more often than did high school teachers. As for subject area, mathematics teachers reported using traditional methods of assessment much less frequently than did teachers in all other areas. This last finding was a surprise and the researchers speculated that the emphasis on problem solving in mathematics may preclude the use of traditional forms of assessment (Bol, Stephenson, and O'Connell, 1998).

This study provides insight into the attitudes of teachers toward alternative assessments. Because alternative assessment is an important component of educational reform, school leaders need to be aware of teacher attitudes, decide what variables affect these attitudes, and select the steps they will take to bring about successful reform efforts in assessment.

What Are the Hopes for the Future in Assessment?

The tug of war between traditional and alternative assessments will no doubt be played out on the field of standards-based reform. Although the push for higher standards offers opportunities for true educational reform, the demand for traditional assessment methods as the sole measure of progress toward those standards could stifle reforms in curriculum and instruction for years to come. To prevent this, I concur with Asp (2000) and suggest that educational leaders, as visionaries, design the action plans that will allow for a future where

- ▶ Performance plays a larger role in assessment as the ability to apply what students have learned in real-world situations becomes a more valued goal
- ▶ Norm-referenced testing decreases as accountability focuses more on what individual students can do than on how much content they have acquired compared with other students

- ▸ More coherent assessment systems (including performance assessment) will be used for both large-scale and classroom assessment
- ▸ The quality of assessment will be determined by its impact on student learning, teaching, and the school as an organization
- ▸ Assessment takes on the new role of providing more and better learning for the student rather than for accountability and classification of students

MAJOR POINTS IN CHAPTER 4

❏ Positive classroom climate is important to improving student learning and retention as well as limiting discipline problems.

❏ Novelty is an effective strategy for getting and maintaining interest. Music, humor, movement, and multi-modality activities are just a few examples of novelty.

❏ In a learning episode, we remember best that which comes first, second best that which comes last, and least that which comes just past the middle of the episode. This pattern is known as the *primacy-recency effect* and has important implications for how and when material is presented during a lesson and for block scheduling.

❏ Closure is used to provide the time for mental rehearsal in the hope that the student will be successful in attaching sense and meaning to the new learning. Sense and meaning are two of the major criteria that the brain uses to determine whether new information (or a skill) should be tagged for long-term storage.

❏ Imagery (or visualization) is a powerful mental function that encourages students to search long-term storage sites for appropriate images and to use them more like a movie than a photograph. Imagery is a survival skill that should become a regular part of classroom strategies as early as kindergarten.

❏ Getting students to stand up, move, and talk is an effective instructional strategy because it is multisensory and emotionally stimulating, increases student engagement, and encourages socialization.

❏ Because practice makes permanent, teachers should avoid giving students independent practice before guided practice. If students unknowingly practice the skill incorrectly, it will be more difficult for them to relearn the correct skill later.

❏ Concept mapping is an effective strategy for remembering details because it requires student engagement, rehearsal, and the association of factual information to a pattern.

❑ Educational leaders have a responsibility to ensure that classroom instruction pushes students to high levels of thinking. The brain is designed to do this well, but it must be challenged and stimulated beyond the rote rehearsal of isolated data.

❑ By using differentiated curriculum and instruction, teachers can help more students of varying abilities become successful learners. Educational leaders can be key figures in making this approach happen, by becoming knowledgeable about the aspects of differentiated curriculum and instruction and by providing teachers with the staff development sessions they need to feel comfortable with its implementation.

❑ Assessment of student progress should include more than written standardized tests. Alternative forms of assessment, such as portfolios, performance assessment, and self-assessment are valuable ways of determining how well students can solve complex problems in a real-world context. Educational leaders should encourage these assessment options despite the strong push to rely solely on norm-referenced tests.

TIPS FOR LEADERS #4.1

Helping Teachers Develop a Classroom Climate Conducive to Learning

Educational leaders can help teachers recognize the importance of purposefully maintaining a positive climate in their classrooms. There are several ways to address this issue. Because positive school and classroom climate is so important, consider posing the following questions for discussion in faculty meetings (Sousa, 2001a):

- What kinds of emotions in our school could interfere with cognitive processing (i.e., have a negative effect on learning)?

- What strategies and structures can our school and our teachers use to limit the threat and negative effects of these emotions?

- What factors in our school can foster emotions in students that promote learning (i.e., have a positive effect)?

- What strategies have you used to encourage the positive emotions that promote learning?

Follow up on these discussions and look for ways to implement the good suggestions that emerge from them. Additionally, specific strategies for enhancing classroom climate can be discussed with teachers collectively or individually.

Learning occurs more easily in environments free from threat or intimidation. Whenever a student detects a threat, thoughtful processing gives way to emotion or to survival reactions. Experienced teachers have seen this in the classroom. Under pressure to give a quick response, the student begins to stumble, stabs at answers, gets frustrated or angry, and may even resort to violence.

Questioning Techniques

There are ways to deal with questions and answers that reduce the fear of giving a wrong answer. The teacher could:

- Supply the question to which the wrong answer belongs:
  "You would be right if I had asked ..."

- Give the student a prompt that leads to the correct answer

- Ask another student to help

Threats to students loom continuously in the classroom. The capacity of a teacher to humiliate, embarrass, reject, and punish constitutes a perceived threat. Many students even see grading more as a punitive than as a rewarding process. Students perceive threats in varying degrees, but the presence of a threat in *any* significant degree impedes learning. Thinking and learning functions operate fully only when one feels physically and emotionally secure.

Teachers can make their classrooms better learning environments by avoiding threats (even subtle intimidation) and by establishing democratic climates in which students are treated fairly and feel free to express their opinions during discussions. In these environments students:

- Develop trust in the teacher

- Exhibit more positive behaviors

- Are less likely to be disruptive

- Show greater support for school policy

- Sense that thinking is encouraged and nurtured

Using Humor

Humor (not sarcasm) has many benefits when used frequently and appropriately in the classroom and other school settings. Is there laughter at your faculty meetings? To help relieve the stress in our schools, let's take our work seriously but ourselves lightly. Here are just some of the benefits of humor.

- *Physiological Benefits*

  ▸ The brain needs oxygen and glucose for fuel. When we laugh, we get more oxygen in the bloodstream, so the brain is better fueled.

> ▸ Laughter causes the release of endorphins in the blood, allowing the person to enjoy the moment in body as well as in mind.

● *Psychological, Sociological, and Educational Benefits*

> ▸ Because the normal human brain loves to laugh, beginning the lesson with a humorous tale (such as a joke, pun, or story) helps the learner to focus.
> ▸ When people laugh together, they bond and a community spirit emerges.
> ▸ We know that emotions enhance retention, so the positive feelings that result from laughter increase the probability that students will remember what they learned.
> ▸ Schools and all their occupants are under more stress than ever. Taking time to laugh relieves that stress and gives the staff and students a better mental attitude for accomplishing their tasks.
> ▸ Good-natured humor (not teasing or sarcasm) can be an effective way of reminding students of the rules without raising tension in the classroom. Teachers who use appropriate humor are more likeable, and students have a more positive feeling toward them. Discipline problems, therefore, are less likely to occur.

● *Using Humor as Part of Lessons.* Humor should not be limited to an opening joke or story. Because of its value as an attention-getter and retention strategy, encourage teachers to look for ways to use humor within the context of the learning objective. Droz and Ellis (1996) give many helpful suggestions on how to get students to use humor in lessons on writing, mathematics, science, and history.

● *Avoiding Sarcasm.* Sarcasm is inevitably destructive to someone. Even some well-intentioned teachers say, "Oh, I know my students very well, so they can take sarcasm." But more students are coming to school looking for emotional support. Sarcasm is one of the factors that can undermine that support and turn students against their peers and the school.

● *Educational Leaders and Humor.* Educational leaders also need to remember the value of humor in their relationships with staff, students, and parents. As leaders, they set the example; in meetings and other settings, they can show that humor and laughter are acceptable in schools and classrooms.

TIPS FOR LEADERS #4.2

Helping Teachers Use Novelty
in the Classroom

Using novelty does *not* mean that the teacher needs to be a stand-up comic or the classroom a three-ring circus. It simply means using a varied teaching approach that involves more student activity along with lesson components that the students did not expect. Appropriately used, novelty can add new interest and fun to learning. Here are a few suggestions to help teachers incorporate novelty in their lessons (Sousa, 2001a).

- *Humor.* There are many positive benefits that come from using humor in the classroom at *all* grade levels. See the **Tips for Leaders #4.1,** which suggests guidelines and beneficial reasons for using humor.

- *Movement.* When we sit for more than twenty minutes, our blood pools in our seat and in our feet. By getting up and moving, we recirculate that blood. Within a minute, there is about 15 percent more blood in our brain. We do think better on our feet than on our seat! Students sit too much in classrooms, especially in secondary schools. Look for ways to get students up and moving, especially when they are verbally rehearsing what they have learned.

- *Multisensory Instruction.* Students are acclimated to a multisensory environment. They are more likely to give attention if there are interesting, colorful visuals and if they can walk around and talk about their learning.

- *Quiz Games.* Have students develop a quiz game or other similar activity to test each other on their knowledge of the concepts taught. This is a common strategy in elementary classrooms, but underutilized in secondary schools. Besides being fun, it has the added value of making students rehearse and understand the concepts in order to create the quiz questions and answers.

- *Music.* Although the research is inconclusive, there are some benefits of playing music in the classroom at certain times during the learning episode.

But a few guidelines are in order (Sousa, 2001a).

▶ Music can be played at different times during the learning episode, but the teacher should choose the appropriate music for the particular activity. It is not advisable to play music when the teacher is doing direct instruction (unless the music is part of the lesson) because it can be a distraction.

▶ Because music can affect a person's heart rate, blood pressure, and emotional mood, the number of beats per minute in the music is very important. Choose music that plays at about 60 beats per minute (the average heartbeat rate) as background to facilitate student work. Music at 80 to 90 beats per minute is appropriate for a fast-paced activity.

▶ Administrators note: To calm down a noisy group as, say, in the school cafeteria or commons area, choose music at 40 to 50 beats per minute.

▶ Using music with or without lyrics depends on the purpose of playing the music. Music played at the beginning or end of class can contain lyrics because the main purpose is to set a mood, not get focus. But when students are working on a learning task, lyrics become a distraction.

▶ Use familiar music to set a mood. However, when working on a specific assignment, use music that is unfamiliar. If the students know the background music, some will sing or hum along, causing a distraction. Choose unfamiliar music, such as classical or new age music, and have enough different selections so that they are each played infrequently.

▶ Students may ask to bring in their own selections. To maintain a positive classroom climate, teachers should tell them that they *can* bring in their music, *provided the selections meet the above criteria!* Explain to them why this is necessary.

TIPS FOR LEADERS #4.3

Helping Teachers With Block Scheduling

More educational leaders are finding themselves in high schools (and some middle schools) that have converted to a block schedule consisting of longer teaching periods, usually 80 to 90 minutes. Although there are various formats for the blocks, the main goal of this change is to allow more time for student participation in the learning process.

The introduction of block scheduling should have been preceded by a staff development program that trained teachers in the many advantages and few disadvantages of a longer instructional period. The block experience is likely to be more successful if the teacher recognizes the value and need for novelty, and resists the temptation to be the focus of the block during the entire time period. Here are some suggestions for helping teachers design a brain-compatible block lesson (Sousa, 2001a):

- *Remember the primacy-recency effect.* Teaching a 90-minute episode as one continuous lesson will mean a down-time of about 35 minutes. Planning for four 20-minute learning segments reduces the down-time to about 10 minutes. This down-time can also be productive if the students are engaged in discussions about the new learning.

- *Be in direct control of just one segment.* The teacher may wish to do some direct instruction during one of the lesson segments. If so, the first segment should be used for this, and then shift the work burden to the students for the other segments. **Remember that the brain that does the work is the brain that learns.**

- *Go off-task between segments.* Going off-task between the lesson segments can increase the degree of focus when the students return to task. This is because of the novelty effect. If it is important to stay on-task, however, then a joke, story, or cartoon that is related to the learning can be used. The students still get the novelty effect but without losing focus.

- *Eliminate the unnecessary.* Block scheduling is designed to give students a chance to dig deeper into concepts. To get the time to do this, teachers should scrap less important items that sneak into the curriculum over time. We all know that everything in the curriculum is not of equal importance. This selective abandonment is necessary on a regular basis.

- *Work with colleagues.* Block activities offer an excellent opportunity for teachers to work together in planning the longer lessons. This collegial process can be very productive and interesting, especially when teachers deliver lessons together. Such planning can be within or across subject areas.

- *Vary the blocks.* Novelty means finding ways to make each of the segments different and multisensory. Here are just a few examples of block activities that can be used for the lesson segments:

> Teacher talk (maximum of two segments of 10 to 15 minutes each)
> Research
> Cooperative learning groups
> Reading
> Student peer coaching
> Laboratory experiences
> Computer work
> Journal writing
> Guest speakers
> Videos/movies/slides
> Audiotapes
> Reflection time
> Jigsaw combinations
> Discussion groups
> Role-playing/simulations
> Instructional games/puzzles

TIPS FOR LEADERS #4.4

Helping Teachers Use Closure

Most lessons should have a closure component to allow the student's working memory the opportunity to attach sense and meaning to the new learning, thereby increasing the probability that the learning will be retained. Remind teachers of the following when using closure:

- *Initiating Closure.* The teacher gives directions that focus the student on the new learning and provides adequate quiet time for the cerebral summarizing to occur. This is followed by an overt activity (discussion) for student accountability. During the discussion, the teacher can assess the quality and accuracy of what occurred during closure and make any necessary adjustments in teaching.

- *Closure Is Different From Review.* In review, the teacher does most of the work, repeating key concepts made during the lesson and rechecking student understanding. In closure, the student does most of the work by mentally rehearsing and summarizing those concepts and deciding whether they make sense and have meaning.

- *When to Use Closure.* Closure can occur at various times in a lesson.

    - It can start a lesson: "Think of the two causes of the Revolutionary War we talked about yesterday and be prepared to discuss them."
    - It can occur during the lesson (called *procedural closure*) when the teacher moves from one sublearning to the next: "Review those two rules in your mind before we learn the third rule."
    - It should also take place at the end of the lesson (called *terminal closure*) to tie all the sublearnings together.

TIPS FOR LEADERS #4.5

Encouraging Student Movement

Remember that students are participating less in physical education programs. Yet physical activity is essential to promoting the normal growth of mental function, to generating positive emotions, and in learning and remembering cognitive material. Here are some suggestions that may encourage teachers to get students moving more (Sousa, 2001a):

- *Synergy*. Synergy describes how the joint actions of people working together increase their mutual effectiveness. This strategy gets students moving and talking while learning. Each participant ends up having a better understanding as a result of this interaction (synergy). It can be used from the primary grades to graduate school. The steps for the teacher are the following:

  ▸ Teach a concept. Ask students to quietly review their notes and be prepared to explain what they have learned to someone else. Allow sufficient time for this mental rehearsal to occur (usually 1 to 3 minutes).

  ▸ Ask students to walk across the room and pair up with someone they don't usually work with. They stand face-to-face and take turns explaining what they have learned. They add to their notes anything their partners have said that they don't have.

  ▸ Move around the room. Answer questions to get them back on track, but avoid re-teaching the lesson.

  ▸ Allow enough time for the process. Start with a few minutes, adding more time if they are still on task and reducing the time when they seem done.

  ▸ To help students stay on task, call on several students at random when the activity is over to explain what they discussed and learned.

  ▸ Ask if there were any misunderstandings or items that need further explanation, and clarify them.

- *Energizers.* Use movement activities to energize students who are at low points in their energy levels (e.g., during early morning periods for high school students or during that downtime just past the middle of the day). For example,

    "Measure the room's length in hand spans."

    "Touch seven objects in the room that are the same color."

    "Go to four different sources of information in this room."

    "In your group, make a poster-sized mind map of this unit."

- *Acting Out Key Concepts.* This strategy uses the body in a physical way to learn and remember a difficult concept. If the lesson objective is to learn the continents, try this: Stand in front of a world map and use body parts to represent the different continents.

- *Role-Playing.* Do role-playing on a regular basis. For example, students can organize extemporaneous pantomime or play charades to dramatize major points in a unit. Have them develop and act out short commercials advertizing upcoming units or to review previously learned material.

- *Vocabulary Building: Act Out the Word.* Look for vocabulary words that lend themselves to a physical movement. Then, say the word, read the meaning, and do the movement that acts out the meaning of the word (Chapman and King, 2000).

- *Verbal to Physical Tug-of-War.* In this activity, students choose a partner and a topic from the unit they have been learning. Each student forms an opinion about the topic and has 30 seconds to convince a partner why his or her own topic is more important (the verbal tug-of-war). After this debate, the partners separate to opposite sides for a physical tug-of-war with a rope.

TIPS FOR LEADERS #4.6

Concept Mapping

Concept mapping uses diagrams to organize and represent the relationships between and among the components of a unit of study. These diagrams are also called *graphic organizers*. Students should discuss the different types of relationships that can exist and give their own examples before attempting to select a concept map. There are dozens of possible organizers (Hyerle, 1996; Sousa, 2001a). Below are some common types.

- *Spider maps* best illustrate classification, similarity, and difference relationships.

- *Hierarchy maps* illustrate defining and/or subsuming, equivalence, and quantity relationships.

- *Chain maps* illustrate time sequence, casual, and enabling relationships.

- *Story maps* are useful for classifying main ideas with supporting events and information from the story.

- *Analogy maps* illustrate similarities and differences between new and familiar concepts.

- *K-W-L maps* illustrate the degree of new learning that will be needed. The " K" is for what we already *know;* "W" is for what we *want* to know; and "L" is for what we *learned*.

- *Venn diagrams* map the similarities and differences between two concepts.

- *Plot diagrams* are used to find the major parts of a novel.

- *Brace maps* show subsets of larger items.

TIPS FOR LEADERS #4.7

Understanding and Using Bloom's Taxonomy

Bloom's (1956) Taxonomy consists of six levels that represent the increasing complexity of human thought. The following are the levels in decreasing order of complexity with terms and sample activities that illustrate the thought processes at each level (Sousa, 2001a).

Levels of Bloom's Taxonomy
Difficulty and Complexity

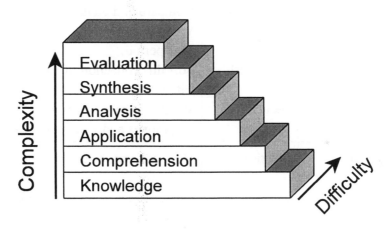

LEVEL	TERMS	SAMPLE ACTIVITIES
Evaluation	appraise	Which of the two main characters in the story would you rather have as a friend? Why?
	assess	Is violence ever justified in correcting injustices? Why or why not?
	judge	Which of the environments we've studied seems like the best place for you to live? Defend your answer.

LEVEL	TERMS	SAMPLE ACTIVITIES
Synthesis	imagine	Pretend you were a participant in the Boston Tea Party and write a diary entry that tells what happened.
	compose	Rewrite *Little Red Riding Hood* as a news story.
	design	Design a different way of solving this problem.
	infer	Formulate a hypothesis that might explain the results of these three experiments.
Analysis	analyze	Which events in the story are fantasy and which really happened?
	contrast	Compare and contrast the post–Civil War period with the post–Vietnam War period.
	distinguish	Sort this collection of rocks into three categories.
	deduce	Which of these words are Latin derivatives and which are Greek?
Application	practice	Use each vocabulary word in a sentence.
	calculate	Calculate the area of your classroom.
	apply	Think of three situations in which we would use this mathematics operation.
Comprehension	summarize	Summarize the paragraph in your own words.
	discuss	Why are symbols used on maps?
	explain	Write a paragraph explaining the duties of the mayor.
Knowledge	define	What is the definition of a verb?
	label	Label the three symbols on this map.
	recall	What are the three branches of government?

Some Tips on Using Bloom's Taxonomy

Teachers are sometimes reluctant to use the higher levels of the taxonomy because they are not sure what to expect from the learner. As an educational leader, you can encourage the faculty to push students to higher levels of thinking. Model the taxonomy in your own meetings and make the following suggestions to teachers about using the taxonomy (Sousa, 2001a):

- *Watch the Behavior of the Learner.* Learning behavior reveals the level of complexity where processing is taking place. Whenever the brain has the option of solving a problem at two levels of complexity, it generally chooses the less complex level. Teachers can inadvertently design activities that they believe are at one level of complexity that students actually accomplish at a different (usually lower) level.

- *Remember That the Levels Are Cumulative.* Each level includes the levels of lesser complexity. Students must deal with the new learnings thoroughly and successfully at lower levels before moving to upper levels. It is very difficult to create a product (synthesis) without a solid knowledge base and sufficient practice in applying the learnings.

- *Beware of Mimicry.* Sometimes students seem to be applying their learning to a new situation (application level) when they are just mimicking the teacher's behavior. Mimicry is knowledge level. For students to be really at the application level, they must understand why they are using a particular process to solve *new* problems.

- *Discuss Core Concepts at the Higher Levels.* Not all topics are suitable for processing at the upper levels. There are some areas in which creativity is *not* desired (e.g., basic arithmetic, spelling, the rules of grammar), but consider taking to the upper levels every concept that is identified as a core learning. This helps students to attach meaning and make connections to past learnings, thereby significantly increasing retention.

- *Choose Complexity Over Difficulty.* Give novel, multisensory tasks to move students progressively up the taxonomy. Reduce their exposure to trivial information and discourage students from memorizing it, a process that many find monotonous and meaningless. Instead, give them divergent activities in analysis, synthesis, and evaluation that are more interesting and more likely to result in a deeper understanding of the learning objectives.

TIPS FOR LEADERS #4.8

Guidelines for Using Performance Assessments

Performance assessment is just one of the different types of alternative assessments. Appropriate assessments of performance require the specification of a task, the devising of a fair plan for scoring, and evidence of test reliability. Here are some guidelines for selecting performance assessment instruments.

The assessment should

- ☐ Require collaboration with others
- ☐ Be free of arbitrary time restraints
- ☐ Identify strengths
- ☐ Include complex, intellectual challenges rather than fragmented tasks
- ☐ Be free of intrusiveness
- ☐ Represent challenges within a specific subject area
- ☐ Be attempted by all students
- ☐ Measure essential knowledge and skills
- ☐ Reflect standards to which everyone in the school can aspire
- ☐ Include authentic (not contrived) problems that reflect the real world
- ☐ Allow for multifaceted scoring systems rather than a single grade
- ☐ Be compatible with the goals of the school
- ☐ Offer opportunities for students to apply what they have learned
- ☐ Complement the curriculum
- ☐ Show evidence of reliability
- ☐ Show evidence of validity

Performance assessments can lower test anxiety and provide students with a challenging, interesting, and active learning environment.

Teacher Evaluation

One area of school reform that has been among the slowest to change is the way educational leaders evaluate their professional staff. No one questions that evaluation of teacher performance is necessary to ensure that the main mission of teaching and learning is being carried out within the school. Such quality assurance is important to all members of the school community, and educational professionals accept this as part of the job. The criticisms of teacher evaluation center on *how* it is conducted.

Most of the traditional evaluation practices stress accountability and are based on teacher-directed activities such as lecture, demonstration, and recitation designed primarily to transmit knowledge and cognitive skills to students. Principals generally use the minimal competencies associated with direct instruction as criteria for judging teacher competence and performance. Teachers generally have had little input into designing the evaluation processes and often resent having their performance judged mainly by short and infrequent classroom visits. This situation leads to a definite mismatch between how the brains of the teachers and principal perceive teacher evaluation (Figure 5.1).

TRADITIONAL MODELS OF TEACHER EVALUATION

Traditional evaluation methods include two categories. One category deals with *formative* processes designed to monitor and improve instruction and enhance professional growth. The other category includes components that are considered *summative* in that they assist leaders in making personnel decisions, such as who stays, who goes, and who changes assignment (Figure 5.2).

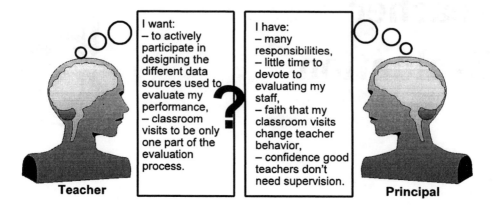

Figure 5.1 Teachers and principals often perceive the evaluation process very differently.

The Formative Process: Clinical Supervision

The most widely used model for formative supervision involves announced visits to classrooms to observe teacher performance. It consists of a pre-observation conference, the observation visit, an analysis of teacher performance, a post-observation conference, and a post-conference analysis. The underlying principle of this approach is that appropriate feedback from a knowledgeable professional over time will encourage teachers to consider alternative classroom strategies. Although this process may be effective with struggling teachers, most educators realize that this format does little to enhance the behavior of competent teachers. The administrators make their observation visits and hold their conferences, and teachers go back to their classrooms and continue to do what they were doing.

The Summative Process: Performance Evaluation

Another form of classroom observation is the unannounced visit. Here the supervisor uses a checklist of desirable teacher behaviors and indicates which behaviors were observed during the lesson. A follow-up meeting may occur for the purposes of signing the completed form. In many cases, however, the form is just handed to the teacher with no formal post-observation conference. These forms become the basis for future personnel actions, such as termination or merit pay. The underlying principle of this approach is that classroom teachers will respond appropriately whether they are commended or criticized for their performance.

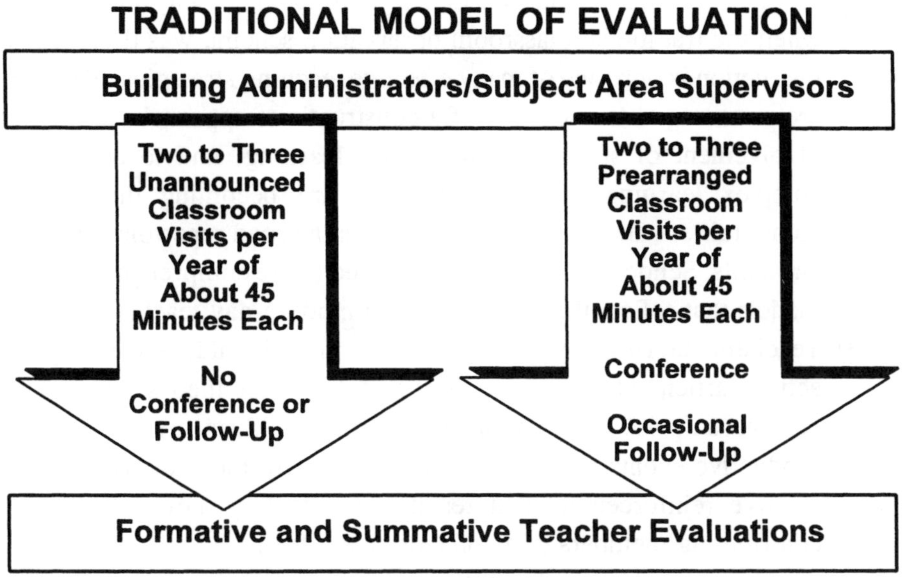

TRADITIONAL MODEL OF EVALUATION

Building Administrators/Subject Area Supervisors

Two to Three Unannounced Classroom Visits per Year of About 45 Minutes Each		**Two to Three Prearranged Classroom Visits per Year of About 45 Minutes Each**
No Conference or Follow-Up		**Conference** **Occasional Follow-Up**

Formative and Summative Teacher Evaluations

Figure 5.2 Traditional models of supervision are based primarily on two to three unannounced and prearranged classroom visits per year.

Although the modern reform paradigm views schools as learning organizations and teachers as knowledge workers within a complex system, there are school leaders who still adhere to this model that evaluates teachers mainly on their classroom performance during two or three 40-minute visits each year. It is no wonder that many teachers view the evaluation process with cynicism and disdain. They rarely object to the classroom visits. What they object to is that the few visits become the *main* criteria for judging their professional competence.

TEACHER EVALUATION FOR THE 21st CENTURY

Dissatisfaction over traditional evaluation methods seems to be growing among both teachers and school leaders. There are several reasons for this trend.

(1) A system based on one or two observations a year does little to help the struggling novice teacher or enhance the professional growth of the experienced teacher. We now accept that effective staff development programs must treat adults as respected professionals, offer them opportunities to master new content and integrate it into their practice, and allow them to engage with other professionals in their field.

(2) The expectations of what constitutes good teaching today are different from when the traditional classroom observation scheme was designed. Direct instruction is only one of many effective teaching strategies. Teachers now are encouraged to use more of a constructivist approach, to increase the involvement of students in their own learning, and to aspire to more complex learning outcomes. Schools are becoming diverse learning communities where teachers must possess a broad repertoire of knowledge and skills. School leaders, therefore, need to use comprehensive evaluation models that reflect the complexities of modern-day teaching.

(3) Teachers entering the profession today in their midtwenties expect to be active participants in the activities that determine their success or failure. Passive surprise observation visits and checklists are not going to be productive events for these teachers. They are more likely to respond to positive reinforcement that results from feeling they are valuable and contributing members of a collaborative effort.

> **LEADER'S QUESTION: What are some new directions for teacher evaluation? SEE TIP #5.1**

(4) Traditional evaluation methods run counter to the principles of reform that are striving to convert schools from a collection of isolated classrooms into an interactive and dynamic learning organization led by a creative and visionary mentor. Evaluation methods that focus on complying with a regimented set of teaching behaviors do not encourage the development of collaborative school cultures.

(5) How we evaluate teachers ought to fit in with how we evaluate students. Teachers certainly would not judge student achievement based on two 40-minute performances a year. Should we not treat teachers at least as well as we treat students?

No one approach to teacher evaluation will please all. But districts should choose a system that all the stakeholders can accept and which is consistent with other reform efforts being undertaken in the schools. Here are a few of the models that researchers are suggesting. It is not the intent of this book to go into great detail about each model. That is best done by looking at the appropriate references.

Linking Teacher Evaluation to Professional Standards

In 1987, the National Board of Professional Teaching Standards (NBPTS) was created to make teaching a profession dedicated to student learning and to upholding high standards for professional performance. The NBPTS developed in 1989 general standards for certifying the quality of performance of experienced teachers. The NBPTS effort raised the standards for teachers, advocated strengthening their educational preparation through the standards, and created performance-based assessments that demonstrate effective application of the standards. The standards were based on the following five core propositions that educators agree are essential to accomplished teaching (NBPTS, 2002):

> ▸ Teachers are committed to students and their learning.
> ▸ Teachers know the subjects they teach and how to teach those subjects to students.
> ▸ Teachers are responsible for managing and mentoring student learning.
> ▸ Teachers think systematically about their practice and learn from experience.
> ▸ Teachers are members of learning communities.

> **LEADER'S QUESTION: What are the INTASC standards for assessing the performance of new teachers? SEE TIP #5.2**

In 1992, the Interstate New Teacher Assessment and Support Consortium (INTASC), a program of the Council of Chief State School Officers, developed 10 performance-based standards that were compatible with the NBPTS core propositions. Although the INTASC standards were designed to define the knowledge, dispositions, and performances of all beginning teachers, they can be applied to teachers at all levels of experience (INTASC, 1992). Nearly 40 states are now translating the INTASC standards into discipline-specific standards in each of the major K–12 content areas.

Linking Teacher Evaluation to Professional Development

One of the major criticisms of the observation-checklist approach is that it treats all teachers alike. Evaluators usually make the same number of visits to highly skilled teachers as to mediocre teachers. Furthermore, there is seldom any connection between the teacher behaviors noted in the observation report and that teacher's professional development.

Danielson and McGreal (2000) have developed a comprehensive design for teacher evaluation which they suggest needs to

> ▸ Be directly linked to the school district's mission
> ▸ Be tied to staff development and viewed as a continuing process,

▶ Emphasize student outcomes

▶ Have sufficient resources allocated to it to be successful

To implement such a system, evaluation programs should

▶ Be built on a research-based set of standards

▶ Allow for a range of data and information sources so that teachers can demonstrate their mastery of the standards

▶ Provide for teachers at different career stages to be involved in different activities and processes

▶ Be heavily focused on the formative aspects of evaluation to promote professional learning

According to Danielson and McGreal (2000), school districts that are adopting this approach of linking teaching evaluation to staff development have designed a three-track model. The first track is for beginning teachers, the second track is for experienced teachers, and the third is for teachers needing assistance. Beginning teachers in Track 1 move to Track 2 in one to three years, depending on whether they had teaching experience before entering the district.

> **LEADER'S QUESTION:**
> **What are the components of the three-track teacher evaluation system?**
> **SEE TIP #5.3**

Each track serves different but complementary purposes, and teachers are evaluated using the effective teaching standards of (1) classroom environment, (2) preparation and planning, (3) instructional techniques, (4) student assessment strategies, and (5) communication and professional responsibilities. Data are collected from a variety of sources to evaluate a teacher's performance in all five areas.

Linking Teacher Evaluation to Total School Reform

Another major problem with traditional teacher evaluation is that it focuses on teachers as individuals acting alone rather than as colleagues working together in a system that dispenses and generates knowledge. One approach to modern teacher evaluation, proposed by Francis Duffy (1997), is to link it with school improvement. If school districts function essentially as educational systems, then the traditional approach to teacher evaluation is not very effective because it attempts to improve the system one teacher at a time. Duffy believes that changing the entire school organization will improve individual teachers much more than changing the behavior of individual teachers will improve the school.

In his ambitious model, Duffy (2003) proposes that teacher evaluation shift from examining the behavior of individual teachers to reforming the entire school system by *simultaneously* improving the work processes of each school, its social architecture, and its relationship with the broader community it serves. He describes each of these three components as follows:

- ▶ *Improving the Work Processes.* The core work of the school district is teaching and learning. Although other work in the district is important, teaching and learning must come first, and all other activities in the district's schools need to serve and support this work.
- ▶ *Improving the Social Architecture.* Social architecture refers to the policies, procedures, methods, values, beliefs, and communication structures that support life in a social system. All of these supports strongly influence the way people interact with each other in an organization. Thus, school leaders also need to redesign these supports to ensure that the new social architecture and the new work processes complement and reinforce each other. The best way to assure this mutual support is to make improvements to both elements of the school system simultaneously.
- ▶ *Improving Relationships With the Community.* School systems need to have positive and productive relationships with community stakeholders whose support is often essential for significant reform initiatives to succeed. Because this support is important during all stages of reform, leaders need to improve their district's community relationships at the same time they start improving the work processes and social architecture.

Duffy calls this approach of linking teacher evaluation to school improvement *knowledge work supervision.* To implement the approach, he suggests the following (Duffy, 1997):

- ▶ Shift the underlying philosophy of teacher evaluation from studying the behavior of individual teachers to a school's overall performance.
- ▶ Evaluate the performance of teachers by how they work within a cluster of schools rather than within an individual school.
- ▶ Replace classroom observations as the main evaluation tool with ways of assessing how teachers contribute to the work processes of teaching and learning, how they improve the social architecture, and how they communicate with the school community.

▶ Designate for each school an administrator, supervisor, or teacher as a Knowledge Work Supervisor who provides the overall coordination of activities and information between grade levels, levels of schooling, school clusters, and the district office.

▶ Replace the view of teachers as colleagues always in need of assistance to semi-autonomous knowledge workers who are stakeholders in the school improvement process.

▶ Improve individual teacher performance through formative evaluation techniques, self-directed inservice training, coaching, clinical supervision on an individual basis when needed, competency modeling, and technology that enhances performance.

DESIGNING A COMPREHENSIVE TEACHER EVALUATION PROGRAM

After reviewing the suggestions of researchers and stakeholders, educational leaders have to decide what type of teacher evaluation program best addresses the needs of their total school community. At the very least, such a program should:

▶ Conform to the requirements of federal and state regulations concerning the evaluation of teachers

▶ Be clearly understood by the entire school community

▶ Be consistent with other aspects of school reform going on in the district

▶ Be consistent with the standards developed by the National Board for Professional Teaching Standards

▶ Allow teachers to be involved in the evaluation process

▶ Include formative, monitoring, and summative procedures

▶ Provide for many sources of objective data to assess teacher performance

▶ Be closely linked to the district's professional development program

▶ Allow for its own evaluation and subsequent refinement

Designing an effective and *modern* teacher evaluation program is a tall order, but possible. A program based on an eclectic approach that includes numerous evaluation procedures is more likely to succeed because it has components that address the interests of all concerned stakeholders. School leaders should consider including multiple components in the evaluation program, such as clinical supervision, mentoring, peer coaching, teacher portfolios, action research, student and parent surveys, and student achievement data (Figure 5.3).

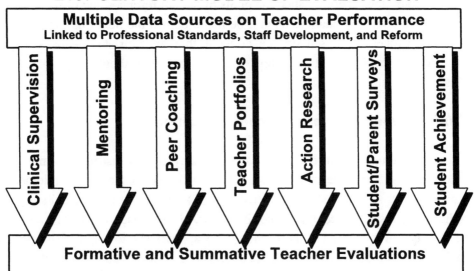

Figure 5.3 Modern evaluation systems contain multiple sources of data on teacher performance.

Clinical Supervision: A Formative Process

Begun in the early 1970s and based on the works of Goldhammer (1969) and Cogan (1973), clinical supervision centers on formal and prearranged classroom visits to observe teacher behavior. It consists of five steps:

(1) *A pre-observation conference with the teacher.* During this session, the supervisor discusses the purpose, identifies the focus, and agrees to a time for the classroom observation.

(2) *An observation of classroom performance.* The supervisor observes the teacher and takes notes describing the actions of the teacher and students.

(3) *An analysis of teacher performance.* The supervisor uses the notes to analyze and interpret performance and decides what approach to take during the post-observation conference.

(4) *A post-observation conference with the teacher.* In this meeting, the supervisor discusses the analysis of the observation and any suggestions for improving instruction. Sometimes, a follow-up visit is planned to observe the teacher using the supervisor's suggestion.

(5) *A post-conference analysis*. The supervisor reviews whether the previous four steps accomplished the goals of the conferences and observation, and whether any changes should be made before the next observation cycle.

This process is based on the concept that appropriate feedback from an experienced professional can help teachers broaden their range of effective classroom strategies.

Clinical Supervision and Teacher Evaluation

Clinical supervision has been used by many school districts to improve and assess the performance of teachers, although the consistency of implementation varies widely among districts. Peterson (2000) insists that for clinical supervision to have any lasting effect on teacher behavior, (1) the observer must be an outsider to the school system; (2) there should be at least six to eight visits per year, including unannounced visits; (3) the observation should focus on a limited number of concrete classroom elements; and (4) the data collected should be analyzed within a consistent, public, and validated framework linked to student learning.

If carried out in a systematic fashion, clinical supervision can be particularly successful with novice and struggling teachers because it results in an instructional improvement plan that the teacher can implement and that the supervisor can observe in future visits. The documented results of these visits and the degree of teacher improvement during the school year become important considerations for educational leaders to use in evaluating teacher competence and potential.

Mentoring Program

Mentoring has existed for thousands of years, but it is only in the last two decades that mentoring has become part of the education profession. Teacher mentoring is a process whereby experienced teachers (called *mentors*) share their professional expertise with less-experienced colleagues (called protégés or *mentees*). The purposes of this mentor-mentee relationship are to

- ▸ Help novice teachers learn their new job
- ▸ Provide moral and emotional support
- ▸ Improve instructional performance through modeling by an experienced teacher
- ▸ Share knowledge about models of teaching, materials, and planning
- ▸ Promote the socialization of new staff into the school community

▶ Assist teachers with classroom management and discipline
▶ Create a collaborative subculture within the school
▶ Encourage teachers to reflect on their practice
▶ Provide veteran staff a setting where their contributions are valued

Value for the Novice Teacher

Mentoring programs have increased dramatically in the last decade, primarily to support and retain novice teachers. Many states now require local school districts to have mentoring programs for new teachers or provide incentives for districts to establish some form of mentoring system. There is plenty of research evidence that carefully developed mentor programs can significantly help novice teachers successfully cope with the challenges they face during their first and second years of teaching (Odell and Huling, 2000). But mentoring can occur whenever someone seeks to learn from another professional who has experience in the topic for learning. Preservice, novice, and experienced teachers can all have mentors.

Value for the Mentor Teacher

Veteran teachers also derive benefits from participating as mentors. Huling and Resta (2001) reviewed the research and found that mentoring contributes to the professional development of experienced teachers in the following ways:

> **LEADER'S QUESTION: What are some guidelines for a mentoring program? SEE TIP #5.4**

▶ *Professional Competency.* As mentors help their protégés, they also improve their own teaching. Mentors benefit by asking questions, applying cognitive coaching skills, providing nonjudgmental feedback, and reassessing their own classroom management techniques.

▶ *Reflective Practice.* Mentoring has forced mentors to be more reflective about their own teaching as well as their beliefs about students and learning. Reflective mentors find that they take more informed action and gain a greater understanding of the complexity of teaching.

▶ *Renewal.* Mentors often experience professional renewal and a strengthening of their commitment to the teaching profession.

▶ *Psychological Benefits.* Mentoring enhances self-esteem and gives mentors a sense of significance in their professional world. They derive satisfaction from helping a colleague and consider mentoring as their contribution back to the teaching profession.

▶ *Collaboration.* Mentors report that mentoring provides some of the richest collegial interactions they have ever had.

▶ *Contributions to Teacher Leadership.* Experiences in mentoring can build in mentors a capacity for leadership through structured professional development, including training and experience in classroom observation and coaching. Studies found that mentors are often sought after for leadership positions and are generally very effective in these new roles.

Mentoring benefits both the novice and experienced teacher. Educational leaders should recognize that creating a structure that allows novice teachers to work with experienced teachers will ultimately benefit not only their students, but the overall school organization as well.

Mentoring and Teacher Evaluation

Mentors should not participate directly in teacher evaluation. The relationship between a mentor and mentee is based on mutual trust and a safe environment for taking risks. Neither of these will occur under the threat of evaluation where teachers believe that what they share with the mentor might be used against them. Nonetheless, mentors can assist novice and experienced teachers by making observations using the same assessments used by the formal evaluator and providing meaningful feedback. In this way, mentors play a collegial and nonjudgmental role in the evaluation process (Danielson and McGreal, 2000).

Mentoring for Principals

Novice principals also benefit from mentoring programs. Some school districts as well as professional and private organizations are sponsoring mentoring programs to help beginning principals by pairing them with experienced principals. Malone (2001) has examined these programs and offers the following advice:

▶ *Matching the Mentor and the Mentee.* Not all leaders make suitable mentors. The best mentors display certain traits, such as their ability to coach and serve as a role model. But the mentor must also personally connect with the mentee or the result will not be productive. The decision to pair a mentor and a protégé should take into account the skills and talents of both, and the locations and characteristics of the schools where the two principals are assigned.

▶ *Length of the Mentor Relationship.* Research studies indicate that mentor relationships should not be limited to just the early stages when training principals. Providing an ongoing relationship allows the new principal to benefit from the mentor when trying to solve the difficult and varied problems that all principals encounter. Eventually, this relationship prepares newer principals to become mentors in their own right.

Mentoring is a developmental and complex process whereby mentors support and guide their mentees through the transitions and challenges that are part of becoming an effective and reflective educator and leader.

Peer Coaching

Mentoring is an all-inclusive process describing everything that mentors do to support mentees. Coaching is one strategy that mentors use to provide feedback to their mentees on classroom performance. Peer coaching can also be a collaborative arrangement between experienced teachers who want to add new instructional skills to their repertoire.

LEADER'S QUESTION: What are some guidelines for a peer coaching program? SEE TIP #5.5

In its simplest form, two faculty members agree to engage in several reciprocal visits during the school year. Before each visit, the two agree on a specific focus for observation during the visit. After the visit, the two meet and the observer presents observations and they discuss any issues that are raised. The process allows the pair to reflect on their classroom style and choice of instructional strategies. It promotes a deeper analysis of teaching and learning and exposes teachers to new ideas and techniques. To be successful, peer coaches must possess the skills of collaboration and of sharing feedback as well as understand the nature of adult learning. Effective peer coaching programs have the following key elements (Danielson and McGreal, 2000):

- ▶ Colleagues observe each other teach.
- ▶ Their observations are data-based in that the observer records information about the class observed.
- ▶ There is collaborative assessment in that each participant tries to identify patterns of teacher and learner behavior.
- ▶ An importance is attached to student outcomes.
- ▶ The collaborative assessment is based on the goals and desired outcomes described in their professional growth plans.
- ▶ The process involves the cycle of observation, conference, and documentation.

Peer Coaching and Teacher Evaluation

Like mentors, peer coaches should not be directly involved in teacher evaluation. Peterson (2000) maintains that peer visits should be avoided in teacher evaluation. He believes that data from such visits are not reliable because of observer bias and the social, educational, or personal relationships that exist with the teacher. Nonetheless, some school districts have implemented a peer assistance and review program in which experienced teachers conduct formative and summative evaluations of their colleagues, based primarily on classroom visits. These peer evaluations may be used by the school district in making decisions about a teacher's employment status.

The peer assistance and review program is in limited use because of both teacher and administrative resistance to this shift of responsibility for evaluating teacher performance. Ironically, the National Education Association supports the program, which it views as teachers taking charge of their own profession by providing expert assistance to teachers who need help and, where appropriate, counseling failing teachers to leave the profession (Chase, 1997). As more teacher associations subscribe to the concept of peer review and assistance, peer coaching will become a valuable component of the total teacher evaluation process.

The Teacher Portfolio

Just as artists use portfolios of collected works to demonstrate their talents, teachers can use portfolios to show their talents. Through portfolios, teachers demonstrate knowledge of their subject matter, their students, and their teaching practices. Although portfolios are used primarily with preservice and novice teachers, they can also be used by experienced teachers who may wish to use the portfolio when seeking a new position or for advancement.

Rather than being laden with teaching artifacts and evaluations, portfolios are concrete products created by teachers that reveal, relate, and describe their duties, expertise, and growth. The portfolio provides a means of reflection and illustrates what a teacher can do.

A portfolio may include some or all of the following items:

- ▸ Teacher's background
- ▸ Results of written examinations, such as the National Teacher Exam and state licensure tests
- ▸ A personal statement of the teacher's philosophy and goals

> ▸ Video- and audiotapes of classroom lessons
> ▸ Implemented lesson plans and classroom handouts
> ▸ Graded student work, such as tests and class projects
> ▸ Documentation of efforts to improve teaching, such as attendance at conferences, seminars, and district professional development activities
> ▸ Written reflections on teaching

The portfolio should *not* be a simple collection of student works, classroom life, or notes of affection from parents and students. Portfolios can be a valuable professional development experience, especially for teachers new to a school district. While constructing their portfolios, beginning teachers should share and discuss them with experienced teachers. This continuing dialogue provides a rich context for collaboration and for experiencing the multifaceted nature of teaching. Burke (1997) contends that portfolios offer teachers a structure and a process for documenting and reflecting on their practice. Over time, portfolios present an authentic view of how a teacher thinks, acts, and grows professionally.

Portfolios and Teacher Evaluation

As a form of authentic assessment, teacher portfolios can be a major component in the overall evaluation of beginning teachers. The portfolio offers the opportunity for critiquing and evaluating the effectiveness of lessons or interpersonal interactions with students and peers. More states and school districts are using teacher portfolios to augment their traditional measures for assessing the performance of beginning teachers.

> **LEADER'S QUESTION: What are some guidelines for implementing teacher portfolios? SEE TIP #5.6**

Evaluating the Portfolio. Portfolios that are used to make personnel decisions get greater scrutiny than if the intended use is professional growth. The open-ended nature of portfolios is an advantage in that each portfolio is unique and tailored to the individual teacher. This is a positive feature when the portfolio is used for professional development. But when the portfolio is used for summative evaluation, where comparability between teachers is desired, the subjectivity of the evaluation and the lack of standardization can be problems.

If a district decides to use portfolios as an important component in summative evaluation, Doolittle (1994) suggests that the lack of standardization can be overcome if all portfolios contain the following five mandated items:

> ▸ Statement of teaching responsibilities
> ▸ Statement of teaching philosophies and methodologies

- ► Description of efforts to improve one's teaching
- ► Representative course syllabi
- ► Summary of teacher evaluations by students

He further suggests that the subjectivity of the evaluation of portfolios can be made more reliable and valid through Likert-type forms that contain predetermined qualities based on the mandated items in the previous list.

Peterson (2000) contends that, in addition to the problems of standardization and subjectivity, teacher portfolios can become unmanageable in size. He suggests a refinement to teacher portfolios that he calls *teacher dossiers*. Dossiers are much more compact because evaluation data are summarized, processed for key information, and subjected to a prior review. This compression greatly reduces the size of portfolios and makes it easier, according to Peterson, to make judgments about their merit and worth.

Action Research

School leaders already know that one component of the reform initiatives is to give teachers opportunities to reclaim the authority and responsibility for their own classroom teaching practices through research. The NBPTS recognizes this teacher-as-researcher role in several of its five core propositions. Action research gives the practitioner a chance to be a researcher and to investigate specific problems that affect teaching and learning.

> **LEADER'S QUESTION: What are some guidelines for implementing action research? SEE TIP #5.7**

Unlike traditional education research, where teachers are studied by outsiders, action research is conducted by teachers themselves to study their own classroom practices. It is a systematic investigation into some aspect of the school pursued by educators out of a desire to improve what they do. Action research expands the role of a teacher as an inquirer into teaching and learning through systematic classroom research.

Action research is well suited to schools because of its democratic methodology, inclusiveness, flexibility of approach, and potential for changing practice. Using a solution-oriented approach, action research is characterized by cycles of problem identification, systematic data collection, data analysis, data-driven actions, and problem redefinition (Figure 5.4). Because the teacher who is responsible for implementing changes also does the research, a real fit is created between the needs of a specific learner and the action taken.

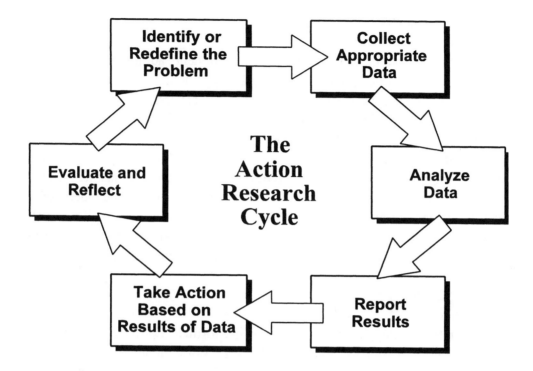

Figure 5.4 The diagram illustrates the six steps in the action research cycle.

The current focus on school restructuring has site-based, shared decision-making as one of its major features. With this newly acquired autonomy come new responsibilities. If school leaders are asking teachers to participate in making building decisions, they should be informed decisions that are driven by data. Thus, it becomes essential for teachers to be much more deliberate in documenting and evaluating their efforts. Action research becomes one means to that end.

Action research also provides teachers with opportunities to gain knowledge and skills in research methods and applications and to become more aware of the possibilities and options for change. Teachers using action research are likely to be receptive and supportive of systemic changes that school leaders may be seeking.

Action Research and Teacher Evaluation

Action research assists practitioners in identifying needs, assessing their own developmental processes, and evaluating the outcomes of the changes they make as a result of their research efforts. This self-evaluation aspect can be part of their individual improvement plans that are included in a comprehensive teacher evaluation process.

Student and Parent Surveys

Student and parent surveys are written instruments administered to students (usually in the classroom) and to parents (usually at home). The surveys have the advantage of looking at teacher behavior from different perspectives. Consequently, the surveys can provide teachers with feedback on items, such as development of motivation, fairness, and communication skills, that might not be obvious through other feedback methods. They also provide educational leaders with information that they might never observe. These types of surveys have been justified from the standpoint that students and parents are consumers and stakeholders of the educational system and should have input into evaluating teachers. To be valid, however, survey questions have to be carefully worded so that they avoid matters of favoritism, personality differences, or other extraneous matters.

Student Surveys

Advantages. Student ratings of teacher performance provide information on important factors, such as motivation, the degree of communication and rapport between the student and teacher, how much was learned, classroom practice, testing, and homework assignments. Students have a good idea of their own needs, observe teachers every day, and are the direct beneficiaries of good teaching. Reliability may be a potential concern, but Peterson (2000) contends that research studies place aggregated class data reliability in the 0.80 to 0.90 range for many kinds of teacher performances. (The closer a reliability score is to 1.00, the better.)

Disadvantages. Peterson (2000) notes, however, that despite the high degree of reliability, some disadvantages exist for using students as judges of teacher quality. (1) The judgments of immature students may differ greatly from those of the school leaders who are ultimately responsible for making personnel decisions. (2) Students are not subject matter experts. (3) Effective teachers can have very different teaching styles and personalities. (4) Some students may be dishonest in their evaluations for personal or trivial reasons. (5) The existence of these surveys may prompt some teachers to pander to students for better ratings. (6) Teachers working with students who dislike school or who are transient may be at a disadvantage because these student ratings could be lower regardless of the teacher's competence.

Teacher Reactions. Student surveys to evaluate teachers have been used in some school districts for years. Although numerous research studies have looked at the effect of student surveys in higher education, few studies have been carried out at the K–12 level. Nonetheless, these studies show that teachers distrust the results of student surveys when they are mandated. Teachers feel that student opinion can be easily swayed by irrelevant factors. Yet, these same studies show that, despite these concerns, student evaluations can be surprisingly accurate if the survey questions are carefully drawn to ask about the class, rather than about the teacher (Peterson, 2000).

Questionable Survey Items. Because of teacher concerns and the disadvantages of using student surveys, questions arise over whether certain items should be included. Not all researchers are in agreement. Peterson (2000), for example, argues that items related to fairness should not be included at all because fairness is subject to such wide interpretation as to be unreliable. On the other hand, Danielson and McGreal (2000) maintain that asking whether all students are treated fairly in the class is an acceptable topic for these surveys.

Parent Surveys

As taxpayers, consumers, and stakeholders in the education of their children, parents (and guardians) are valid observers and reporters of certain school-related factors that relate to teacher quality.

| LEADER'S QUESTION: What are examples of student and parent surveys? SEE TIP #5.8 |

Advantages. Parents are in a good position to know how their children respond to their teachers. Although parents cannot be expected to comment on classroom activities, they can evaluate the nature and extent of their communications with teachers, and the degree to which they feel in a partnership with teachers in the education of their children. They would know, for example, whether their children had the skills to complete their homework assignments.

Disadvantages. Teacher complaints about parental interference in school and classroom matters are common. Consequently, teachers fear that parental responses on surveys could be influenced by misrepresentations of classroom events or personal differences over teaching methodologies. Some excellent teachers often have little need for parental communications and thus may be at a disadvantage if parents give a low rating for teacher contacts.

Like student surveys, the items on parental surveys need to be carefully constructed to ask about those things that only parents can reasonably judge.

Surveys and Teacher Evaluation

On a personal note, I have been a believer in student surveys and used them in the high school and university classes I taught. I still believe that most students and parents will be forthright in assessing the experiences they had with a particular teacher. But such surveys have to be carefully worded so that they focus on the teaching and learning processes. This is particularly important given the high degree of public accountability and media attention that currently hover over schools and teachers.

Although parent and student surveys can provide valuable insights, school leaders must remember that survey responses are based on perceptions and, therefore, are not entirely reliable sources of evidence. If they are used, a few guidelines are in order. (1) Teachers should have input in the design of the surveys and how they will be conducted. (2) The surveys should be distributed, scored, and reported by a third party, probably from the district office. (3) Teachers should be able to review the survey results and decide if they are to be included in their portfolios or dossiers (Peterson, 2000).

Student Achievement Data

> **LEADER'S QUESTION: What are the conditions for using student achievement data to evaluate teachers? SEE TIP #5.9**

I have intentionally saved this item for last because it is currently a hot topic for debate. Should student achievement data be used to evaluate teacher performance? Advocates of this idea say that it does not matter what the teacher does in the classroom if those actions do not result in student learning. Therefore, measures of student learning are appropriate data to be included in evaluating teacher performance. In some states, such inclusion is now mandatory as part of initiatives to raise student achievement. Furthermore, the argument that good teaching results in good learning makes a great deal of sense to parents and non-educators who can conceive of no other benchmark for measuring teacher quality. Critics argue that there are too many variables affecting student achievement, some of which are beyond the control of the teacher. Consequently, it is unfair to include student test data in the performance evaluations of classroom teachers.

Research Findings

Research findings (Archer, 1998) support what I have personally believed for a long time: **The quality of learning seldom exceeds the quality of teaching.** From that perspective, I support adding student achievement outcomes into the mix of data used to evaluate teachers. I also recognize, however, that many factors influence student learning, some of which are outside the control of teachers.

Problems at home may prevent a student from finding the time or a quiet place to do homework. In other families, parents ensure that homework time is available and add support, assistance, and encouragement to the efforts of their children. Some students have a job where they work late hours after school to support the household and are too exhausted to study when they come home. These, and a variety of other factors, affect student performance in the classroom.

Danielson and McGreal (2000) point out that factors within the school can also affect student performance. Apart from teacher quality, the curriculum, the type of school organization, and the extent of support available for troubled learners, can all have an impact on student achievement. Classes with large numbers of ESL students and students with special needs, for example, will pose additional challenges for teachers and affect the progress of some students.

If student achievement data are to be used for teacher evaluation, it is essential to develop a methodology that tracks what students have learned during the school year. Known as the *value-added approach*, it measures the growth in individual student achievement from one point in time to another and takes into account background factors that affect learning but are outside the control of the school. Such factors include academic support in the home as well as the income and education levels of the parents. These data are aggregated across a grade level or classroom to provide an overall index of growth for those students (Asp, 2000).

The index also allows schools to determine how much value they have added in terms of student achievement by eliminating the inherent unfairness of comparing the absolute achievement of students who come from widely different socio-economic backgrounds. It would also provide a legitimate comparison of student achievement across classrooms where the entry achievement level varies significantly from one school year to the next. This approach judges more fairly the true impact of individual teachers on student achievement (Evans, 1999).

One such system is known as the Tennessee Value-Added Assessment System (TVAAS), developed by William Sanders and his colleagues at the University of Tennessee (Sanders, Saxton, and Horn, 1997). Although there are critics of value-added methodology, the current accountability climate is likely to maintain interest in this approach for years to come.

EVALUATING PRINCIPALS AND DISTRICT OFFICE ADMINISTRATORS

"I meet with my superintendent twice a year for a formal evaluation. In August, we talk about my goals for the year and in April, we review how well I met them, and he writes a report." Those comments from a high school principal may reflect how many building and district office administrators are formally evaluated. Although this arrangement may seem inadequate, in reality, these administrators are being constantly evaluated. When I was a school superintendent, I interacted with principals and district office staff every day and was able to make frequent judgements about their decision-making and interpersonal skills. Granted, I gathered these impressions on the run and while I was involved in making my own decisions. This daily contact gave me a good sense of the leadership and management skills of these administrators, but they deserve more and better.

Many of the components used for the evaluation of teachers can also be used to evaluate the performance of building and district office administrators. Mentoring, peer coaching, professional portfolios, action research, and surveys are all valid data sources for the evaluation of administrative staff. Mentoring and peer coaching are particularly valuable for leaders new to their position. A program with guidelines similar to those for teacher mentoring can be effective in helping new leaders cope with their responsibilities and obligations. Portfolios can include summaries of their success in designing and implementing action plans. Action research can focus on building or district-wide topics. Surveys can be any mix that includes students, faculty, or parents.

> **LEADER'S QUESTION: What are the steps in conducting a three-party supervisory conference? SEE TIP #5.10**

A modified form of clinical supervision, called the *three-party supervisory conference*, is a useful evaluation method. As a superintendent, I used this technique with my building principals to give them feedback on their supervisory and conferencing skills when observing their teachers. Beside improving the skills of building leaders, three-party conferencing strengthens the credibility of the overall evaluation program because teachers see that their principals are working regularly to improve their own skills.

MAJOR POINTS IN CHAPTER 5

❑ Traditional models of teacher evaluation based primarily on classroom visits are not compatible with current initiatives that are reforming schools into learning organizations where teachers and school leaders work collaboratively instead of in isolation.

❑ Newer models link teacher evaluation to national professional standards, staff development, and total school reform.

❑ Teacher evaluation today should be based on a comprehensive process that includes clinical supervision, mentoring, peer coaching, teacher portfolios, action research, student and parent surveys, and student achievement data.

❑ Many of the components of teacher evaluation can also be used as data sources for the evaluation of principals and other district administrators. Three-party conferencing is an effective method of adapting clinical supervision to evaluate principals.

TIPS FOR LEADERS #5.1

New Directions for Teacher Evaluation

Effective teacher evaluation in the 21st century needs to move away from traditional models and be based, instead, on methods that convince teachers that it can be a beneficial process. For this to happen, researchers are calling upon educational leaders to implement evaluation systems that are more consistent with the changing nature of schools, teachers, and students. Peterson (2000) offers some new directions for consideration, compared with current practices. Put a check in the box next to your district's practices.

New Direction	✔	**Current Practice**	✔
✅ One function of teacher evaluation should be to seek out, document, and acknowledge the good teaching that already exists.		✗ Emphasizes minimum competency, control, feedback, accountability, and future improvement.	
✅ Use good reasons to evaluate, such as recognizing good teaching practices and offering meaningful professional development programs.		✗ Reasons for evaluating are mainly to improve teaching and to monitor minimal performance for retention.	
✅ Place teachers at the center of the evaluation process by allowing them to collect the data that will evaluate their duties and responsibilities. Teachers should also be involved in evaluating each other.		✗ A brief visit by a supervisor who has little meaningful contact with the students and who summarizes the results of the visit on a generalized checklist.	
✅ Use several persons to judge teacher quality and performance, such as a panel that reviews a teacher's practice and background.		✗ Performance rated by a single administrator.	

New Direction	✔	Current Practice	✔
✅ Limit the role of building administrators in teacher evaluation because it is difficult for them to be summative judges and educational leaders at the same time.		✗ Building administrators have many tasks including monitoring minimal performance, judging overall teacher quality, inducting new teachers, deciding on teacher retention, and remediating poor practice.	
✅ Use many data sources to judge teacher quality, such as student and parent surveys, peer review of materials, teacher tests, and student performance data.		✗ Teacher quality is reviewed in an annual administrative report.	
✅ If possible, use student achievement data where they are defensible and where teachers agree to them.		✗ Administrators use rough ratings (e.g., satisfactory, below standard), and some states require linking test results to all evaluations.	
✅ Use different data sources for teachers in different settings who should be judged by data appropriate to those settings.		✗ Use the same standard information for all teachers in the district.	
✅ Devote sufficient time and resources necessary to recognize good teaching. Money is needed for student and parent surveys, and for collecting and securing data.		✗ Short amount of time for one or two classroom visits (usually 40 to 45 minutes each). Time and money devoted to teacher evaluation process are minimal.	
✅ Use research on teacher evaluation correctly. For example, research shows that principals' reports do not accurately reflect teacher competence. Seek out research from peer-reviewed journals.		✗ To ignore direct research on teacher evaluation, but to use teacher behavior checklists and clinical supervision as the primary basis for evaluation.	

New Direction	✔	Current Practice	✔
✓ Pay attention to the sociological forces that influence school districts. Teachers do not trust the current evaluation system. Review the school's reward structure as well as teacher isolation. Find ways to make teachers take greater control of their own evaluation.		✗ To ignore the powerful effects of rewards, sanctions, roles, expectations, and relationships in the workplace. Evaluation is seen mainly as observation, feedback, and decisions on retention, rather than as a complex process in a human organization.	
✓ Use teacher evaluation results to encourage personal professional dossiers and to assure the community that quality education is occurring. Aggregated evaluation results should be shared at public and legislative gatherings to promote the successes of the professional staff.		✗ To file away administrative reports into storage losing the opportunity to make public the valued and successful efforts of the teaching staff.	

Analysis

Review the placement of the check marks in the survey. What statement can you make about the extent to which your district has incorporated evaluation practices that reflect new directions in assessing the performance of professional educators? _____

_____

_____

What steps will you take as a result of your analysis of the current evaluation program? _____

_____

_____

TIPS FOR LEADERS #5.2

The INTASC Performance-Based Standards for Beginning Teachers

The Interstate New Teacher Assessment and Support Consortium (INTASC) developed 10 core performance-based standards for states to consider as part of their teacher licensing process. The standards describe the knowledge, dispositions, and performances that beginning teachers should possess when entering the profession. Although designed for beginning teachers, the standards are applicable to teachers at all levels of experience.

An important attribute of these standards is that they are performance-based; that is, they describe what teachers should know and be able to do rather than listing courses that teachers should take in order to be awarded a license or a teaching position. This approach should clarify what the criteria are for assessment, placing more emphasis on the abilities teachers develop than on the hours they spend taking classes.

About 40 states are now adapting the INTASC standards as part of a broader teacher licensing and evaluation system that is more consistent with the dynamics of contemporary schools. School leaders need to examine how closely these nationally accepted standards compare to the standards their school district is using to assess the performance of new and experienced teachers. Review the 10 standards (INTASC, 1992) and note how your district uses each standard.

INTASC Standard	How My District Uses This Standard
1. The teacher understands the central concepts, tools of inquiry, and structures of the discipline(s) he or she teaches and can create learning experiences that make these aspects of subject matter meaningful for students.	
2. The teacher understands how children learn and develop, and can provide learning opportunities that support their intellectual, social, and personal development.	

INTASC Standard	How My District Uses This Standard
3. The teacher understands how students differ in their approaches to learning and creates instructional opportunities that are adapted to diverse learners.	
4. The teacher understands and uses a variety of instructional strategies to encourage students' development of critical thinking, problem solving, and performance skills.	
5. The teacher uses an understanding of individual and group motivation and behavior to create a learning environment that encourages positive social interaction, active engagement in learning, and self-motivation.	
6. The teacher uses knowledge of effective verbal, nonverbal, and media communication techniques to foster active inquiry, collaboration, and supportive interaction in the classroom.	
7. The teacher plans instruction based upon knowledge of subject matter, students, the community, and curriculum goals.	
8. The teacher understands and uses formal and informal assessment strategies to evaluate and ensure the continuous intellectual, social, and physical development of the learner.	
9. The teacher is a reflective practitioner who continually evaluates the effects of his or her choices and actions on others (students, parents, and other professionals in the learning community) and who actively seeks out opportunities to grow professionally.	

INTASC Standard	How My District Uses This Standard
10. The teacher fosters relationships with school colleagues, parents, and agencies in the larger community to support students' learning and well-being.	

Analysis

How well did the teacher evaluation standards in your district compare with those of INTASC? _____

_____

_____

_____

What action(s) will you take as a result of this analysis? _____

_____

_____

_____

TIPS FOR LEADERS #5.3

A Three-Track Teacher Evaluation Program

Danielson and McGreal (2000) suggest a three-track evaluation program closely tied to the experience level and professional development plan of each teacher. The evaluation of teacher performance starts with the standards of effective teaching, which include:

- *Classroom Environment:* The skill of creating an environment conducive to learning and mutual respect, including managing student behavior and classroom procedures, and organizing physical space.
- *Preparation and Planning:* The skill of understanding the content to be taught, knowing the backgrounds of students, and designing coherent instruction.
- *Instructional Techniques:* The skill of engaging students in learning, using questioning and discussion techniques, and providing feedback.
- *Assessment Strategies:* The skill at designing a variety of methods to assess student achievement and using assessment results to design subsequent instruction.
- *Communication and Professional Responsibilities:* The skill at communicating with parents, reflecting on practice, contributing to the school and district, and growing professionally.

Teachers should be allowed to demonstrate their mastery of the above standards through a broad range of information and data sources, consistent with their levels of experience and competence.

The following diagram summarizes the components of the three tracks. Novice teachers in Track 1 move to Track 2 in one to three years, depending on whether they had teaching experience before entering the district.

Three Tracks of the Teacher Evaluation Program		
(Adapted from Danielson and McGreal, 2000)		
TRACK 1 **Beginning Teachers**	**TRACK 2** **Experienced** **Teachers**	**TRACK 3** **Teachers Needing** **Assistance**
Includes all teachers new to district for 1 to 3 years, depending on teaching experience before entering district.	**Includes** tenured teachers who demonstrate the standards for effective teaching.	**Includes** tenured teachers needing specific professional guidance in identified area(s) of the standards for effective teaching.
Purposes are to ensure that standards for effective teaching are understood and demonstrated, and to provide data for decisions to continue or end employment.	**Purposes** are to enhance professional growth, improve student achievement, and focus on school improvement initiatives.	**Purposes** are to give the teacher an opportunity to seek assistance in any area of the standards, to offer greater structure and support for the teacher, and to provide due process for disciplinary action.
Methods include classroom observations, reviewing portfolios, discussing professional practices, and getting feedback from mentor.	**Methods** include discussing teacher performance, developing individual growth plan, establishing indicators of progress, and getting administrative input.	**Methods** include observing and giving feedback focused on the area(s) identified as needing improvement.

TIPS FOR LEADERS #5.4

Guidelines for a Teacher Mentoring Program

Although mentoring programs are valuable for evaluating the performance of novice teachers, they also benefit experienced teachers as well as the overall school organization. Here are some guidelines to help educational leaders successfully implement a mentoring program (Danielson and McGreal, 2000; Sweeny, 1994).

- Building administrators must be committed to the concept of the mentoring program by ensuring that the mentors get adequate planning time, monetary and material resources, and other support that permits them to carry out their role.

- Participation as a mentor should be voluntary.

- Mentors should be experienced teachers who are continual, visible learners and who maintain a high level of expertise. They should be active listeners who are responsive to the needs of others.

- The role of the mentor must be clearly defined in terms of what function (e.g., support, encourage) the mentor serves and what activities (e.g., coach, observe, plan) the mentor will conduct. The focus at first should be on helping with activities that new teachers value the most: classroom management and curriculum.

- Matching mentors and mentees should be based first on the similarity of their job assignments, proximity, and ability to have common planning times. An age difference of five or more years seems to work best. Ask the mentee whether gender matching is important.

- Mentors and their mentees should participate in a planned and validated training session that makes expectations clear and that models the key mentoring attitudes and skills necessary for effective collaborative practice.

- Guard against overloading either the mentor or the mentee. Both are busy with regular duties and should plan their mentoring sessions carefully to avoid trying to do too much.

- Mentors should have opportunities to get together periodically to share experiences, develop supportive relationships, and remain accountable to each other and to the expectations of the program. These support groups should uncover, refine, and record their growing knowledge base about mentoring practices.

- Provide a stipend for mentors or other benefit (e.g., compensatory time off, conference attendance, release from lunch or hall duty, or an end-of-the-year award) in recognition of the responsibility they assumed and the many hours that were required.

- Develop a mentoring program for administrators. Novice leaders are often more isolated than teachers and need the support of experienced mentors.

TIPS FOR LEADERS #5.5

Guidelines for a Peer Coaching Program

A well-structured peer coaching program can be a valuable component of an overall teacher evaluation process because it gives teachers opportunities to talk to each other in depth about ways to improve their selection and implementation of instructional strategies. Glickman (2002) suggests that educational leaders consider the following steps when implementing a peer coaching program:

- *Purpose of Program.* The first step is to meet with teachers to decide the purpose of the program. A program designed just to acquaint teachers with different teaching styles, for example, can be less formal than one designed to help teachers progress toward specific learning standards as part of their professional action plan.

- *Preliminary Training.* Before peer coaching begins, teachers should be involved in a training program that helps them understand (1) the purpose and procedures of peer coaching, (2) how to conduct the pre-conference and determine the focus of the peer visit, (3) how to analyze an observation to determine the difference between observing and interpreting classroom events, and (4) how to conduct two post-conferences with different approaches for developing a teacher's personal improvement plan.

- *Standardized Forms for the Post-conference.* There should be a standard form that all peer coaches use in the post-conference to help teachers develop their personal improvement plans. The form should include the objective to be worked on, the activities the teacher will use to achieve those objectives, the resources needed, and the time and date of the next pre-conference.

- *Scheduling the Peer Coaching Visits.* All attempts should be made to pair coaches so that the pre- and post-conferences can occur during the school day.

- *Arranging the Peer Teams.* Teachers should be teamed together who are comfortable with each other but not at the same level of experience or competence. Avoid matching colleagues who are too much alike or too different. The aim is to find colleagues who are different enough to learn from each other.

- *Monitoring Peer Progress.* A peer coaching facilitator should be available to the peer teams. This person can provide resources, such as instruments on clinical supervision, books, and videotapes, and be available to answer questions, monitor the peer teams, and help where needed.

Analysis

If your district already has a peer coaching program, how does it compare with the guidelines outlined above? _____
_____
_____

What changes, if any, might you consider making to your current peer coaching program? _____
_____
_____

TIPS FOR LEADERS #5.6

Guidelines for Implementing Teacher Portfolios

Used primarily with novice teachers, portfolios are educational tools that are used to provide feedback to teachers so that they can improve their teaching and level of professionalism. Portfolios can also be used as a means of authentic assessment in evaluating the effectiveness of a teacher. The content of teacher portfolios depends on how the portfolio is actually used.

Key Features

At the very least, teacher portfolios should have the following key features (Wolf, Lichtenstein, and Stevenson, 1997):

- A portfolio should be structured around sound professional teaching standards, and individual and school goals.

- A portfolio should contain carefully selected work samples of the teacher and the students that illustrate important features of a teacher's practice.

- The portfolio should be framed by captions and written commentaries that explain and reflect on the portfolio's contents.

- For beginning teachers, a portfolio should be part of a mentoring or coaching experience in which the portfolio is used as a basis for ongoing professional conversations with colleagues and supervisors.

Steps for Implementation

Here are some steps to consider for implementing a portfolio program (Doolittle, 1994):

- *Start Slowly*. Allow one to two years to develop, implement, regulate, and evaluate a portfolio program.

- *Gain Acceptance.* Both school leaders and teachers must accept the use of portfolios. If leaders do not relate the importance and usefulness of portfolios, then the process will fail. Likewise, if teachers do not value the portfolio approach, then they will not contribute the effort needed for success.

- *Instill Ownership.* Teachers must be involved from the beginning so that they feel ownership over the program's direction and use.

- *Communicate Implementation.* Teachers need to know explicitly how the portfolios will be used. If portfolios are used for advancement, then the structure and intended scoring methods must be explained in detail.

- *Use Models.* Collect and show models used by other districts. The models provide examples for teachers who are developing their own portfolios.

- *Be Selective.* Portfolios should contain carefully selected items that are in conformity with guidelines and that substantiate the expertise and achievements of the teacher.

- *Be Realistic.* Use portfolios as only one form of authentic assessment in conjunction with other measures.

Dossiers

Some districts are shifting to dossiers that compress much of the information contained in portfolios. As a result, they are less bulky and easier to standardize. Peterson (2000) offers the following sample of district guidelines for compiling teacher dossiers:

- Limit dossiers to 15 pages (8½ in. × 11 in.), bound in a heavy paper cover.

- Dossiers should contain at least four data sources.

- Each data source must follow the guidelines established by the district office's evaluation unit for that source.

- District-approved forms must be used. Any alterations to the form must be explained so that they are noted.

- The following data sources must be collected and authenticated by the evaluation unit: student surveys, parent surveys, peer reviews, systematic observations, and administrator reports.

- The evaluation unit will keep no records of data recalled by the teacher.

- The following are guidelines for quality control on certain data sources:

  ▸ Parent surveys and student surveys: one standard deviation below the mean.
  ▸ Teacher tests: above 40th percentile on national norms.
  ▸ Peer reviews and administrator reports: "contributing, well functioning."

- Backup documents must be kept in accordion folders.

TIPS FOR LEADERS #5.7

Guidelines for Using Action Research

Educational leaders should encourage and facilitate action research projects in their schools. Action research gives teachers opportunities to conduct systematic investigations into classroom practices by collecting and analyzing data to determine whether action needs to be taken to improve those practices.

General Considerations

- Action research is almost always conducted as a voluntary and collaborative venture.

- Conducting the research should not undermine the researcher's primary job of teaching, and the data collection must not interfere with instructional processes.

- A project is usually researched during one school year.

- The researchers should have opportunities to share what they have learned with their school and district colleagues, professional associations, journals, and at conferences.

Steps in the Process

According to Sagor (1992) and Glickman (2002), action research should include the following steps and questions:

(1) *Problem Formulation*. The area of research chosen should focus on student learning objectives. This focus requires the teachers to scrutinize the learning environment, including curriculum and instruction. The teachers reflect on what the students are doing, or not doing, that they find troubling. The teacher may ask questions such as:

- What student learning objective is of the highest priority in this situation?

- What else do we need to know about how our students are currently performing related to this goal?

(2) *Data Collection.* The teachers gather data that they believe will shed light on the issue they are examining. Data should be gathered from at least three sources to ensure a valid picture of reality. This phase usually lasts two to three months. One important question is:

- What do we now have as baseline data on student learning that can be used for later comparisons?

(3) *Data Analysis.* The teachers sift through the collected data, categorizing and sorting, to determine what patterns or trends emerge and what conclusions they can draw.

(4) *Reporting of Results.* The teachers find forums, such as professional journals, conferences, and Web sites, to share what they have discovered, thereby playing a role in expanding the knowledge base about teaching and learning.

(5) *Action Planning.* The teachers plan and implement improvements based on what they have learned through their research. They address questions such as the following:

- What changes will we make in our classrooms?
- What assistance will we need from each other?
- What will be the actions and the completion dates for changes in our own teaching and learning?

(6) *Evaluation and Reflection.* The teachers discuss evaluation strategies that will assess whether the changes are successful. They also need to discuss if and how the action research plan can be improved the next time it is used. They address questions such as the following:

- After the implementation period, what data will we collect to determine progress, or lack of it, and to use for further action research cycles?
- How do we improve upon the process next time?

TIPS FOR LEADERS #5.8

Examples of Student and Parent Surveys for Evaluating Teachers

The Davis School District (2002) in Farmington, Utah, has used these types of surveys for about five years. Teachers decide if they want to use the surveys and whether to report the results to their building principal as part of their evaluation. Principals, however, can request surveys for teachers in need of improvement. The samples are reprinted with the permission of the Davis School District (2002).

Student Surveys

K–2 Non-reader Student Survey. The Non-reader Survey is used in K–2 classrooms where a large number of students cannot independently read and complete the items. The surveys are administered verbally, using a three-point scale: *No, Sometimes,* and *Yes.*

(1) My teacher shows me how to do new things.
(2) My class is a good place for learning.
(3) I like to come to this class.
(4) My teacher is a good teacher.
(5) I know what I am supposed to do in this class.
(6) My teacher's rules are fair.
(7) My teacher is nice to me.

Elementary Student Survey (Grades 3–6). The Elementary Survey is for students who can read and mark the survey independently, using a three-point scale: *No, Sometimes,* and *Yes.*

(1) I learn new things in this class.
(2) My class is a good place for learning.
(3) I like to come to this class.
(4) My teacher is a good teacher.
(5) I know what I am supposed to do in this class.
(6) I understand the rules in my class.
(7) My teacher treats me fairly.

(8) I know how well I am learning in this class.

(9) My teacher is nice to me.

Secondary Student Survey (Grades 7–12). Administered to students in grades 7 through 12, the students respond using a three-point scale: *No, Sometimes,* and *Yes.*

(1)   I learn new things in this class.

(2)   This class is a good place for learning.

(3)   This teacher treats me with care and respect.

(4)   This is a good teacher.

(5)   I know what I am supposed to do in this class.

(6)   I understand the class rules.

(7)   This teacher treats me fairly.

(8)   I know how well I am doing in this class.

(9)   I usually understand how to do my assignments.

(10)   This teacher maintains class discipline.

Parent Survey. The Parent Survey asks parents to respond using a four-point scale: *No opinion, No, Sometimes,* and *Yes.*

(1)   My son/daughter is learning in this class.

(2)   This classroom is a good place for learning.

(3)   This teacher treats my son/daughter with care and respect.

(4)   I am satisfied with my son's/daughter's experience in this class.

(5)   The learning activities in this class are appropriate for my son/daughter.

(6)   My son/daughter knows what is expected in this class.

(7)   The teacher treats my son/daughter fairly.

(8)   This teacher is accessible.

(9)   Homework in this class helps my son/daughter learn.

(10)   The amount of homework in this class is about right.

(11)   I have reviewed the class content and goals for this class.

(12)   I attended a parent-teacher conference with this teacher.

(13)   I know how my son/daughter is doing in this class.

TIPS FOR LEADERS #5.9

Guidelines for Using Student Achievement Data to Evaluate Teachers

If we accept that student learning is relevant to the evaluation of teacher performance, the question then is: Under what conditions should student achievement data be used as part of the teacher evaluation process? At the very least, the following should be considered:

- Teachers need to have substantial participation in the design and implementation of any process that uses student achievement data to measure teacher performance.

- The process has to take into account student baseline data. That is, the achievement data must measure changes that occurred as a result of the teacher, adjusted for prior achievement. This is sometimes referred to as the "value-added" concept: What value did being in this classroom add to the knowledge or skill base of the student?

- The process should be phased in over several years to give all members of the school community time to discuss and reflect on teacher quality and to find ways to implement the process with the least disruption to classroom instruction.

- The process should apply only to those teachers where there are valid measures of student achievement. For example, there are objective and standardized tests that can measure student achievement in a mathematics course. But what objective test would measure student progress in a music or art course?

- Consider whether the process should apply to teachers of classes that have high student turnover during the course of the school year, because the baseline achievement data would be constantly changing.

- The student achievement data should be analyzed and interpreted by review panels composed of teachers and administrators, rather than by individuals.

This format allows for greater objectivity and for controlling bias. Some districts use educators from neighboring school districts to assist in the analysis and interpretation of achievement data.

- The process should be just one of several sources of data to evaluate teachers. Peer review, portfolios or dossiers, mentoring, peer coaching, and administrator reports are just some of the other sources of data for evaluating teacher quality.

- Some states and local districts are offering financial incentives to teachers and building administrators in schools where student achievement exceeds certain levels. This plan can be very divisive in a school by fostering unhealthy competition, disrupting the school climate, and diverting resources away from other problems that need attention.

TIPS FOR LEADERS #5.10

Steps for Conducting a Three-Party Supervisory Conference

In a three-party supervisory conference, the superintendent (or other district office administrator) observes a lesson and the post-observation conference between a principal (or other evaluator) and a teacher in order to provide feedback to principals on their supervisory and conferencing skills. Using a building principal as an example, the following steps outline how to carry out the three-party conference:

- *Setting Up the Observation.* Ask the principal to arrange for you to be included during a formal supervisory observation visit to a class. The principal should select a teacher who will participate voluntarily and who fully understands the three-party conference process. Be sure the principal alerts the teacher that you will also be observing the class and taking notes in order to gather data for assessing how the principal conducts the post-observation conference.

- *Observing the Teacher.* During the classroom visit, write down significant teacher and student behaviors, especially those related to the focus of the observation (e.g., wait time, classroom management, retention techniques). Also observe the degree to which the principal is recording information.

- *Sitting In on the Post-Observation Conference.* Sit in on the post-observation conference as a nonparticipating observer. Before the conference begins, you may wish to remind the teacher that you are there to observe the principal and will not be involved in the discussion. Take notes on (1) the conference strategy that the principal used, (2) any teacher skills that the principal reinforced through compliments, and (3) any recommendations the principal made for improvement.

- *Between the Post-Observation Conference and the Conference With the Principal.* Before meeting with the principal, analyze your conference notes to determine which of the supervisory and conferencing skills should be complimented. If any skills need improvement, decide on your approach and on what suggestions you will make. You can prepare a written evaluation report either before or after the conference with the principal, depending on district procedures for handling teacher observation reports.

● *The Principal's Conference.* Start with questions, such as
  – What went well in the conference?
  – Did the conference go as you expected?
  – Would you do anything differently next time?
  Your hope is that the principal will lead into those areas of strength and even into the area(s) needing improvement. Offer your suggestions and provide any material or other resources the principal will need to successfully improve the skill.

Besides being a valuable component of the administrator evaluation process, the three-party conference process serves to improve the supervisory and conferencing skills of principals and other evaluators. Furthermore, the process strengthens the credibility of the overall evaluation program because it demonstrates to teachers that their principals are working regularly with their own supervisors to improve their skills.

Ethical and Spiritual Leadership

When I took courses in educational administration several decades ago, almost nothing was said about ethical or spiritual leadership. The course work focused mainly on curriculum development, clinical supervision, personnel and legal issues, school finance, and relationships with school board members and the community. We used lots of inbox scenarios to demonstrate how we would apply our learning in situations that school leaders were likely to encounter. These would include items such as dealing with an incompetent teacher, interpreting a school policy, and placating an angry parent. The occasional ethical issue usually centered on teacher-student relations as, for example, whether teachers should tutor their own students outside of school.

Ethical and spiritual issues have always been in schools. Until recently, however, they stayed in the background, lingering in some gray area where they were shunned or ignored. School reform initiatives have now shed light on these issues, prompting educational leaders to recognize that some of the decisions they make and conflicts they resolve have ethical and, occasionally, spiritual ramifications. (Note: For the purposes of this book, I use the terms *moral* and *ethical* interchangeably. Despite the slight nuances that exist between them, both concepts are primarily concerned with principles of right or wrong conduct.)

Schools are, after all, moral institutions in that they promote social norms. Principals are moral agents who are often called upon to make decisions that favor one moral value over another, a situation known as an *ethical dilemma*. For example, should parents be informed if a counselor learns that their daughter is considering an abortion? Should the student council be allowed to invite an assembly speaker whose ideas will offend some members of the community?

When making decisions involving ethical dilemmas, principals exercise moral authority and teachers need to be convinced that the moral perspective of the principal reflects values they support. Yet I suspect that even today, few principals have been trained to analyze these types of conflicts because ethical issues have been given little attention in preparation programs for administrators.

Earlier in this book, I suggested that individual classroom teachers can be the instrument of change in school reform while the individual school can be the unit of change. Thus, school principals are in a unique position in the administrative hierarchy. Not only do they lead an identifiable community of teachers, students, parents, and other stakeholders, but they also conduct daily personal interactions and make decisions that can, more than those of any other district leader, advance the school organization little by little toward higher ethical and spiritual levels.

To that end, Fullan (2002) suggests that the role and responsibilities of principals today go far beyond those of an instructional leader. The new role, he continues, gives principals opportunities to lead enduring reform if they

- ▸ *Make a difference in the lives of students.* This is perhaps the most important aspect of ethical leadership for the building principal.
- ▸ *Commit to reducing the gap between high- and low- performing students.* Principals need to disaggregate testing data to address the needs of all student subgroups in the school and to consistently monitor all aspects of the school population.
- ▸ *Contribute to reducing the achievement gap among schools within the district.* School leaders should also be concerned about the success of other schools within the district. This helps develop the social/moral environment in the district so that improved achievement can be sustained.
- ▸ *Transform the working environment so that it fosters the commitment, growth, engagement, and spawning of leadership in others.* Leaders need to transform the learning conditions so that there is an enduring sense of moral purpose and commitment for all members of the school organization.

Moral and ethical leadership are closely linked and often difficult to separate as distinct concepts. We will discuss them together. Spiritual leadership, on the other hand, has its own characteristics and will be explored separately.

ETHICAL LEADERSHIP

In the last decade, much has been written about the ethical aspects of leadership in the private sector. Ironically, recent revelations about business practices at Enron, Worldcom, and Adelphia raised questions not only about whether the behavior of their top leadership was legal, but also about whether their activities were ethical. Despite the enormous interest in ethical behavior in the business world, little attention has been paid to what impact ethics have on school leaders as they carry out their daily responsibilities.

Two disturbing trends have now emerged that require an examination of the importance school leaders give to their own ethical behavior and that of their students. The first trend is the increase in incidents of school violence, cheating, and bullying. The second trend is the recognition that some building principals mistreat their teachers in abusive and unethical ways.

Ethics of American Youth

There was a time when children learned about ethical behavior at home and through the practice of their religions. But families and churches seem to be having less influence in instilling ethical values in our children. Changing family patterns and the powerful influence of television and other technology have loosened family ties. One result is the widespread decline in ethical standards.

Although teachers have been saying for some time that student lying and cheating are on the increase in schools, a recent study of the ethical behavior of youth conducted by the Josephson Institute of Ethics (2002) revealed the extent of these ethical lapses. The survey sample included more than 12,000 students from 43 high schools across the country in urban, suburban, and rural areas.

Figure 6.1 compares the percentage of student responses to four questions asked in both the 1992 and 2002 surveys. (Note: The percentages are of those students who responded *strongly agree/agree*.) The results showed a marked increase in unethical behavior. During the ten-year period, cheating on a test increased from 61 percent to 74 percent. Lying to a teacher increased significantly from 69 percent in 1992 to 83 percent in 2002, while lying to a parent went from 83 percent to 93 percent during the same time period. The percentage of students who stole an item from a store rose from 33 to 38. Clearly, students today are more likely to cheat, lie, and steal than the students of 10 years ago.

Other interesting findings from the study were the following:

▸ *Private Religious Schools*. Students attending private religious schools were less likely to shoplift (35 percent vs. 39 percent), but were more likely to cheat on exams (78 percent vs. 72 percent) and lie to teachers (86 percent vs. 81 percent).

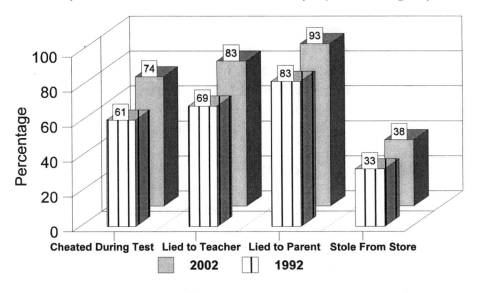

Comparison of 1992 and 2002 Student Responses to Ethical Questions (in percentages)

Figure 6.1 The graph compares the percentage of students who responded "strongly agree/agree" to ethical questions in 1992 and 2002 (Josephson Institute of Ethics, 2002).

▶ *Varsity Sports Players.* Casting some doubt on whether playing sports builds character, students participating in varsity sports cheated on exams at a higher rate than students who were not varsity players (78 percent vs. 73 percent). Could this be because varsity players feel the pressure to maintain a certain grade point average to remain on the team?

▶ *Gender Differences.* In general, girls cheat and lie as much as boys but are less likely to engage in shoplifting. Girls also have more positive attitudes toward ethics.

▶ *College and Honors Classes.* Students who indicated that they intended to go to college and attended honors classes said they cheated, lied, and stole less than others.

Ethical Changes, 2000 to 2002. Some items in the Josephson survey were added only in recent years. Table 6.1 compares the percentages of student responses (of *strongly agree/agree*) for certain items in 2000 and 2002. The percentage of students willing to lie to save money or to get a job jumped dramatically in 2002 (36 percent to 46 percent). An increase in adolescent cynicism was apparent by the sharp rise in the percentage of students agreeing that lying or cheating was sometimes necessary to succeed (28 percent to 37 percent).

Table 6.1 Comparison of Student Survey Responses on Ethics
(Percentage Responding "Strongly Agree/Agree")

Survey Item	2000	2002
I would be willing to lie to save money.	36	46
I would be willing to lie if it would help me get a job.	28	37
A person has to lie or cheat sometimes in order to succeed.	34	43
When it comes to doing what is right, I am better than most people I know.	73	76
It's important to me that people trust me.	96	95
It's not worth it to lie or cheat because it hurts your character.	83	79
My school tries hard to help students develop good character.	70	74
My parents always want me to do the right thing, no matter what the cost.	87	84
My parents would rather I cheat than get bad grades.	5	7

Source: Josephson Institute of Ethics (2002)

Despite these increases in lying and cheating, 76 percent of the students indicated high self-esteem by agreeing that they are better than most people when it comes to doing things right. Furthermore, 95 percent agreed that being trusted was very important to them, while 79 percent agreed that lying or cheating hurts character.

Nearly three-quarters of the students thought that their school tries hard to help students develop good character. Concerning parents, 84 percent said their parents want them to do the right thing, and only 7 percent thought their parents would rather have them cheat than get bad grades. According to the student responses, the increases in lying and cheating apparently cannot be attributed to omissions in the school curriculum or to mixed messages from parents. Nonetheless, the data make it clear that school leaders have to try harder to develop character in students and to provide good role models through their own exercise of ethical leadership.

Ethics in the Curriculum

The Josephson and other similar studies have caused educators to consider incorporating programs that teach ethics into the school curriculum. Such programs are known by a variety of names, including character education, life skills education, ethics/moral philosophy, and values education. The core content of all these programs is to address the moral dimensions of the individual and society, explore how standards of right and wrong are developed, discuss the components of character, and examine the basic attitudes and values of society. The school community identifies the core values of the school, and teachers use the program to reinforce those shared values within the students' lives.

Several programs are now available that are designed to teach students about character, ethics, and ethical behavior. One of particular note is called Character Counts!, sponsored by the Josephson Institute of Ethics. Character Counts! is a voluntary coalition that was formed in 1993, following the 1992 Josephson survey, to promote and support character education nationally. Six pillars of character were identified by the coalition. They are:

- ▶ Trustworthiness
- ▶ Respect
- ▶ Responsibility
- ▶ Fairness
- ▶ Caring
- ▶ Citizenship

Now composed of more than 500 schools, communities, and education and human-service organizations, the program builds a consensus that there are universally accepted values that define human beings at their best, however diverse their views, backgrounds, and religious beliefs.

But does Character Counts! work? Although school administrators and teachers offered testimonials about improvements in student behavior after introducing the program, harder evidence was needed for the skeptics. More than 20 studies have been conducted to date to examine the effect of Character Counts! on student behavior. The most extensive study was done by researchers at South Dakota State University with nearly 8,500 student participants (Character Counts!, 2002).

The results showed that Character Counts! sharply cut crime and drug use in just a two-year period from 1998 to 2000. Students who said they had

- ▶ Broken into another's property dropped 50 percent.
- ▶ Used a fake ID dropped 56 percent.
- ▶ Taken something without paying dropped 46 percent.
- ▶ Drunk alcoholic beverages dropped 31 percent.
- ▶ Taken illegal drugs dropped 32 percent.
- ▶ Defaced or vandalized property dropped 46 percent.
- ▶ Used force against someone who insulted them dropped 33 percent.

The program led to other improvements. Students who said they had

- Cheated on an exam dropped 30 percent.
- Received a detention or suspension dropped 28 percent.
- Missed class without a legitimate excuse dropped 39 percent.
- Teased someone because of race or ethnicity dropped 45 percent.
- Borrowed money without repaying it dropped 34 percent.

Among the other findings in the study

- Students reported improvement in every category of misdeed assessed.
- Teachers reported better student behavior toward others and authority.
- Character Counts! was especially effective for students in grades 1–6.
- The more exposures per month students had to Character Counts!, the better they behaved.

Other character education programs that are available include the following:

- The Giraffe Project is a national program that challenges participants to "stick their necks out" for good character. The program offers examples of real heros who displayed ethical behavior by showing care and concern for others.

- The Character Education Project is a nonpartisan coalition that recognizes National Schools of Character that serve as models of exemplary character education practice in the nation.

- Nearly 20 states have legislation regarding character education, and more are expected. As an example of one response to state legislation mandating good citizenship education for all its students, the Indiana Department of Education developed a curriculum guide, *Partners for Good Citizenship: Parents, Schools, Communities,* based on 13 characteristics of good citizenship.

Increases in school violence and disaffected students, coupled with declining test scores and diminished interest in community involvement have all contributed to renewed interest in ethical/character/values education. School leaders need to give serious thought to the efforts they are making to support and encourage ethical behavior among the students and staff in schools.

Not all members of the school community agree that schools should be teaching character and values. Critics worry about whose values will be taught and whether they will conflict with values taught at home. Other criticisms are that character education does little to improve scores on standardized tests, and it is difficult to measure whether the program is working.

Mistreatment of Teachers by Principals

Organizational researchers have been studying the issue of workplace abuse for two decades. Numerous books and articles have been written about how employers mistreat their employees. Although Congress and many state legislatures have passed laws to curb sexual harassment and other forms of abuses in the workplace, not much has been done to legally curb workplace bullying.

Until recently, little attention was paid to the nature and extent of workplace abuse in public schools. In a revealing and ground breaking study, Blase and Blase (2003) conducted in-depth interviews with 50 teachers from elementary, middle, and high schools who experienced long-term (6 months to 9 years) abusive conduct by their principals. The range of abuses ran the gamut from moderate (e.g., withholding and denying resources to teachers, discounting their needs and feelings, and offensive personal conduct) to serious (e.g., spying, sabotage, and public criticism). More severe forms of mistreatment included threats, unwarranted reprimands, and lying.

> **LEADER'S QUESTION: What are some questions for reflecting on ways to prevent the mistreatment of teachers? SEE TIP #6.1**

In effect, this disturbing study found that the same types of employer-employee abuses that exist in private organizations are also present in some schools. Such behavior took its toll on teachers and on the school organizations as well. Teachers felt trapped, humiliated, angry, stressed, and a diminished sense of professionalism. Schools suffered because mistreated teachers withdrew from all discretionary activity and lost the motivation necessary to prepare exciting lessons for their students (Blase and Blase, 2003).

The researchers in this study admit that the sample was small and that it would be difficult to extrapolate their data to determine the extent of mistreatment of teachers throughout the country. Regardless of the pervasiveness of the mistreatment, this problem needs to be addressed in the open. Ethical leadership in schools means providing an environment where ethical principles are encouraged, honored, and modeled. At the very least, it means that principals must ensure that their teachers are not being mistreated as a result of their behavior or that of other administrators in the building.

Attributes of Ethical Decision Making

School leaders will not always recognize ethical issues when they encounter them. Kidder and Born (2002) suggest that the following four attributes are common to decisions involving ethics:

(1) *The decision is rooted in core, shared values.* Core values are those shared by nearly everyone worldwide and that transcend place and time. Acting as the glue that holds diverse societies together, they include *truth, respect, responsibility, fairness,* and *compassion.* Their wide acceptance provides a solid basis for making ethical decisions. For public school organizations, it is important to note that these same values are held by people with deep religious differences. Even people who claim no religious affiliation still identify these five core values as having great importance to them.

> **LEADER'S QUESTION: What are ways to resolve right-versus-right dilemmas? SEE TIP #6.2**

(2) *The decision centers on right-versus-right dilemmas rather than right-versus-wrong temptations.* Right-versus-wrong dilemmas are common in schools, such as when the value of honesty is violated by dishonest behavior. In this situation, most people avoid the temptation and choose what is right. The tough dilemmas are those when two morally clear options are placed in a situation where they are mutually exclusive.

Kidder and Born (2002) identify four types:

(A) Truth versus loyalty: Personal integrity and honesty conflict with responsibility, allegiance, and promise-keeping (e.g., Do I tell a colleague interviewing a former teacher why we dismissed that teacher?).

(B) Individual versus community: The interests of the individual conflict with those of a larger entity (e.g., Do I accept an attractive job offer now or keep my commitment to the community and wait until my contract ends?).

(C) Short-term versus long-term: The important concerns of the present conflict with investment in the future (e.g., Do we keep the budget increase to a minimum now or raise money for a new school to handle future enrollment increases?).

(D) Justice versus mercy: Fairness conflicts with compassion (e.g., Do I suspend the student for truancy or relent because he was taking care of a sick sibling?).

(3) *The decision provides clear and compelling principles for resolving the problem.* The leader needs to have a resolution plan in mind rather than acting impulsively or not acting at all.

(4) *The decision is infused with moral courage.* Individuals display moral courage by facing mental challenges that could harm their emotional well-being, self-esteem, or reputation. Nonetheless, they pursue the challenge, using the five core values to guide their actions.

Factors Influencing Ethical Decisions

The factors that influence the making of ethical decisions fall into three categories: philosophical, psychological, and sociological.

Philosophical Factors

The ethical forces that drive decision making have been studied for many years. In reviewing the literature on philosophy, three domains of ethical thought emerged that suggested ways for school leaders to process moral decisions (Covrig, 2000):

▸ *Formalism (Do what is right, no matter what).* In this domain, ethical decisions are based on universal imperatives and principles that apply to all individuals. Ranging from the abstract ("Do no harm") to the specific ("Never tell a lie"), they are used to guide moral choices in a wide variety of situations.

▸ *Utilitarianism (Do what is right for this particular situation).* Based on the writings of Aristotle, this domain focuses on the nature and context of the situation and ethical decisions are based on the good of the outcomes. Good outcomes are those that provide the greatest good for the greatest number of people, even though others may be adversely affected.

▸ *Virtue (Do what will best help the people I care about).* This approach focuses on the role of virtue in ethical judgment and decision making. Ethical decisions are understood in light of the impact they will have on the well-being of those affected by the decisions. Thus, the care, respect, and relationship that the decision maker has for the affected group are the most important factors.

Each of these domains reflects a different reference point for leaders to justify a decision to their constituents: "My decision preserves the basic principle of honesty" (formalism); "Good only comes if I keep telling the truth" (utilitarianism) and "I do not lie to others" (virtue). The philosophical factors are based on feelings that help individuals rationalize ethical choices.

Denig and Quinn (2001) offer a simpler philosophical model of just two moral approaches: *justice* and *care*. These educational practitioners have combined formalism and utilitarianism into the singular approach they call justice. In practice, they say, most of the ethical decisions made by leaders of public schools are constrained by law and policy (formalism) and are generally aimed to bring about the greatest good for the greatest number of people (utilitarianism). This approach envisions ethical decision making as the rational and objective application of universal principles. By getting the facts, the decision maker focuses on doing what is right for the greater good, rather than for the individual. Equity is the desirable outcome. Using the caring approach, on the other hand, the decision maker steps into the frame of reference of the individual being affected by the decision and examines the situation subjectively. By showing care, the decision maker hopes to establish a relationship that will endure.

When making ethical decisions in practice, Denig and Quinn contend that these two approaches need not be mutually exclusive. Ethical dilemmas can be ambiguous and the best decision is likely to be made by leaders who discuss ethical decisions and their moral perspectives with others. Through collaborative decision making, leaders can analyze the ethical dimensions of dilemmas and be prepared to work together within a school system to make decisions that are ethical. Moral decision making should not be reasoning versus relationships. The enlightened leader should allow the approaches of justice and care to complement and not oppose each other.

Psychological Factors

Cognitive Development. Psychology contributes to our understanding of ethical decision making in several ways. Jean Piaget (1965), for example, tied moral development to the processes of *cognitive* development within the child. A five-year-old child, for example, lacks the cognitive development to understand the rationale for not telling lies.

Building on the work of Piaget, Lawrence Kohlberg (1983) proposed that cognitive development led to several stages of moral reasoning (Figure 6.2). During the early stages (egocentric), moral decisions were based on personal needs, progressing from avoiding physical harm to satisfying an immediate interest. In the middle stages (interpersonal), the focus was on relationships and personal or

Kohlberg's Stages of Moral Development

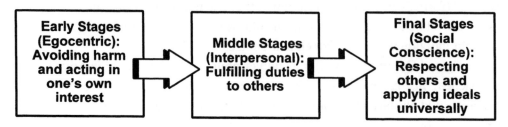

Figure 6.2 Basing his work on Piaget, Kohlberg (1983) suggested several stages of moral development. Most people, he thought, were at the middle stages, but leaders progressed to the final stages.

professional commitments. Fulfillment of duties to others guided moral reasoning. Kohlberg thought that most people were at the middle stages. Leaders, however, were more likely to be in the final stages (social conscience) of moral development where they recognized that people hold a variety of values, that individual rights must be preserved, and that there were ideals that could be universally applied to every decision-making situation.

The cognitive development of leaders may play a key role in how these leaders categorize the kinds of decisions they make. Furthermore, the cognitive development of the school's faculty and students may also contribute to how administrators view their decisions. The psychological factors emphasize the influence that cognitive development has on the way a person processes moral issues.

Emotional Development. Some psychologists insist that emotions, and not cognitive processing, are the basis for moral action. A child will tell a lie about a situation, such as breaking a lamp, for fear of punishment and to avoid unpleasantness. The thought of the lie being discovered is off in the future and unlikely to affect the child's immediate response.

Research in Cognitive Neuroscience. Although it is possible to explain moral growth through either the cognitive or emotional approach, newer research in cognitive science suggests that neither approach fully explains moral behavior. The normal human brain is constantly balancing emotional and cognitive information as it analyzes situations and decides on a course of action. As discussed in Chapter 2, the frontal lobes play a major role in rational thought while the limbic area controls emotional responses. Despite these distinctive roles, the two regions do not act independently of each other. Their neural circuits overlap and both systems are activated and interact with each other whenever we make cognitive decisions that contain emotional issues.

Sociological Factors

The social structure in which we live tends to reduce our individualism, making us more a part of a group. It plays an important role in constraining individual moral action by creating taboos, setting norms, and building shared values that individuals incorporate into their thinking and decision making. Thus, social context greatly influences how we make ethical decisions.

Ethical Leadership in Schools

Schools are complex human organizations where several different moral codes exist, affecting all members of the organization and making conflicting demands for personal and group action. The leader, however, is in a position to arbitrate between these moral codes in order to avoid creating moral ambiguity within the school. Through this process, leaders fill an important role by helping the organization identify the moral code that will clarify its mission and shape the organizational practices to match that mission. As a result, both leaders and their constituents should bring each other to a higher moral ground. This collaborative effort to establish a firm moral system is the essence of ethical leadership and becomes an important factor in the making and breaking of the most difficult decisions within the school—those involving ethical dilemmas.

> **LEADER'S QUESTION:** What steps are involved in ethical decision making? SEE TIP #6.3

Dealing With Ethical Dilemmas

Educational leaders make all kinds of decisions in the course of their work. The types of decisions they make, however, are based on the nature of the problem at hand, and generally fall into three categories (Covrig, 2000).

Routines. Most decisions involve minor adjustments to established school or district rules, policies, and procedures, known as routines:

- ▸ Should we use alphabetical order or grade level in assigning teachers to lunch and bus supervision?
- ▸ When should we mail out the district calendars?

Challenges. Fewer decisions are more challenging because they may alter routines or established precedent. The challenge comes in estimating the implications and ramifications of making the change, even though it may be temporary:

- Should veteran teachers get first choice in selecting which duty they prefer?
- Should the district calendar include the dates that report cards are mailed or will this also alert students to watch the mails?

Dilemmas. The most difficult decisions are those which involve ethical dilemmas because they require the leader to violate one cherished value while trying to respond to another cherished value.

- Should veteran teachers be relieved of lunch and bus supervision in recognition of their seniority? (This dilemma pits the value of *rewarding years of service* against the value of *equitable treatment of all staff.*)
- Should we include in the district calendar the activities of nonprofit, religiously affiliated organizations who use our schools? (This dilemma pits the value of *informing the school community* against the value of *separation of state from religion.*)

The proportion of routines, challenges, and dilemmas varies from one organization to another. Some organizations will have a balanced mix of the three types of decisions while others may be heavily weighted with one type or another. Covrig (2000) suggests that the different mixes produce three basic types of organizations: the routinized organization, the stable organization, and the unstable organization (Figure 6.3).

Routinized Organizations. Routinized organizations, such as schools, universities, and banks, are highly institutionalized and are governed by policies and protocols. Dilemmas are rare or ignored. These types of organizations often attract workers who thrive on routines and, therefore, are resistant to change. Educational leaders who are trying to implement change have a difficult time in those schools where nearly all administrative decisions are defined by locally imposed and tightly written regulations. Leaders have little leeway, the faculty is comfortable with routines, and change is extremely slow. Ethical leadership in highly routinized schools requires that leaders resist the temptation to get lulled into the status quo. They may need to raise moral dilemmas with the staff by asking questions such as "By maintaining the status quo, are we effective in serving the needs of a rapidly changing and increasingly diverse student population?"

To promote change in routinized schools, some school districts have recognized the need to replace entrenched administrators and faculty, especially in consistently underperforming schools. If doing more of the same is not working, new leadership

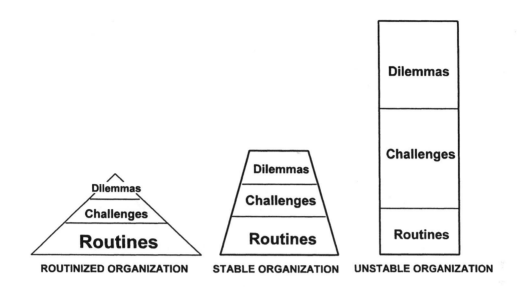

Figure 6.3 The proportion of decisions involving routines, challenges, and dilemmas affects the degree of routinization and stability of an organization. (Adapted with permission of the author from Covrig, 2000.)

and personnel are needed to break up the routines, tackle the challenges, and create or deal with dilemmas.

Stable Organizations. Other organizations have a balance of routines, challenges, and dilemmas. Although policies exist, they are not so limiting or relied

on to fully guide the organization in dealing with its employees and clients. Processes are usually in place to support modest change. This type of school organization is likely to exist in states that have few or no collective bargaining agreements for teachers. The lack of another set of rules, procedures, and limitations found in teacher contracts may provide a less restrictive environment where change can occur more readily.

Unstable Organizations. In some organizations, there are few routines and traditions to guide organizational behavior. This scenario seldom exists in public school organizations because of the myriad of federal, state, and local regulations. But it can occur to some degree in individual schools where the faculty is diverse or transient, making routinization difficult. Although this might seem like a desirable environment for innovation, there is great potential for instability in the school as administrators get consumed dealing with an endless round of decisions involving challenges and dilemmas.

Regardless of the type of school organization, effective ethical leadership involves crafting the routines and dilemmas necessary to move the school toward accomplishing its mission by serving its students. It includes developing an environment that fosters moral sensitivity, promotes the motivation to do good, and keeps the school faithful to its central identity, a place for teaching and learning. Ethical leadership begins with ethical leaders. Those who write about ethics offer somewhat different composites of what makes an ethical leader. But most seem to agree that ethical leaders are those who display honesty, courage, and a willingness to take responsibility for their decisions. They use their power with restraint and acknowledge their own limitations without hiding behind their power and status.

BRAIN RESEARCH AND ETHICAL BEHAVIOR

Most parents encourage in their children character traits, such as honesty, respect, integrity, and responsibility, to help them lead successful and ethical lives. But how does the young brain learn, assess, and internalize the components of ethical behavior? Recent research studies have given us some insights into the moral development of the brain.

The Cognitive-Emotional-Somatic Connection

As discussed in Chapter 2, the neural networks of the frontal lobe play a major role in planning and decision making. Studies with brain-damaged patients show that the frontal lobe is critical for higher cognitive processes, including concept formation, reasoning, and resolving ethical dilemmas. The limbic area is associated primarily with emotions, but there is evidence that some cognitive processing also occurs here. Although these two areas have different functions, they work closely together to provide the individual with a complete set of cognitive and emotional data in order to respond appropriately to a particular situation.

In studies of how the brain makes judgments, Damasio (1994) discovered that when faced with making difficult choices, an area called the *somatosensory cortex* was activated, in addition to the cognitive and emotional areas. (The somatosensory cortex responds to touch or pressure, temperature, pain, and limb position and movement.) Thus, the subjects experienced a bodily sensation (called a *somatic marker*) in addition to an emotional tone. Apparently, these three areas work together as part of a judgment circuit when processing situations involving ethical decisions (Figure 6.4).

This frontal lobe-limbic-somatosensory connection suggests that the brain processes ethical dilemmas cognitively, emotionally, and somatically. The cognitive

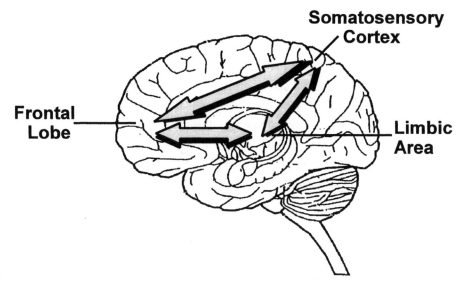

Figure 6.4 Connections between the brain's frontal lobe, limbic area, and somatosensory cortex form a circuit that appears to make possible the learning of ethical principles in an emotional context (Livingston, 1999).

component reflects on the future consequences of an action, the emotional component deals with immediate feelings, and the somatic response involves bodily awareness. For example, if a principal in another school district calls you for a recommendation on a teacher who was a constant complainer, what do you say? As you mentally process this dilemma, the cognitive systems alert you to the future consequences of giving the principal a good recommendation (This teacher might do better in another environment) or a bad one (The teacher might sue me). Meanwhile, processing in the limbic area conjures up emotional responses such as collegial loyalty (I should tell him how I really feel about this teacher) or fear (I better keep quiet about my feelings).

Eventually, the adult brain sorts through the cognitive and emotional data and suggests a course of action that is likely to be more rational than emotional. You might say to your colleague, "Although we did not always agree on things, his teaching skills were fine." This rational statement will very probably be followed by a bodily feeling of relief (perhaps a deep sigh) or pleasure (a sense of euphoria) that you told the truth, further evidence of an integrated cognitive-emotional-somatic packet (Livingston, 1999).

Developing Ethical Behavior in Children

The cognitive-emotional-somatic process is somewhat different in young brains. A child who breaks a lamp and denies responsibility is reacting to the fear of punishment (an immediate emotional response) because the young frontal lobe is not mature enough to understand that lying is wrong and can cause problems in future relationships or employment (a cognitive response). By lying (and acting against an ethical principle), the child avoids immediate punishment; future consequences are not even a consideration.

If lying is the most likely cerebral response of children caught in situations like this, how can parents encourage proper ethical development? Livingston (1999) suggests that parents have to recognize the cognitive-emotional link in moral reasoning and then focus on getting the child to understand and internalize that immoral behavior has future undesirable consequences. This is not easy, although some parents do it intuitively. According to Livingston, the first step is to get the child to feel the unpleasantness of being dishonest (some form of punishment such as withdrawing a privilege). Next, explain to the child the moral principle at hand, (in this case, honesty) and why the act of lying was dishonest. Finally, if the child lies again, the punishment should be more severe but also delayed for a short time, during which the child is asked to anticipate what will occur. This way, the child makes the internal link between the cognitive (dishonesty is not good), the emotional (dishonesty has consequences), and the somatic (the unpleasant bodily feelings of awaiting punishment).

As children respond to ethical dilemmas, parents, and eventually teachers and principals, are faced with finding ways to explain ethical principles to children in a way they can understand. Such explanation is essential for the child's brain to make the cognitive-emotional connection needed for the development of an acceptable code of ethical behavior.

SPIRITUAL LEADERSHIP

Spiritual leadership is a way of guiding school organizations so that spirituality is encouraged and supported. Until recently, the idea of even discussing spirituality in the context of public schools would have been considered unwise. Educational leaders would no doubt have argued that such discussions were prohibited by the First Amendment to the Constitution of the United States, which requires the separation of church and state. Others would have argued that, regardless of the legal barriers, spirituality is a topic best left to the family. But one of the outcomes of our rapidly changing society has been a recognition that our culture overemphasizes the importance of accumulating material possessions and financial wealth, thereby creating a spiritual void.

Some argue that the lack of spirituality is having a serious effect on students and their educators. Many students feel an emptiness and disconnection with their environment. The rash of teen suicides and campus massacres has awakened educators and the community to how much we have neglected the spiritual development of our youth. **When adolescents have no spiritual compass to guide them in times of crisis, they are likely to take irrational and immoral action.** Teachers, especially at the secondary level, report that students are asking more questions than ever about personal spiritual matters, and many teachers are unwilling to help for fear that they may be crossing into forbidden territory. A way has to be found to fill the spiritual void. Ideally, spirituality should be nurtured in the home during the early years of childhood. But this seems to be occurring less. If schools ignore opportunities to support spirituality, where else will our youth get it? The question is whether schools can provide students and staff with spiritual support without violating their religious beliefs or the Constitution.

What Is Spirituality?

One way to accomplish this task is to separate spirituality from religion. This is not easy, especially because many adults associate spirituality with their own religious faith. Yet it is possible to examine components of spirituality that are not tied exclusively to any one religious doctrine. Howard Gardner (2000) has attempted to do this with his concept of existential intelligence. He describes this intelligence as the ability to locate oneself with respect to the significance of life, the meaning of death, and the ultimate fate of the psychological and physical worlds.

Spirituality is closely related to existential intelligence, but goes a step further. It involves our deepest emotions and yearnings as well as our sense of connection to larger forces such as nature. Spirituality describes grappling with the meaning and purpose of life and being consciously aware of those meanings.

Spirituality in Schools

Nel Noddings (Halford, 1999) suggests that spirituality is a way of life that recognizes something called spirit. Religion is a specific way of exercising that spirituality, usually through some institutional affiliation. Because of this difference, she continues, a discussion of religions and spiritual values can be safely conducted in schools without violating any laws. School leaders should not be afraid to encourage the discussion of religions and spirituality. The key to success is open communication. The principal, teachers, and parents know that these discussions are going on in the classrooms, that they are age-appropriate, and that the focus is on analysis, not proselytizing.

Educators now are suggesting that the keep-religion-out-of-schools pendulum is beginning to swing the other way. This may be because schools have become such complex organizations where an enormously overcrowded curriculum pushes teachers to deliver cognitive information at a faster pace than ever to beat the high-stakes testing. In many schools today, the curriculum remains cognitive-based, teacher-controlled, fragmented, and textbook-oriented. Students feel swamped with schoolwork at the same time they are trying to deal with sex, drugs, alcohol, AIDS, and their own ethical dilemmas.

Even as members of the school community act out their various roles, there is a growing feeling that the current school plan, based on the industrial model and agrarian calendar, is less relevant to the changing needs of modern society. As a result, students feel no sense of connectedness to other members of the school community or the world around them. They long for something more. Rachael Kessler (2000) believes that schools ignore the soul of education. Schools have little or no time in the curriculum to help students understand about themselves, about each other, and about the universe, just when they need it most. Some of the questions that Kessler reports students asking most frequently are:

- ▸ Why am I so alone?
- ▸ How do I know I'm normal?
- ▸ Why do I feel scared and confused about becoming an adult?
- ▸ Why do people hate others—black, white, Hispanic?
- ▸ What is our purpose in life?
- ▸ Why have we ruined our earth?
- ▸ How come people kill other people?

Educators are concentrating so heavily on transferring cognitive information that they are ignoring the fears, worries, and wonderment that percolate within our youth. These feelings can no longer be neglected.

Spirituality in the Curriculum

Schools offer an environment where spirituality can be recognized in many ways such as through music, poetry, biography, history, and science. Infusing spirituality in the curriculum starts with convincing school leaders and teachers about the importance of exploring bigger questions with students at appropriate times in and out of the classroom. Many opportunities abound. Here are a few examples (Kessler, 2000):

> ▶ In a biology class, a discussion of ecosystems could include questions such as these: *Does every organism have a part to play in the ecosystem or is life random? And where is our place? Has mankind contributed to our ecosystems or ruined them? If we have ruined the earth, why are we here?*

> ▶ A history class would offer opportunities to address the following questions: *Why do people hate others? Why do people kill others?*

> ▶ Poetry and literature open the door to many spiritual questions: *Why am I so alone? Is there anyone else in the world like me? Why do people who love you hurt you? What makes people evil? When will I know what being myself really is? What is my destiny?*

Kessler believes that there are certain kinds of experiences, apart from religion, that nourish the spiritual development of young people. These experiences fall into seven categories that she calls gateways. School leaders need to recognize the importance of these gateways and encourage experiences that fulfill the spiritual yearnings of students.

Solomon and Hunter (2002) suggest that curriculum and spirituality ought to go hand in hand. The curriculum should develop the capacity of students to think critically *within* various subjects and *about* them as well. They should personally engage with, respond to, and assess what they are studying. By doing so, students produce deep and rich understandings about different subjects and build complex neural networks between them. Spirituality and education share an ongoing search for understanding, connections, and meaning about the human experience.

Mindfulness

Questions involving spirituality encourage the learner to move beyond rational and analytic thinking to emotional and intuitive thinking in order to find focus and to grasp meanings that are important for the individual. This approach is referred to as *mindfulness*. Being mindful means focusing completely on the task at hand, becoming fully aware of each moment, and searching within oneself to interpret that moment.

Studies conducted by Ellen Langer (1997) have shown that students remember much more of what they learn through mindfulness. Mindfulness does not mean ignoring rational

LEADER'S QUESTION: How can schools address the spiritual needs of students? SEE TIP #6.4

thinking, but rather, *adding* the intuitive approach so that students can reflect on deeper meanings and identity. A spiritual curriculum supports mindfulness when it avoids meaningless activities and old routines while encouraging creativity, flexibility, reflection, and an atmosphere where intuitions lead to deeper understandings. Integrating spirituality into the curriculum not only helps those within the school, but helps bring compassion and fair-mindedness to those outside the school community by extending this climate of mindfulness.

Spirituality and School Leadership

> **LEADER'S QUESTION: How can I address my own spiritual needs? SEE TIP #6.5**

Spirituality has a broad-ranging impact on how we think and act in our daily routines. How connected we feel to things beyond and within ourselves, and how well we can align our public and private work lives with our values, are all a part of spirituality. School leaders are driven by the forces of spirituality, regardless of whether they consider themselves to be spiritual. Recently, the American Association of School Administrators asked researchers in leadership and spirituality to suggest ways of integrating spirituality into educational leadership. Here are a few of their suggestions that appeared in the September 2002 Web edition of *The School Administrator*.

- Solomon and Hunter (2002) suggest that school leaders convey to their staffs that our understandings about the deeper meanings of life can help us be more effective in carrying out our professional responsibilities as educators. Leaders do not impose their spiritual system on others, but rather acknowledge that drawing on personal spirituality is a valid method for framing, conceptualizing, and approaching our work. Furthermore, leaders set an example of how spirituality guides their work when they interact with others. When leaders show respect and humility toward their colleagues, for example, they model spiritual values that set a tone throughout the school organization.

- If school leaders feel a strong sense of vocation in what they do, they can avoid being overwhelmed and discouraged by knowing there is a meaning to their lives. Also, by believing in a power greater than their own, they can be more courageous in their decisions and resilient in their actions.

Wheatley (2002) believes that the following principles, based on spiritual thinking and traditions, describe the work of current leaders.

▸ *Life is uncertain.* Nowadays, change is a constant. Many people resist change. But if leaders give people time to reflect on their personal experiences, they realize that they have changed many times throughout the years. School leaders, then, can gently guide their faculty to discover their own wisdom about life.

▸ *Life is cyclical.* Throughout life, we move from peace to chaos and then to peace again. When chaos occurs, leaders should help people stay with the chaos, help them walk through it together, and look for new insights as a result of the experience.

▸ *Meaning is what motivates people.* Most people want their work to serve a greater good. Leaders, therefore, must create time for people to recall the initial motivation and enthusiasm they had when they began their work and to remember who still benefits from it.

▸ *Service brings us joy.* Many people discover profound happiness through their work, especially when that work involves helping others.

▸ *Courage comes from our hearts.* Leaders are courageous champions when they are willing to open their hearts to an issue or a person, and when they tell stories that open other people's hearts.

▸ *We are interconnected to all life.* Leaders recognize this interconnectedness when they understand how a decision may affect others in the future.

▸ *We can rely on human goodness.* Leaders need to rely on the good qualities in others.

▸ *We need peace of mind.* Leaders need to find ways to help people avoid unnecessary frantic activity and find a sense of inner peace. When a meeting has a particularly serious issue on the agenda, start with a few minutes of silent contemplation.

> **LEADER'S QUESTION: What are some practices that can help me maintain inner peace as a leader? SEE TIP #6.6**

● Hoyle (2002) maintains that the spiritual and administrative sides are of equal importance in educational leadership. The spiritual side provides the breadth of vision and deep understanding of human motives that leaders need to inspire all members of the school community. Believing that spiritual leadership can be taught, Hoyle offers the following suggestions as part of preparation programs for school leaders:

▶ *Conduct spiritual discussions.* Students of educational leadership should discuss real-life ethical dilemmas and propose alternative solutions and actions. The solutions should center on the core values of honesty, fairness, compassion, respect, and responsibility.

▶ *Create the spiritual self.* School leaders should generate a vision of the ideal person they wish to become and determine what spiritual habits of mind they need to fulfill that vision.

▶ *Assign books on spiritual leadership.* Students of educational leadership can learn about spiritual leadership by reading and debating the concepts developed by prominent writers in the field. The stories of great spiritual leaders can inspire school leaders to infuse spiritual leadership into their own work.

● Kessler (2002) argues that spiritual leadership is even more important today, given a climate where administrators feel threatened and intimidated by a system of accountability that is measured almost exclusively by high-stakes testing. Furthermore, principals feel like they are competing with each other when their building test scores get published and ranked. Trying to lead with soul is not easy when school leaders are worried about their livelihood. Yet most administrators remember times in their careers when their compassion and caring turned around a troubled student. To keep this spiritual leadership alive, Kessler suggests that school leaders create teams of school community members that adhere to the following principles:

▶ *Personalize.* Team members need to articulate their own goals, perhaps by sharing what motivated them to enter teaching. Getting this perspective helps the team members to recognize the value of spiritual values, especially those of honesty, fairness, respect, commitment, and genuine listening.

▶ *Pacing.* Move slowly to allow people time to get to know each other gradually. Introduce information that connects spiritual values to successful learning.

▶ *Permission.* Take time to listen to team members to find out where they are. If some people prefer to opt out of discussions, the leader can ask them to serve as witnesses who can later share their observations, if they wish.

▶ *Protection.* Protect team members from interruptions, put-downs, disrespect, or the pressure to participate. This approach fosters trust and a sense of community by demonstrating that, for some topics, team members may want to pass and just listen.

▸   *Paradox*. Be willing to entertain ideas that contain opposites, such as privacy and community, authority and collaboration, standards and spirituality. This last combination may be the most difficult because either extreme is undesirable. A school based solely on standards creates an arid, test-driven organization. On the other hand, a school based exclusively on spirituality can get lost in tending to the inner world of students and no real learning is accomplished. But when both standards and spirituality are together in balance, a productive and compassionate learning environment emerges.

In practice, ethical and spiritual leaders make decisions and take actions that respond to, clarify, and preserve the core values of the school community. At the same time, these leaders must move themselves, their teachers, and students to recognize the importance of ethical sensitivity, judgment, and action in order to maintain a high moral and spiritual ethos within the school.

MAJOR POINTS IN CHAPTER 6

❑ Little attention has been paid as to what impact ethics have on school leaders as they carry out their daily responsibilities.

❑ Recent surveys show that unethical behavior in American youth is increasing. School leaders have to try harder to develop character in students and to be good role models through their own exercise of ethical leadership. Character education programs are available and should be considered.

❑ Incidents of the mistreatment of teachers by principals can no longer be ignored. Treating staff with respect and dignity is part of ethical leadership.

❑ Ethical decision making is influenced by philosophical, psychological, and sociological factors.

❑ Several models exist that can help school leaders identify and resolve ethical dilemmas. Success at resolving these dilemmas often depends on whether the school organization is routinized, stable, or unstable.

❑ Brain research is providing some insight into how people learn ethical behavior and deal with ethical issues. This information may help parents and educators be more successful in encouraging a child's moral development.

❑ Spiritual leadership is a way of guiding school organizations so that spirituality is encouraged and supported. It is possible to have spirituality in school without violating the religious beliefs of others or the U.S. Constitution. The increase in teen suicides and campus massacres has awakened educators and the community to how much we have neglected the spiritual development of our youth.

TIPS FOR LEADERS #6.1

Preventing Mistreatment of Teachers

The mistreatment of teachers by school leaders is not always an intentional, premeditated act. It can be the result of a series of inadvertent acts that accumulate and eventually result in abuse. Blase and Blase (2003) suggest that building principals reflect on the following questions that may be helpful in preventing the mistreatment of staff. Read each question and record your response.

- How do I encourage or discourage a supportive and respectful climate in my school? _____
  _____
  _____

- How can I raise my awareness and understanding about abuse in the workplace? _____
  _____
  _____

- Do I know what the local, state, and federal policies and regulations say about teacher mistreatment? _____
  _____
  _____

- How can I become more aware of the impact of my behavior on teachers?
  _____
  _____
  _____

- Do stress and anger drive my behavior toward teachers, and do I tend to be authoritarian? _____
  _____
  _____

- Have I unfairly blocked the professional growth of a teacher or withheld or denied resources to certain teachers? _____

  _____

  _____

- Have I been guilty in using teacher evaluation procedures to punish a teacher for matters unrelated to school? _____

  _____

  _____

- What opportunities exist for counseling and guidance with respect to the issue of teacher mistreatment? _____

  _____

  _____

What actions will you take as a result of your responses? _____

_____

_____

_____

TIPS FOR LEADERS #6.2

Resolving Right-Versus-Right Dilemmas

Right-versus-right ethical dilemmas are difficult to resolve because they involve two morally valid options in a situation where they are mutually exclusive. Kidder and Born (2002) suggest that there are four types: truth versus loyalty, individual versus community, short-term versus long-term, and justice versus mercy. They further suggest that individuals tend to select one of three principles (ends-based, rules-based, and care-based thinking) when resolving these dilemmas. Respond to the questions below and decide which approach works best for you in resolving a right-versus-right dilemma.

- *Ends-Based Thinking.* This principle is concerned with the results of a decision. It is a utilitarian approach, commonly summarized as the greatest good for the greatest number. In essence, the consequences of the decision determine its moral rightness. If everything turns out well, then it was the correct decision.
  What do you think will happen if you make this decision? _____
  _____
  _____
  *How many people will benefit from this decision compared with other options?*_____
  _____

- *Rule-Based Thinking.* In contrast to ends-based thinking, this principle denies that the end results of any decision can really be known or even estimated in advance. Consequently, the rule-based thinker identifies and selects the rule that can be applied anywhere. The consequences are of little interest. What matters is the fundamental and universally applicable precept that underlies the decision.
  What fundamental principle is applicable to this dilemma? _____
  _____

- *Care-Based Thinking.* This principle is based on the Golden Rule of doing to others as you would have them do to you. Care-based thinkers put themselves in the position of the other person to understand that perspective. The decision is based on the notion of reciprocity: What would I prefer to have done to me if the situation were reversed?

If you were in the position of those affected by this decision, is this what you would want? Why? _____

_____

Who else do you need to be concerned about with this decision?

_____

_____

Finally, you might consider whether there is a possible third way out of the dilemma. By their nature, most right-versus-right dilemmas do not offer a third option, but the search for one is worth considering. For example, a parent might object to a homework assignment on religious grounds. Here, the principal might negotiate an alternative assignment with the teacher and parent, thereby preserving academic integrity without trampling on the parent's rights.

Is there a third option to consider here? _____

_____

TIPS FOR LEADERS #6.3

Steps Involved in Ethical Decision Making

Several models of ethical decision making exist. In his search of the literature, Duane Covrig (2000) suggests an eclectic model originally developed by Jones (1991) that includes six aspects to help define whether an issue or incident is a candidate for ethical decision making, and outlines four steps in that process.

Aspects for Defining an Ethical Issue

Clearly, issues can have different degrees of ethical intensity. To decide whether a case, issue, or incident is a candidate for ethical decision making, an educational leader should first respond to the following six questions.

- *What is the magnitude of the consequences resulting from this decision?*

  _____

- *What social consensus already exists about this issue?* _____

  _____

- *What is the probability that something critical will result from this case or issue?* _____

  _____

- *How important is the immediacy of this decision to other stakeholders?*

  _____

- *How closely is the ethical question tied to this case/issue?* _____

  _____

  _____

- *How concentrated will the effects of this decision be on any one individual?*

  _____

  _____

Although your responses are subject to bias, taken in their totality, they are sufficiently accurate to help you make critical distinctions about the degree of ethical intensity of your impending decision.

Steps in the Process

The process consists of four steps. The level of cognitive development and emotional makeup will influence how an individual navigates through the four areas. Although the decision may be made by a single individual, the process occurs within cultural, social, and organizational contexts.

Step 1. Recognizing an Ethical Issue After reviewing the answers to the above six questions, the leader decides on the nature and intensity of the ethical case or issue.	What is the ethical issue?
Step 2. Making Moral Judgments About the Issue The leader needs to make moral judgments about the issue. Several factors, such as the opportunity to reach a personal or financial goal, the presence of significant others, as well as the rewards or sanctions of an action, will influence these judgments.	What moral judgments have you made about this issue?
Step 3. Intending an Action In this step, the leader selects an action (or actions) for implementation.	What action(s) do you plan to take?
Step 4. Implementing the Action This step includes the planning necessary to implement the action in a timely manner.	How will you implement your decision?

TIPS FOR LEADERS #6.4

Addressing the Spiritual Needs of Students

Educational leaders can address the spiritual needs of students by first recognizing the kinds of experiences that nourish those needs. Kessler (2000) suggests that such experiences can be placed into seven categories, called *gateways,* that begin with a yearning. Examine the following seven gateways and review what opportunities are available in your school for experiences that nurture these yearnings.

- *The Yearning for Deep Connection.* This gateway describes the nature of relationships that have deep meaning and are profoundly caring. Students may make these connections to themselves, to each other, to nature, or to a higher power.
  In my school, the yearning for deep connection can be met by _____
  _____
  _____

- *The Longing for Silence and Solitude.* This gateway takes a respite from the business of modern life, offering students an opportunity for reflection, rest, and contemplation.
  In my school, the longing for silence and solitude can be met by _____
  _____
  _____

- *The Search for Meaning and Purpose.* This gateway explores the big questions: Why am I here? What is my purpose in life? What is in my future? These questions often arise when discussing powerful literary works.
  In my school, the meaning and purpose of life are discussed in _____
  _____
  _____

- *The Hunger for Joy and Delight.* Activities such as play and celebrations can address this yearning. Joy can come when students encounter power, brilliance, beauty, and the sheer pleasure of being alive.

In my school, the hunger for joy and delight can be met by _____

_____

_____

- *The Creative Drive.* This gateway is the most familiar for nourishing the spirit in school and is part of all the other gateways. Students feel the awe and mystery of creating when they produce a work of art, develop a new idea, make a scientific discovery, or acquire a new view on life.
In my school, the creative drive is nourished by _____

_____

_____

- *The Urge for Transcendence.* This gateway describes the urge of young people to go beyond their perceived limits and to experience the extraordinary in academics, athletics, the arts, or human relations. Transcendence is a powerful urge that educators should channel to productive ends.
In my school, the urge for transcendence is met by _____

_____

_____

- *The Need for Initiation.* The rights of passage for the young as they move from childhood to adulthood are at the center of this gateway. This need can be met when adults give young people tools for dealing with transitions. Ceremonies with parents and educators that welcome youth into the community of adults can also help meet this strong desire.
In my school, the need for initiation is met by _____

_____

_____

Spirituality-Integrated Curriculum

Spirituality can become an overt part of school life through an integrated, thematic curriculum that helps school leaders, teachers, and students address the connectedness of life that is inherent in spirituality. Review the eight characteristics suggested by Clark (1997) of a spirituality-integrated curriculum and rate where you believe your school or district stands in giving priority to each of the following:

Category	Rating
	1 (Low)---2 --- 3 --- 4 --- 5 (High)
● Context over content	1 ------- 2 ------- 3 ------- 4 ------- 5
● Concepts over facts	1 ------- 2 ------- 3 ------- 4 ------- 5
● Questions over answers	1 ------- 2 ------- 3 ------- 4 ------- 5
● Imagination over knowledge	1 ------- 2 ------- 3 ------- 4 ------- 5
● Intuition over rational logic	1 ------- 2 ------- 3 ------- 4 ------- 5
● Developmental intent over graded content	1 ------- 2 ------- 3 ------- 4 ------- 5
● The learning process over the product of learning	1 ------- 2 ------- 3 ------- 4 ------- 5
● Quality of information over quantity of information	1 ------- 2 ------- 3 ------- 4 ------- 5

Analysis

Based on these characteristics, how would you summarize the extent to which your school addresses spirituality through the curriculum? _____

_____

_____

What steps, if any, will you take to increase the integration of spirituality in the curriculum? _____

_____

_____

TIPS FOR LEADERS #6.5

Addressing Your Own Spiritual Needs

Spiritual renewal is an important part of spiritual leadership. Take some time to ponder the questions below and then write a short response. Revisit the questions periodically and expand or change your response accordingly (Kaiser, 2002).

- *What am I here to do?* _____
  _____
  _____

- *Who am I here to serve?* _____
  _____
  _____

- *What am I here to learn?* _____
  _____
  _____

- *What are my genetic strengths and weaknesses?* _____
  _____
  _____

- *What are my spirituality-based strengths and weaknesses?* _____
  _____
  _____

- *How can I best expand my spiritual awareness?* _____
  _____
  _____

- *How is my persona different from who I really am?* _____
  _____
  _____

- *What is my greatest barrier to spiritual progress?* _____
  _____
  _____

- *Where am I in my unfolding life story?* _____
  _____
  _____

- *Where am I currently stuck?* _____
  _____
  _____

- *What can other people learn from studying my life?* _____
  _____
  _____

- *How can I increase my happiness?* _____
  _____
  _____

- *What are some of my unrealized spiritual potentials?* _____
  _____
  _____

- *Am I spending too much time and effort maintaining my present work situation?* _____
  _____
  _____

- *What is my most probable future if I continue living as I am now living?*
  _____
  _____
  _____

TIPS FOR LEADERS #6.6

Practices for Maintaining Inner Peace

As a school leader, your daily life is filled with hectic, disjointed, and tense situations that often require immediate decisions and conflict resolution. Maintaining this frenzied pace takes a toll on your spiritual equilibrium, upsetting the delicate balance of compassion and justice that you need to make sound decisions. Wheatley (2002) suggests some simple practices that you can use to restore your focus and sense of inner peace.

- *Start your day off peacefully.* Use silence, soothing music, reflection, or meditation to start your day.

- *Learn to be mindful.* Mindfulness means avoiding an instant response to a situation and giving yourself time to determine all the options you have available before acting.

- *Slow things down.* If a group or meeting is moving too fast, slow yourself down by sitting back, reflecting, and taking a deep breath.

- *Create your own measures.* Create personal measures you can use to determine if you are becoming a better person. These measures help you evaluate positive changes in your behavior such as telling the truth more often, getting angry less, or becoming more patient.

- *Expect surprise.* Accept surprise as a fact of life and do not get thrown by it.

- *Practice gratefulness.* Find the time to count your blessings and be grateful for what you have. Expressing your gratefulness to colleagues can improve professional relationships dramatically.

Transforming School Culture

Educational leaders cannot transform schools without a deep and thorough understanding of the nature of school culture. Although hard to define, culture is a powerful force that shapes the opinions, attitudes, and behaviors of all people connected to an organization. In a school, culture influences what students and teachers talk about, their emphasis on teaching and learning, how they dress, and their willingness to change.

Deal and Peterson (1999) describe culture as the norms, traditions, values, and beliefs that build up over time as people work together within an organization, face challenges, and solve problems. Culture also includes the ceremonies, rituals, symbols, myths, and stories that bind the school together, reinforce the school's mission, and communicate its core values. School cultures are unique and they can either encourage or stifle change.

TYPES OF SCHOOL CULTURE

No two schools have the same culture. Yet there are some characteristics common to cultures that support teaching and learning, called positive or collegial cultures, and those that hinder teaching and learning, often referred to by Deal and Peterson (1999) as *toxic cultures*.

Supportive cultures are characterized by

- Honest, open communication
- High expectations
- Trust and confidence
- Recognition and appreciation
- Teacher involvement in decision making

- ► Collegiality
- ► Caring and humor
- ► Traditions that strengthen school culture

Schools with positive cultures have a sense of cohesion and collaboration, numerous opportunities for professional development, and stories that celebrate student success. They value the involvement of teachers, administrators, parents, and when appropriate, students in solving problems.

Toxic school cultures, on the other hand,

- ► Blame students for lack of progress
- ► Lack a clear sense of purpose
- ► Have few traditions to celebrate what is good
- ► Avoid seeking new ideas because they believe they are doing the best they can
- ► Rarely have collegial gatherings to share materials, ideas, or solutions to school problems
- ► Share stories that are discouraging and demoralizing

Toxic cultures focus on failure and generate feelings of hopelessness and hostility. New ideas are squelched and new teachers with positive attitudes are quickly resocialized into the negative culture. Stress levels are high because much energy is spent maintaining negative values. Toxic subcultures can lurk even in good schools, usually in the form of small groups of staff or parents who want to spread hopelessness and frustration.

MONITORING SCHOOL CULTURE

Demographics play an important role in school culture. Variations in the culture occur as the staff and students change from year to year. Sometimes educational leaders are so focused on raising test scores and meeting state standards that they lose track of how the culture is evolving in a particular school.

School Culture Surveys

Wagner and Masden-Copas (2002) suggest that school leaders conduct periodic self-assessments to determine the status of school culture. They recommend two instruments. The first is a survey that looks at the culture of the staff, particularly in the areas of professional collaboration, collegiality, and self-determination. The second instrument is a 13-item survey that is given to different members of the school community, including teachers, students, parents, administrators, custodians, teacher aides, secretaries, and bus drivers. Both surveys are tabulated and the results are useful in determining the quality and health of the school culture.

> **LEADER'S QUESTION: What surveys can I use to assess my school's culture? SEE TIP #7.1**

Much has been written about school cultures and the many factors that contribute to their development. The purpose of this book is to look at how recent discoveries in brain research may inform the decisions that educators make in schools and classrooms. Therefore, rather than discuss all aspects of school culture, this chapter will focus mainly on those components that need to be reconsidered in light of newer discoveries in brain research and cognitive neuroscience.

ATTITUDES AND BELIEFS ABOUT SCHOOLING

Because attitudes and beliefs shape school culture, many innovations do not come to fruition because they conflict with widely held internal notions about how schools work. These ideas confine individuals to familiar ways of thinking and acting, resulting in a state of mind that supports the status quo and opposes change. School leaders who expect to be successful in implementing change will need to use those components of their culture that can support the change and determine how to modify those components that resist it.

In my opinion, one way to alter deeply rooted attitudes and beliefs is to show objective evidence that suggests a change in beliefs may be beneficial to the teaching and learning processes. Despite the power of culture, I believe that all teachers want to succeed and that they are willing to change their beliefs given sufficient proof that it is in their interest to do so. Some teachers adhere to a belief, rightly or wrongly, that any suggestion from a school leader stems from ulterior motives that support the bureaucracy and may not be supportive of teachers or the learning environment. When school leaders present scientific evidence, however, teachers become less skeptical because they can go to the research sources themselves and make their own judgments about the implications of the research for their practice.

School Start Times

The Traditional School Day

In many of the 16,000 K–12 public school districts in the United States, high schools start earlier than the other schools in their community, some as early as 7:00 a.m. Elementary schools are usually the latest to start. This cultural tradition began many decades ago for a number of reasons. High school students could be up early to help their parents tend to younger siblings and to ensure that the older students had plenty of time after school for working on the farm before nightfall. Elementary schools started later so that the younger children could walk to school in the safety of daylight. Society, of course, has changed dramatically throughout the decades, but this tradition continues despite growing scientific evidence that students of high school age should start school later in the morning. Here is what science has been discovering.

Circadian Rhythms

Many of our body functions and their components, such as temperature, breathing, digestion, hormone concentrations, and so forth, go through daily cycles of highs and lows. These daily cycles are called *circadian* (from the Latin, "about a day") rhythms. One of these rhythms regulates our ability to focus on incoming information with intent to learn. It can be referred to as the psychological-cognitive cycle. This cycle has drawn the attention of researchers who study the awake-and-asleep cycles of students (Carskadon, Acebo, Wolfson, Tzischinsky, and Darley, 1997). Their findings show that the cognitive rhythm is about the same for a preadolescent and an adult, but starts later in an adolescent. This is because the onset of puberty shifts this particular cycle roughly an hour later than in the preadolescent. It returns to its previous level when the adolescent enters adulthood.

Figure 7.1 shows a comparison of the preadolescent/postadolescent and adolescent cycles. Note the trough that occurs for both groups just past the middle of the day. This is a low point of focus. Learning can still occur during this 20- to 60-minute period, but it will require more *effort*. Note also that the adolescent cycle has shifted and that these students do not reach their peak ability to focus in the morning until about an hour later. Furthermore, the second peak is flatter than for the other groups. This graph explains why adolescents are sleepier in the morning and likely to stay up later at night.

The different rhythms among preadolescents, adolescents, and their teachers have important implications. Preadolescents reach their morning cognitive peak

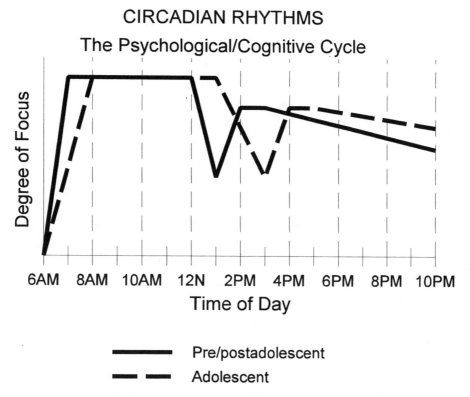

CIRCADIAN RHYTHMS

The Psychological/Cognitive Cycle

——— Pre/postadolescent

— — Adolescent

Figure 7.1 A comparison of the pre/postadolescent and adolescent cognitive cycles during a typical day (Sousa, 2001a).

earlier than adolescents. Therefore, elementary schools should start earlier and secondary schools, later. Many questions will arise: Can we reverse the bus runs without inconveniencing too many households? Will high school students be playing afternoon sports in the dark? Will elementary school children be walking to school in the morning before the light of dawn, and will they get home in the afternoon before their older siblings or parents? Despite these concerns, about 200 school districts across the country, from Bellevue, Washington to Gwinnett County, Georgia, have overcome these seemingly insurmountable problems and start their high schools later.

Getting More Sleep

An added benefit of later start times for high schools is that adolescents get the opportunity for more sleep. Most teenagers need eight to nine hours of sleep each night. The encoding of

LEADER'S QUESTION: What impact do circadian rhythms have on schools and classrooms? SEE TIP #7.2

information into long-term memory occurs during sleep, more specifically, during the rapid eye movement (REM) stage. Adequate sleep is vital to the memory storage process, especially for young learners. Several factors are responsible for eroding their sleep time. Because of the shift in the cognitive cycle explained above (Figure 7.1), teens tend to stay up later in the evening. Many high schools start so early that the average sleep time for teens is five to six hours, resulting in sleep deprivation. This condition not only disturbs the memory storage process but can lead to other problems as well. Students may nod off in class or become irritable. Worse, their decreased alertness due to fatigue can lead to accidents in school and on the road (Acebo, Wolfson, and Carskadon, 1997).

Some studies show that students who get less sleep are more likely to get poorer grades in school than students who sleep longer. Sleep-deprived students also had more daytime sleepiness and depressed moods (Wolfson and Carskadon, 1998). It is important to remind students of the significance of sleep to their mental and physical health and to encourage them to reexamine their daily activities to provide for adequate sleep.

Research Studies

Some studies are now under way to determine what effect the later high school start times have had on student performance and school climate. The largest study to date is in the Minneapolis Public Schools (49,000 students), which moved their high school start time from 7:15 a.m. to 8:40 a.m. in 1997. Conducted by the Center for Applied Research and Educational Improvement at the University of Minnesota, the researchers collected data for four years and reported the following benefits of the later start times (Viadero, 2001):

- ▸ Students got an average of five hours more sleep per week.
- ▸ Attendance rates improved at all grade levels, but the gains were greatest for students who had been the most transient when school started earlier.
- ▸ The number of transient students dropped.
- ▸ Although there was no statistically significant effect on grades, teachers reported that students seemed more alert and more ready to learn.

Year-Round Schools

When school calendars were originally set, about a hundred years ago, agriculture accounted for nearly one-half of our gross national production.

Consequently, it was important to have schools closed during the summer months so that students could work full-time on farms. Although agriculture now accounts for merely 2 percent of our national output, most school districts still adhere to the agrarian calendar. In many instances, schools are in session about 180 days per year and summer vacation time with the family has replaced planting time on the farm. This tradition is firmly entrenched in our society. Many businesses and summer camps rely on students being free for the summer.

The Year-Round Calendars

During the 1920s and 1930s, some schools experimented with the idea of keeping schools open the entire year for vocational training, but that ended during World War II. The idea, known as *year-round education*, resurfaced in the late 1960s when some districts were overwhelmed by large and sudden increases in their school populations.

Year-round education reorganizes the school calendar by breaking up the summer vacation into shorter, more frequent vacations so that instructional time and vacation breaks are more evenly distributed across 12 months. Students go to the same classes and receive the same curriculum as those on a traditional calendar. Although there are some economic benefits to keeping schools open 12 months, the major pedagogical reason is to minimize the learning loss that occurs during the typical three-month summer break. By 2002, more than two million students in about 3,000 public schools were on some form of year-round calendar (Figure 7.2). It should be noted, however, that several hundred schools in California that were among the first to resort to year-round scheduling because of increased enrollment, reverted back to a traditional calendar during the mid-1990s (NAYRE, 2002).

Year-round schools may be on a single-track or multi-track schedule. In the single-track format, the instructional period of 180 days is typically divided into four terms consisting of 45 days of instruction followed by 15 days of vacation (intersession). This is known as the 45/15 schedule, but other variations, such as 45/10 or 60/15, exist. A multi-track format staggers the instructional and intersession periods of each track throughout the year, so that some students are in school while others are on intersession. Thus, multi-track scheduling allows for a one-third increase in school enrollment or a reduction in class size.

Perceived Advantages/Disadvantages

Year-round education offers some perceived advantages and disadvantages (Kneese, 2000; Palmer and Bemis, 1996). First, the advantages:

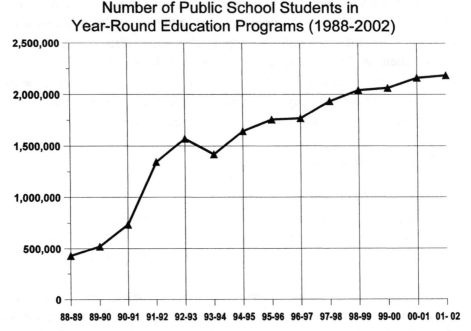

Figure 7.2 The graph shows the number of public school students enrolled in year-round education programs from the 1988-89 to the 2001-02 school years (NAYRE, 2002).

▶ Decrease in student discipline problems because of reduced stress.
▶ Improved teacher and student attendance.
▶ Increased availability of enrichment activities during intersessions.
▶ Improved student achievement due to shorter vacation periods.
▶ More opportunities for teachers to increase their earnings by working when they are on break during intersessions.
▶ Reduced stress as those teachers who prefer more personal time can work less than a full school year.
▶ Greater continuity of instruction leads to a better school climate.
▶ Less review time at the beginning of each instructional term because of the shorter intersessions.
▶ Greater sense of professionalism because the opportunities for higher earnings reduce the need for teachers to moonlight in other jobs.

Some perceived disadvantages of year-round education are:

▶ Increased burnout among administrators because they get less time off.
▶ Organizational issues can be annoying in the multi-track format. Four different teachers might share the same classroom throughout the year,

requiring teachers to pack up their materials before each intersession. Some teachers move constantly and feel alienated from the rest of the school.

▸ Teacher involvement in extracurricular activities can also be problematic. These activities continue even when the sponsors are on break, necessitating sharing the activity or working during their vacation.

▸ Professional development may be difficult to schedule because many of these courses are offered during the summer when teachers may still be working.

▸ Teachers in year-round schools may run into personal scheduling problems if, for example, their own children go to schools on traditional schedules.

Do Year-Round Schools Enhance Retention?

Although some schools resorted to year-round scheduling because of unexpected jumps in student enrollment, most schools have made the change primarily to increase student achievement by reducing learning loss and providing more continuity of instruction. Other benefits, such as enabling increased enrollment or smaller class size, are generally of lesser importance.

Before we look at what research studies have found regarding year-round calendars and retention of learning, let us look first at the basic premise presented here: *that students are likely to remember more of what they learn if they experience shorter breaks in the learning cycle.* Chapters 2 and 4 discussed the nature of learning and retention. Learning is the act of acquiring information into immediate or working memory. Without rehearsal, the information will most likely decay and be lost. Retention, on the other hand, involves processing the information for sense and meaning and building conceptual frameworks for eventual consolidation into long-term memory. The major factors affecting retention include extent of emotional response, amount and quality of rehearsal or practice, perception of whether the learning makes sense, and degree of relevancy. Less important factors include sensory modality used, amount of time devoted to rehearsal, and class size.

Note that the major factors affecting retention can be controlled by the teacher, who ultimately decides how much emotion to infuse into a lesson, the nature of the rehearsal, and the strategies for convincing students that the new learning makes sense and has meaning. If these teacher actions are successful, there is a high probability that students who processed the learning will retain a good portion of it. Recall and rehearsal during the subsequent days will serve to further clarify and consolidate the new learning into neural networks located at the long-term storage sites. After such consolidation, the memory is not likely to decay just because the ensuing vacation period is three weeks or 10 weeks. **It seems, then, that the**

instructional strategies selected by the teacher have a far more powerful impact on retention of learning than the length of the vacation period. Let us now look at the studies that measured whether moving to a year-round schedule had a significant positive impact on student achievement.

Research Studies

Student Achievement. Of 75 statistical studies examined by Palmer and Bemis (1996), 42 revealed no significant effect on achievement for students attending year-round schools. Twenty-seven studies indicated significant positive effects, of which 11 were in reading, nine in mathematics, five in language and writing, one in science, and one in combined studies. From these results, the researchers concluded that students attending year-round schools are likely to achieve as well if not better than their peers in traditional nine-month programs, especially in the upper elementary grades. Despite this positive conclusion, the researchers warned that the studies they examined had four limitations.

- ▶ Research design varied greatly, and some studies covered a span of just one year. A few studies tried to control for other variables such as the students' gender, socioeconomic status, and ethnicity.
- ▶ In many studies, statistical data were not complete, so additional analyses could not be carried out.
- ▶ Studies did not always identify the type of year-round calendar and whether instruction during intersessions was included.
- ▶ Studies did not address any changes in curriculum and instruction that might have accompanied the conversion to a year-round calendar.

Related Outcomes. Palmer and Bemis (1996) looked at studies that assessed other advantages and disadvantages of year-round education. Many of the topics here are part of the school culture. Here is what they found.

- ▶ **Student Attendance.** Studies did not find a *significant* increase in student attendance at year-round schools compared with the traditional calendar.
- ▶ **Teacher Absenteeism.** Studies found a reduction in teacher absenteeism in year-round schools, but the decrease was not statistically significant.
- ▶ **Student Attitudes.** Studies showed mixed findings regarding how students felt about year-round education. Some studies found that students felt more positive, other studies showed no difference in attitudes, and others reported that students in year-round schools had a lower self-concept than those in traditional schools.

▸ **Teacher Attitudes.** Studies indicated that the more teachers participated in year-round schools, the more they liked it. Teachers in these schools also had a very positive feeling about their school's culture.

▸ **Teacher Professional Development.** Teachers in year-round schools reported more difficulty in attending classes and college courses during the summer months.

▸ **Administrative Burnout.** The very few studies that have examined this question found no significant difference in the emotional exhaustion, personal accomplishment, or depersonalization of elementary principals in year-round schools compared with those on a traditional schedule.

▸ **Parent Attitudes.** Studies showed that the attitudes of parents toward year-round education became more positive over time.

▸ **Impact on Families.** The results were mixed. Some studies found that arrangements for child care and vacations were not as difficult as the parents had anticipated, while other studies showed no differences.

Additional studies of year-round schools continue to emerge. North Carolina has had some year-round schools since 1990. Nearly 150 schools in almost 50 districts are on a year-round calendar. Most of these schools use the 45/15 format and more than 80 percent are elementary schools. A recent study of almost 28,000 students in grades 3–8 found no significant achievement differences in reading and mathematics between students attending year-round schools and those on a traditional calendar (NCDPI, 2000).

> **LEADER'S QUESTION:** What are some key points to consider about year-round schools? SEE TIP #7.3

In summary, the studies to date seem to indicate that year-round schedules can have a small positive impact on student achievement and other factors. On the other hand, moving to year-round scheduling does not in and of itself significantly accelerate achievement. Positive benefits from year-round schooling accrue when the change includes a major reform in curriculum so that the intersessions offer productive learning opportunities, including remediation and enrichment.

Extending School Calendars

Some school districts are exploring ways to increase the amount of instructional time during the school year without implementing a year-round schedule. The high-stakes testing required by the "No Child Left Behind" Act of 2001 is putting pressure on school leaders to find creative ways of adding instructional hours to the traditional 180-day calendar. Such creative endeavors include starting school earlier or ending later in the year, a longer school day, and more curricular options for after-school programs and during the summer. Just adding time, however, is of little value if it is not accompanied by a concrete plan to enhance instruction and student learning. More of the same will not raise student achievement if the same refers to poor instruction, low motivation, and minimal expectations.

School leaders realize that changing the school calendar can be controversial. A measured approach to calendar change should include the following:

▸ Ensure that all stakeholders are involved in discussions, planning, and implementation.
▸ Plan for no less than two years of lead time.
▸ Consider piloting the new calendar before full district implementation.
▸ Remember that teacher resistance usually wanes and they begin to prefer the new schedules over time.

Changes in school calendars should be undertaken only when there is a clear, well-thought-out plan and an expectation that the change will result in meaningful improvements in both teaching and learning.

ATTITUDES AND BELIEFS ABOUT STUDENTS

School culture includes the attitudes and beliefs that school leaders and teachers hold toward their students as well as how students of one ethnic, social, or intellectual group feel about students in a different group. Although much progress has been made in the last few decades toward expanding educational opportunities for all types of learners, cultural biases persist among students and, in some cases, teachers, administrators, and parents. Three particularly enduring biases in the school culture are those regarding students with learning disabilities, students who are considered gifted, and the motivation of minority students.

Students With Learning Disabilities

Cases of autism, Attention-Deficit Hyperactivity Disorder (ADHD), and speech and language problems seem to be growing to nearly epidemic proportions. Add in the number of students whose learning problems are substantial but not serious enough for formal classification, and the result is disturbingly high. As these totals grow, educational leaders are blanching at the increasing portion of the school budget that must be devoted to special education and remedial programs.

How students and staff interact with and treat students with learning disabilities are powerful measures of the culture and moral condition of any school. Too many misconceptions remain about students with learning disabilities. Teachers who base their assumptions about students with learning problems on these misconceptions may blame the family for the disability, affect their choices of classroom activities, and slant their evaluation of student performance. School leaders have an obligation to provide staff and parents with programs that help to dispel these myths so that students with learning problems can enjoy all the benefits of a positive school culture. Table 7.1 lists some of the prevailing misconceptions about the causes and implications of learning disabilities (Sousa, 2001b).

Cultural differences can affect expectations and thereby contribute to the failure of students. If a school professes to be egalitarian but in fact demands that all students follow a white, middle-class script, then students with very different cultural backgrounds, skills, languages, and values will be perceived as not meeting the requirements of the school. This is not to imply that students with learning problems should be held to lower standards. On the contrary, educational leaders should ensure that the culture of their school supports rather than hinders the efforts of all its students to reach their full potential.

Gifted Students

Gifted students may have as much difficulty succeeding in some school cultures as students with learning problems. As strange as that may seem, some parents, educators, and politicians object to any special programs for gifted children on the grounds of *elitism*. This word has acquired the negative connotations of snobbishness, selectivity, and unfair special attention at a time, critics say, when educators should be emphasizing egalitarianism.

The reality is that gifted students are elite in the sense that they possess skills to a higher degree than most people in their class. The same is true for professional athletes, musical soloists, inventors, or physicians. Parents and schools must provide children with equal opportunity, not equal treatment. Treating all students as though they learned exactly the same way is folly. Therefore, schools have a responsibility to challenge gifted students to their fullest potential while, at the same time, challenging those who cry elitism to rethink the true meaning of the word and the real purpose of education (Sousa, 2003).

Table 7.1   Misconceptions About Learning Disabilities

Misconception	Explanation
Learning disabilities are common and therefore easy to diagnose.	Although common, learning disabilities are often hidden and thus difficult to diagnose. Brain imaging shows promise in the diagnosis of some learning disabilities, but no X-ray-type imaging at this time can definitively reveal a brain defect that causes a specific learning problem. Thus, diagnosis needs to result from extensive observation and testing by a clinical team.
Children outgrow their learning disabilities.	Most learning disabilities last throughout life. However, many adults have devised strategies to cope successfully with their disabilities and lead productive lives.
Learning disabilities are caused by poor parenting.	No definitive association exists between the child-rearing skills of parents and the presence or absence of permanent learning disabilities in their children. However, home discipline, the degree of parental interaction, learning resources, and other factors may affect a child's self-image and enthusiasm for success in school. Physical abuse *can* cause permanent changes in the brain.
All students with learning disabilities will attend special education classes.	Many students with learning disabilities can have their problems addressed in the regular classroom. However, students who are classified typically have an Individualized Education Plan (IEP) that specifies how certain interventions will be implemented.
Medication, diet, or other treatments can cure learning disabilities.	No quick fix exists to cure learning disabilities. Even medication given to ADHD children acts by mediating the symptoms and does not cure the disorder. Because most learning disabilities are considered lifelong, the support and understanding of, and attention to the child's needs are basic to long-term treatment.
Students with learning disabilities don't try hard enough in school.	Ironically, brain scans show that many students with learning disabilities are working harder at certain tasks than other students, but the result is less successful. Students with learning disabilities often give up trying at school because of their fear of failure.
Learning disabilities affect everything the child does at school.	Some learning disabilities are very specific. Thus, a student's weakness may affect performance in one classroom setting but not in another, or at only a particular grade level.
Children with learning disabilities are just "slow."	Most learning disabilities are independent of cognitive ability. Children at all intellectual levels—including the gifted—can have learning problems.

Source: Sousa (2001b)

Motivation of Minority Students

In an attempt to explain the persistent achievement gap between white and minority students, some researchers have argued that many minority students, especially African American and Hispanic students, have self-defeating attitudes about school. These attitudes lower their motivation to learn, resulting in poor performance on achievement tests. In the last decade, these statements have been heard so often that many educators have assumed them to be valid.

A recent study, however, punctures a hole in this assumption. A survey of 40,000 suburban middle and high school students was conducted during the 2000-2001 school year by the Minority Student Achievement Network (MSAN, 2002). The network is a national consortium of 15 relatively affluent and racially diverse school districts that are looking for ways to close the achievement gap between their white and minority students. Not surprisingly, the survey found that African American and Hispanic students have lower grade point averages and report less understanding of their lessons. They also have lower homework completion rates than their white counterparts but report spending about the same amount of time doing their homework.

But the survey also had two unexpected findings. The first was that skill gaps and differences in home support for academics, not effort or motivation, were the primary explanations of why the African American and Hispanic students got lower grades and completed less homework than white students. Second, nonwhite students, especially African American students, reported that teacher encouragement was their main source of motivation to learn. The special importance of teacher encouragement shows the impact that strong teacher-student relationships have on the achievement of minority students (MSAN, 2002).

One lesson to be learned from this survey relates to the growing number of professional development activities designed to prepare educators to teach to new content standards. If the main goal of these initiatives is to close the achievement gap, then the MSAN study highlights the importance of including professional development strategies that discuss building strong student-teacher relationships. These strategies should prepare teachers to elicit the cooperation, stimulate the ambition, and inspire the trust to help minority students succeed.

PARENTS AND SCHOOL CULTURE

School leaders recognize that parents affect school culture in many ways. Their attitudes about teachers and administrators can determine their degree of support for a school. The lack of strong parent support tends to inhibit high student and teacher performance. On the other hand, schools where parents and teachers are supportive of each other acquire more of an atmosphere of community. Rather than be isolated from the school, parents need to be involved as co-teachers in their children's education. They can do that in several ways. For the purposes of this book, however, I am particularly interested in ways school leaders and parents can work together to ensure that the child's brain and body are ready each day for the school's learning environment and challenges.

A school-parent partnership should begin almost immediately after the birth of a child. Educators are learning more about the emotional and cognitive development of a brain during the early years. This knowledge should be shared with new parents so that they can provide an environment that nurtures the young mind as well as the body. The early years are so important for cognitive development that some states (e.g., Michigan, Missouri, and Kentucky) have instituted state-supported birth-to-school programs whereby new parents are given resources, such as books, music, and manipulatives, to help them develop an age-appropriate and sensory-rich environment for their toddlers.

School leaders who meet with parents of preschool children should share the following information with them about the emotional and cognitive development of young brains.

Developing the Preschool Brain

After birth, the neurons in the young brain make connections at an incredible pace as the child absorbs its environment. Information is entering the brain through "windows" that emerge and taper off at various times. The richer the environment, the greater the number of connections that are made; consequently, learning can take place faster and with greater meaning. Thus, at an early age, experiences are already shaping the brain and designing the unique neural architecture that will influence how it handles future experiences in school, work, and other places (Sousa, 2001a).

Windows of Opportunity

Windows of opportunity represent important periods when the brain responds to certain types of input to create or consolidate neural networks. Figure 7.3 shows just a few windows. Some windows are critical. For example, if even a perfect brain does not receive visual stimuli by the age of two or so, the child will be

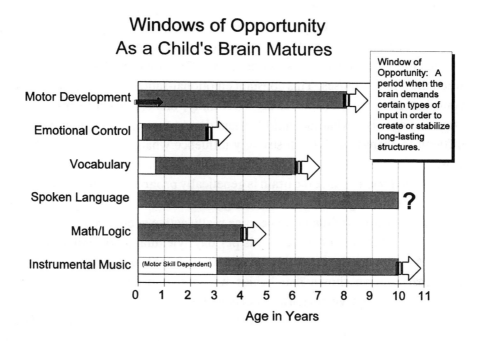

Figure 7.3 The chart shows some of the sensitive periods for cognitive, emotional, and motor development in children.

forever blind, and if it fails to hear words by the age of ten, the child is unlikely to learn a language. When these critical windows close, the brain cells assigned to those tasks lose their ability to perform them (Diamond and Hopson, 1998).

Other windows are more plastic, but still significant. It is important to remember that learning can occur in each of the areas for the rest of our lives, even after a window tapers off. However, the skill level probably will not be as high. Let us examine a few of these windows to understand their importance.

Motor Development. This window opens during fetal development. The ability to learn motor skills appears to be most pronounced in the first eight years. Such seemingly simple tasks as crawling and walking require complicated associations of neural networks, including integrating information from the balance sensors in the inner ear and output signals to the leg and arm muscles. Of course, a person can learn motor skills after the window closes. However, what is learned while it is open will most likely be learned masterfully. For instance, most concert virtuosos, Olympian athletes, and professional players of individual sports (e.g., tennis and golf) began practicing their skills by the age of eight.

Emotional Control. The window for developing emotional control seems to be from two to thirty months. During that time, the limbic (emotional) area and the frontal lobe (rational area) are evaluating their ability to get their owner what it wants. The emotional area will almost always try to gain control, and that is normal. But whether the emotional area will *retain* control is largely determined by the response of the adult. If, for example, tantrums almost always get the child satisfaction when the window is open, then that is the method the child will use when the window closes. This constant emotional-rational battle is one of the major contributors to the "terrible twos." Certainly, one can learn to control emotions after that age. But what the child learned during that open window period will be difficult to change, and it will strongly influence what is learned after the window closes.

Vocabulary. Because the brain is genetically programmed for spoken language, babies start uttering sounds and babbling phrases as early as the age of two months. The language areas of the brain become really active at eighteen to twenty months. A baby can learn ten or more words per day, yielding a vocabulary of about 900 words at age three, increasing to 2,500 to 3,000 words by the age of five. Researchers have shown that babies whose mothers talked to them more had significantly larger vocabularies. Further, talking can also raise a child's IQ.

Language Acquisition. The newborn brain is not the *tabula rasa* (blank slate) we once thought. Certain areas are specialized and prewired for certain stimuli, including spoken language. The drive to acquire spoken language is so strong that children found in feral environments often make up their own language. Opening soon after birth, the window for acquiring spoken language closes around the age of ten or eleven. Beyond that age, learning any other language becomes far more difficult. There is also evidence that the human ability to acquire grammar may have a specific window of opportunity in the early years. As discussed in Chapter 3, it seems illogical that many schools still *start* foreign language instruction in middle and high schools rather than in the primary grades.

Mathematics and Logic. How and when the young brain understands numbers is uncertain, but there is mounting evidence that infants have a rudimentary number sense that is wired into certain brain sites at birth. The purpose of these sites is to categorize the world in terms of the "number of things" in a collection.

Using PET scans and MRI, researchers have located the exact areas in the brain where mathematics takes place, mostly in the left parietal lobe. It is uncertain exactly when these areas begin functioning, but one study showed that children as young as five months have a number sense and reasoning ability that could be called baby arithmetic (Wynn, 1995).

Instrumental Music. There appears to be a window for creating music that emerges around the age of two or three. Mozart was playing the harpsichord and composing at age four. In a famous study, Gordon Shaw and Frances Rauscher showed that children at ages three to four who received piano lessons and group singing lessons scored significantly higher in spatial-temporal tasks than a group who did not get the music training. Further, the increase was long-term, that is, it lasted more than a day. Brain imaging reveals that creating vocal or instrumental music excites the same regions of the left frontal lobe responsible for mathematics and logic. This finding is not surprising if one thinks of music as an artistic expression of mathematics.

Research on how the young brain develops suggests that an enriched home and preschool environment during the early years can help children build neural connections and make full use of their mental abilities. As mentioned earlier, some school districts are now working with the parents of newborns and offer their birth-to-school services and resources to help parents succeed as the first teachers of their children. We need to work faster toward this important goal.

Emotional Connections at Home

The human brain does not process all incoming information with equal interest. There is a hierarchy of response to sensory input. To put it bluntly, the brain is genetically programmed primarily for survival and sex. Its job is to learn how to keep its owner alive long enough to meet an individual of the opposite gender, mate, and thus perpetuate the species. These are powerful reflexive (i.e., requiring little thought) responses.

To fulfill its main missions, the brain gives the highest priority to processing survival information. Thus, data interpreted as posing a threat to the survival of the individual, such as the odor of something burning, a snarling dog, or someone threatening bodily injury, are processed immediately. Upon receiving the stimulus, the brain stem sends a rush of adrenaline throughout the brain, shutting down all unnecessary activity and directing its attention to the source of the stimulus. The emotional areas are activated as well.

Emotional data also take high priority. When an individual responds emotionally to a situation, the older limbic system (stimulated by the amygdala) takes a major role and most of the higher-order cognitive processes are suspended (Sousa, 2001a). **When children fear for their survival at home because of drug problems, impending divorce, or physical abuse, their emotions run high. They cannot concentrate on schoolwork and their long-term memory processes are disrupted.** Sometimes, children feel physically safe at home but get no sense of emotional belonging. Either intentionally or through neglect, their parents have failed to establish an emotionally secure home environment. Consequently, the children worry about their emotional well-being and, not surprisingly, they find it difficult to concentrate on the school curriculum through reflective thought. When

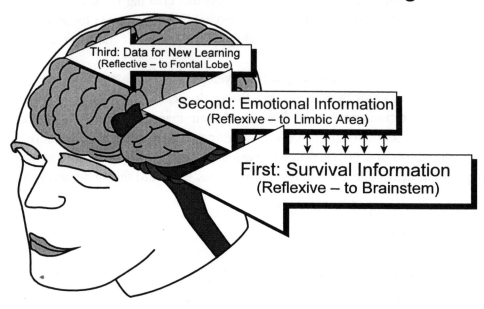

Priority of Information Processing

Figure 7.4 Survival information immediately gets the brain's attention and generally triggers emotional and bodily responses (brainstem). Emotional information also has a high priority (limbic area). Academic information would be processed in the frontal lobe only after survival and strong emotional stimuli are addressed.

a child feels physically safe (i.e., survival needs are met and there is no physical abuse) and emotionally secure (home and family attachments are firm), then the brain is ready for academics (Figure 7.4).

More and more children are awakening on school mornings without an adult in the home. These students are thus inclined to sleep as late as possible and often rush out of the house with little or no breakfast. As mentioned earlier, many of these children are already suffering from sleep deprivation. The lack of sleep and food shifts the body into survival mode, characterized by physical and mental sluggishness. In this condition, learning will be very difficult.

A recent survey by the MetLife Insurance Company revealed the home life of students in secondary schools. Table 7.2 shows the responses of more than 2,000 students in grades 7–12 (MetLife, 2002). Note the high number (54 percent) who wish they could spend more time with their parents. Half the students (50 percent) feel that their parents do not know what they worry about, and almost a third (29 percent) report that their parents do not know what is important to them. As for breakfast, 39 percent report that they eat breakfast only two days a week or less.

Table 7.2 Students Responding on MetLife Survey Questions About Situations at Home	
Percentage of students who report that...	
They spend time on a school day at home when no parent is present	75
Wish they had more time to be with their parents	54
Their parents do not know what they worry about	50
Their parents do not know who their favorite teachers are	35
Their parents do not know what is important to them	29
They eat breakfast two days a week or less	39
They get seven hours of sleep a night or less	33

Source: The MetLife Survey of the American Teacher (2002)

When talking with parents, school leaders should emphasize the importance that parental oversight can have on the success of their child in school. Of particular importance is the recognition that emotional security plays a vital role in stabilizing the home environment. By spending quality time with their children, parents can reinforce emotional bonds and stress the need for adequate sleep and a healthy breakfast, especially on school days.

TRANSFORMING THROUGH COLLABORATION

To transform school culture, school leaders should remember three steps: (1) understand the present culture, (2) articulate and model core values, and (3) support the positive and modify the negative. In the first step, the principal acquires a thorough understanding of the current culture. Who are the stakeholders and what roles do they assume? Who are the teacher leaders willing to explore, take risks, and bring about change? Who are the people willing to follow the teacher leaders by being open to change? Who are the people content with the present situation and with doing the same thing year after year? It is also important to identify the core values and beliefs that provide both stability and direction for the school. The core values provide stability by representing the unchanging beliefs within a school, and direction by guiding behavior.

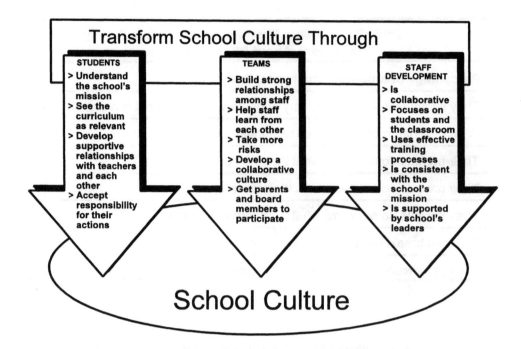

Figure 7.5 Educational leaders can transform school culture by supporting student initiatives, work teams, and staff development that enhance the school's mission.

Next, the principal articulates and models the core values that support the main mission of teaching and learning. Finally, the principal reinforces the positive elements of the culture while modifying those that are negative. Because the various components of school culture are so intertwined, school leaders should not expect to transform culture unless they take a multifaceted approach that centers on collaboration. Students, teachers, and parents are the major influences on school culture and need to be included in any efforts to transform it. Student and teacher support can come from collaborating on a curriculum that is personal and meaningful. Teacher and parent support can arise by working together on teams and through effective staff development (Figure 7.5).

Developing Collaborative Cultures

The vision for a school district is set by the school board and superintendent. Within that context, principals work with the staff to set a particular vision for their individual schools. That vision is rooted in the history, beliefs, and values of what the school should be. As the school culture changes, so must the vision. The principal who works collaboratively with teachers, staff, parents, and students to adjust the vision when new challenges emerge will be more successful in building a strong school culture.

Making School Experiences Relevant

When school experiences are irrelevant, the culture is damaged by poor student performance, strained relationships, cynicism, and alienation. A collaborative school culture provides curricular and other experiences that are relevant to the students and to society. This culture encourages teachers, staff, parents, and students to work together to embrace the world beyond the school so that experiences within the school are meaningful.

Fostering Teacher and Student Relationships

School cultures must be more client-oriented to meet the needs of individual students living in the 21st century. This orientation to client service evolves from productive relationships within the school that are based on the belief that all students can learn and that teachers are responsible for student learning. Relationships between teachers and students are marked by mutual respect, concern, and collaboration. Teachers provide full support for their students and hold high expectations for their performance and behavior.

In traditional schools, teachers usually work in isolation from each other and from the real world outside of school. No teacher can meet the needs of all students in a classroom. Consequently, school leaders should encourage teachers to form new relationships and partnerships, both within and outside the school, that will provide productive, real-world experiences for their students.

Recognizing Responsibility

In a collaborative school culture, all members of the school community are responsible to each other. They accept responsibility for their actions without making excuses or blaming others. Students who violate rules are expected to repair any relationships they have damaged while classmates accept the responsibility for supporting offenders to prevent future violations. As a collaborative team, the school community recognizes its responsibility to continually study, research, and analyze the culture and to recognize needs. The community formulates or reformulates the mission and, over time, identifies and overcomes barriers that impede school improvement.

Shaping the Culture

Principal's Influence

Members of a collaborative school community all contribute in their own way to shaping school culture. But as educational leaders, principals are a powerful force in molding and influencing the culture of a school community. Deal and Peterson (1999) argue that principals are shaping school culture whenever they

- ▶ Articulate core values by their words and actions
- ▶ Observe traditions and rituals to support the soul of the school
- ▶ Honor and recognize those who have worked to serve students and the mission
- ▶ Recognize heros and heroines and the work these exemplars accomplish
- ▶ Speak eloquently of the deeper mission of the school
- ▶ Celebrate the accomplishments of the staff, students, and community
- ▶ Preserve the focus on students by recounting stories of their achievements

WORKING WITH TEAMS

The notion of using teams rather than a single manager to make important decisions began in the American private sector several decades ago and is now a common practice. But the bureaucratic structure of school districts has resisted the implementation of work teams as a permanent part of its culture. Decision making in traditional schools and districts generally occurs at the top administrative levels with little input from teachers and staff. Yet, schools are more productive for staff and students when they support a culture of collaborative decision making, especially through the use of work teams.

Teachers in traditional schools, however, have little experience working in teams. They are accustomed to working and making decisions alone, with few links to other teachers. Thus, collaborative teaming can be difficult for professionals trained to autonomously carry out their teaching and other responsibilities in their own classrooms. If two brains are better than one, imagine how much better four or five brains can be for decision making and problem solving. Teams offer the opportunity to capitalize on the diverse and specialized knowledge of educators who have had different training and experience. But adopting a collaborative mode of interaction requires that school leaders modify existing organizational structures so that they are compatible with the roles and responsibilities of all team members.

Types and Benefits of Teams

Teams vary in mission, duration, and size. In school districts, there are generally two types of teams. The first is the management team, usually composed of the superintendent and other district office administrators, principals, and perhaps a school board member or parent. This team is ongoing and is responsible for implementing district-wide policies although it may delegate some of its tasks, such as curriculum development, to other teams. Management teams can also be formed at the building level where they make decisions involving their individual school.

LEADER'S QUESTION: What are some strategies for forming effective teams? SEE TIP #7.4

The second type of team is formed to achieve certain goals. It may be a permanent structure or exist only long enough to carry out a specific task. They are usually made up of individuals from different levels of the district who possess the expertise or organizational status needed to accomplish the goals of the team. These work teams may be formed to take on a variety of tasks as, for example, to recommend student grading procedures, homework policies, and professional development activities.

When trying to build a strong, positive school culture, here are some of the benefits of work teams over individuals working alone.

- ▸ Teamwork builds stronger relationships among the staff that ultimately benefit students.
- ▸ Teams get more people involved in making a decision, so it is more likely to be implemented.
- ▸ Team members learn from each other's new ideas.
- ▸ Better actions and results come from a group of people with a variety of resources and skills.
- ▸ There is a better chance that mistakes will be detected and corrected.
- ▸ Risk-taking is more likely because of the collective power of the group.
- ▸ By working together, the team develops communication, understanding, and a sense that something can happen.

Teamwork allows teachers to develop new understandings about the purpose of their work, how to accomplish it, and how to connect with others.

The Culture of Teams

Teams develop a culture of their own as they bond and form a sense of community through their work. The bonding builds loyalty and enthusiasm, ensuring that the team members will commit the time, effort, knowledge, and skills to the team. Bonding can begin when the team first meets and reviews its purpose, goals, and individual and group responsibilities. The sense of community builds cohesiveness in the group so that members feel like they relate to the team and want to belong to it.

> **LEADER'S QUESTION: What steps should school teams use in their meetings to solve problems? SEE TIP #7.5**

To be successful, the culture of the team must reflect certain rules of behavior. Members should listen actively and not interrupt, ask questions to elicit the views of others, allow others to be silent if they wish, respect the opinions of others, and support those who are unfairly attacked.

In a school whose culture focuses on student achievement, teams can fulfill many roles. They can be used to address specific problems (e.g., homework policies and professional development choices) or be constituted to effect curricular goals, such as dealing with widely heterogeneous classes and students with learning disabilities.

Interdisciplinary Teams for Heterogeneous Classes

Classrooms today typically include students with limited English proficiency and learning problems. Class sizes are growing, and teachers today are faced with difficult situations as the student body becomes more heterogeneous. These teachers need the group support and advice that collaborative work teams can offer. Collaboration fosters a sense of shared responsibility for educating these students and increases communication across the subject area disciplines. Moreover, by collaborating with their colleagues, teachers establish more professional and long-lasting social and professional relationships than those who work in isolation.

Interdisciplinary teams usually consist of three to five teachers representing different content areas. Sometimes, students are part of the team. The team's focus is to find strategies that teachers can use to deal with current classroom situations. Teachers learn to apply the same problem-solving techniques they are using in the team to their classroom, thereby eliminating ineffective instructional practices and the problems that result from using them. Because they meet regularly and are constituted for at least an academic semester or year, meetings of the interdisciplinary teams require structure and a set of guidelines to ensure that they operate efficiently and effectively. Members should have specific roles, and procedures should be in place for resolving differences in opinion and to deal with personal conflict that may emerge. Gable and Manning (1999) suggest a ten-step process for solving problems at interdisciplinary team meetings.

Role of the School Leader

Educational leaders are often cast in the role of facilitating the work of school teams. The facilitator's main job is to ensure that the team is focused on the appropriate tasks and to reduce or eliminate internal and external distractions. McFadzean and Nelson (1998) suggest that an effective facilitator uses the following guidelines to foster success:

- ▶ *Preplanning the activities.* Working with the client (superintendent, parent, teacher, student) whose issue is at hand, the facilitator discusses the agenda, goals, and issues, and selects potential team members. This session lays the foundation of what is to come and greatly increases the chance of overall success when the team first meets.
- ▶ *Conducting the sessions.* The facilitator guides and supports the team members while remaining flexible and encouraging. Goals are clarified, meeting objectives are met, and all members are encouraged to participate.
- ▶ *Producing a post-session report.* The facilitator may work with the recorder to produce a report after the team has completed its task. The report should include any recommendations from the team, action plans to be implemented, and whether further data need to be gathered.
- ▶ *A post-session review.* After the team completes its goals, a post-session should be held where the team can discuss how their meetings went, evaluate the team processes, and make recommendations as to how the work of this and future teams could be more efficient. This component keeps the energy and enthusiasm for work teams alive by communicating, promoting, and implementing the actions developed by the team.

STAFF DEVELOPMENT

School culture cannot be successfully transformed without the support and participation of the faculty. Teachers are a considerable influence in school culture, and often form subcultures of their own. Hargreaves (1994) identifies four forms of teacher cultures:

- ▸ *Individualism:* Teachers act and are treated autonomously, and there are few opportunities for interaction or the building of relationships. Change is extremely difficult because there is no focus of effort.

- ▸ *Balkanization:* Teachers form significant relationships with others in small subgroups, such as a department. Their loyalty and commitment are to the subgroup rather than the school, effectively blocking any substantive change that may have a negative impact on the subgroup's culture.

- ▸ *Contrived collegiality:* This culture looks like collaboration, but external mandates and administrative goals regulate the work load and make mandatory demands on teacher time. This inflexible environment makes the implementation of change difficult, mainly because teachers feel the proposed change was the administrative will and was going to occur regardless of their input.

- ▸ *Collaboration:* This culture relies on consensus building and on relationships that are voluntary, spontaneous, and focused on professional and organizational development.

Hargreaves (1994) argues that collaboration is the ideal form, not only because it reinforces a healthy school culture, but also because it is flexible by allowing for shifting and overlapping relationships as the context changes. Teachers interact authentically and collegially with other departments and subgroups as the situation changes.

Staff development affords opportunities to build collegial and collaborative relationships among faculty members. The modern notion of staff development moves away from the traditional model whereby administrators decide which training all teachers receive to a model in which teachers and administrators collectively formulate development plans to meet individual faculty and organizational needs.

Relating Staff Development to School Culture

In one of the most extensive studies of its kind, the Georgia Council for School Performance (1998) examined the relationship between staff development and school culture. The Council found clear differences in staff development between a sample of lower and higher achieving schools. Although the staff development at both categories of schools included the same content given by similar sources at similar times during the day and year, professional development in the higher achieving schools included:

- ▸ More collaboration on decisions about staff development
- ▸ A greater focus on students
- ▸ A greater focus on the classroom
- ▸ More use of effective training processes, and
- ▸ More support from school leaders.

Researchers reported an obvious excitement in these schools when teachers and school leaders talked together about ways in which staff development could have a greater impact on students. Their approach was professional and collaborative.

On the other hand, staff development in lower achieving schools was characterized by:

- ▸ An individualistic and haphazard approach
- ▸ A greater emphasis on certification renewal and stipends
- ▸ Less use of effective training strategies
- ▸ Less support from school leaders

Teachers in the lower achieving schools tended to sign up for courses or conferences to meet their own individual needs and desires, rather than to meet the collective needs based on school data. The job of the school leader here was primarily to process the paperwork needed to enable teachers to participate in activities for inservice credit or stipends.

Table 7.3 shows the percentage of higher and lower achieving schools that demonstrated each practice related to staff development. It is worth noting that just 3 percent of teachers in lower achieving schools reported that their involvement in the decision-making process was a motivator for their participation in staff development activities. Lack of collaboration apparently takes a heavy toll on the nature of staff development and the culture of the school.

This study implies that a collaborative school culture can have a very positive effect on student achievement. Of course, a professional development plan should be consistent with the vision and mission of the school community. Although the Georgia study did not assess school vision, it seems clear that to collaborate people need to share a vision, be committed to it, and communicate effectively with each other.

> **LEADER'S QUESTION: What are the attributes of staff development programs in high-achieving schools? SEE TIP #7.6**

**Table 7.3 Percentage of Schools Where
Professional Development Practices Existed**

Practice	Higher Achieving Schools	Lower Achieving Schools
School leader's desire to improve performance influences professional development.	72%	46%
Teachers emphasize a change in student performance as an outcome of professional development.	63%	35%
Teachers cite impact on students as a motivator for participating in professional development.	41%	13%
Teachers cite state, district, and principal requirements as motivators for participating in professional development.	69%	90%
Teachers cite summer stipends and compensatory time as motivators for participating in professional development.	28%	53%
Teachers are involved in collaborative professional development decision process.	52%	20%
Department, grade level, or cluster teams have professional development responsibilities.	41%	13%
School improvement or building leadership teams have professional development responsibilities.	59%	27%
Teachers cite involvement in decisions as a motivator for participating in professional development.	34%	3%

Source: Georgia Council for School Performance (1998).

MAJOR POINTS IN CHAPTER 7

❏ School culture is a powerful force that influences what students, teachers, and parents talk about, their emphasis on teaching and learning, and their willingness to change. The culture of a school can be monitored through student and staff surveys.

❏ Changing traditional school start times and calenders may help overcome the problem of sleep deprivation that afflicts so many middle and high school students.

❏ School culture is often imbued with misconceptions about gifted students and students with learning disabilities, and the motivation of minority students. These myths can hamper the efforts schools should be making to meet the needs of all types of students.

❏ Schools should do more to connect with parents of newborns to help them understand the nature of the developing brain and how they can be more successful as their child's first teacher.

❏ Principals and other school leaders can transform school culture when they understand the present culture, articulate and model core values, and support the positive and modify the negative aspects of that culture.

❏ Students perceive the school culture as positive when their school experiences are relevant, they maintain supportive relationships with each other and their teachers, and they recognize their responsibilities.

❏ School leaders can use different types of management, interdisciplinary, and subject-specific teams to help in transforming school culture.

❏ Staff development that is collaborative, that is consistent with the vision and mission of the school, and that focuses mainly on student needs can have a strong positive impact on culture by improving student achievement.

TIPS FOR LEADERS #7.1

Surveys to Assess School Culture

Wagner and Masden-Copas (2002) suggest that school leaders conduct periodic surveys of their schools to determine the quality and health of their cultures, and to use the results as a basis of discussions with various members of the school community.

PART 1
Staff Self-Assessment: School Culture Triage

This survey is intended for the teaching staff at the same school. After they complete the form, have them add up their individual scores. Then add up all the individual scores and divide by the number of surveys to get an average score. Compare the average score with the scoring guide below.

	Never	Rarely	Some-times	Often	Always or Almost Always
PROFESSIONAL COLLABORATION					
1. Teachers and staff discuss instructional strategies and curriculum issues.	1	2	3	4	5
2. Teachers and staff work together to develop the school schedule.	1	2	3	4	5
3. Teachers and staff are involved in the decision-making process with regard to materials and resources.	1	2	3	4	5
4. The student behavior code is the result of collaboration and consensus among staff.	1	2	3	4	5

	Never	Rarely	Some-times	Often	Always or Almost Always
5. The planning and organizational time allotted to teachers and staff is used to plan as collective units/teams rather than as separate individuals.	1	2	3	4	5
AFFILIATIVE COLLEGIALITY					
1. Teachers and staff tell stories of celebrations that support the school's values.	1	2	3	4	5
2. Teachers and staff visit/talk/meet outside of the school to enjoy each other's company.	1	2	3	4	5
3. Our school reflects a true "sense" of community.	1	2	3	4	5
4. Our school schedule reflects frequent communication opportunities for teachers and staff.	1	2	3	4	5
5. Our school supports and appreciates the sharing of new ideas by members of our school.	1	2	3	4	5
6. There is a rich and robust tradition of rituals and celebrations, including holidays, special events, and recognition of goal attainment.	1	2	3	4	5

	Never	Rarely	Some-times	Often	Always or Almost Always
SELF-DETERMINATION/ EFFICACY					
1. When something is not working in our school, the faculty and staff predict and prevent rather than react and repair.	1	2	3	4	5
2. School members are interdependent and value each other.	1	2	3	4	5
3. Members of our school community seek alternatives to problems/issues rather than repeating what we have always done.	1	2	3	4	5
4. Members of our school community seek to define the problem/issue rather than blame others.	1	2	3	4	5
5. The school staff is empowered to make instructional decisions rather than waiting for supervisors to tell them what to do.	1	2	3	4	5
6. People work here because they enjoy it and choose to be here.	1	2	3	4	5

Source: Penelope Masden-Copas (Wagner and Masden-Copas, 2002). Reprinted with permission of the authors and the National Staff Development Council. All rights reserved.

Scoring Guide: The lowest score is 17 and the highest score is 85. Compare your school's average score as follows:

17–40: Critical and immediate attention necessary. Conduct a full-scale assessment of the culture and invest all available resources in repairing and healing that culture.

41–60: Modifications and improvements are necessary. Begin with a more intense assessment of the culture to determine which area is most in need of improvement.

61–75: Monitor and continue to make positive adjustments.

76–85: Amazing! The authors report no score in earlier trials that was higher than 75. Continue monitoring during each school improvement planning cycle, or at least every two years, to be sure you stay in top shape.

PART 2
School Culture Survey

Directions. This survey is intended for individuals representing various components of the school community. Participants should be assured that the responses are anonymous. The surveys take 10 to 15 minutes to complete and should be distributed and collected in person. The faculty survey should be handled by a faculty member. School secretaries can distribute and collect the survey for aides, custodians, bus drivers, and other clerical staff. Parent surveys can be distributed during open house, parent/teachers conferences, or at a PTA/PTO meeting.

Tabulating the Results. A school improvement committee should tabulate the results and provide an average score for what each group (teachers, aides, students, etc.) perceived to be present and important for each of the cultural components. The committee should then review the averages for gaps in the two numbers on each question. In general, a question with a gap of 3.0 or more needs to be addressed. For example, if the average *presence* score for survey question #1 is 3.8, but the average *importance* score is 7.9, the 4.1 difference in the scores indicates that this school needs to address the issue of democratic decision making.

Background: The 13 items in this survey have been identified as key components of a school's culture. Your opinion and ranking of these factors are important and will be valuable in assessing your school's culture. What is culture? For this survey, culture is defined as the beliefs, attitudes, and behaviors that characterize the school in terms of:

- How people treat and feel about each other
- The extent to which people feel included and appreciated
- Rituals and traditions reflecting collaboration and collegiality

Directions: Please rate each item twice. First, rate the item by circling an appropriate number reflecting its PRESENCE in your school. Second, rate the item by circling the appropriate number relative to its IMPORTANCE to you.

I am a (Please circle one)   Student   Teacher aide   Custodian   Parent   Secretary
Administrator   Teacher   Bus driver   Other

---

1. Democratic and participatory decision making.

Not present   1   2   3   4   5   6   7   8   9   10 Always present
Not important   1   2   3   4   5   6   7   8   9   10 Extremely important

---

2. Strong leadership from administrators, teachers, or teams of both.

Not present   1   2   3   4   5   6   7   8   9   10 Always present
Not important   1   2   3   4   5   6   7   8   9   10 Extremely important

---

3. Staff stability–low turnover from year to year.

Not present   1   2   3   4   5   6   7   8   9   10 Always present
Not important   1   2   3   4   5   6   7   8   9   10 Extremely important

---

4. A planned, coordinated curriculum supported by research and faculty.

Not present   1   2   3   4   5   6   7   8   9   10 Always present
Not important   1   2   3   4   5   6   7   8   9   10 Extremely important

---

5. Schoolwide selected and agreed-upon staff development.

Not present   1   2   3   4   5   6   7   8   9   10 Always present
Not important   1   2   3   4   5   6   7   8   9   10 Extremely important

---

6. Parental involvement, engagement, and support.

Not present   1   2   3   4   5   6   7   8   9   10 Always present
Not important   1   2   3   4   5   6   7   8   9   10 Extremely important

---

7. Schoolwide recognition of success for students and staff.

Not present   1   2   3   4   5   6   7   8   9   10 Always present
Not important   1   2   3   4   5   6   7   8   9   10 Extremely important

---

8. An effort to maximize active learning in academic areas.

Not present   1   2   3   4   5   6   7   8   9   10 Always present
Not important   1   2   3   4   5   6   7   8   9   10 Extremely important

9. District support for school improvement efforts.

| Not present | 1 | 2 | 3 | 4 | 5 | 6 | 7 | 8 | 9 | 10 Always present |
| Not important | 1 | 2 | 3 | 4 | 5 | 6 | 7 | 8 | 9 | 10 Extremely important |

10. Collaborative instructional planning and collegial relationships.

| Not present | 1 | 2 | 3 | 4 | 5 | 6 | 7 | 8 | 9 | 10 Always present |
| Not important | 1 | 2 | 3 | 4 | 5 | 6 | 7 | 8 | 9 | 10 Extremely important |

11. Sense of community, family, and team.

| Not present | 1 | 2 | 3 | 4 | 5 | 6 | 7 | 8 | 9 | 10 Always present |
| Not important | 1 | 2 | 3 | 4 | 5 | 6 | 7 | 8 | 9 | 10 Extremely important |

12. Clear goals and high expectations for students and staff.

| Not present | 1 | 2 | 3 | 4 | 5 | 6 | 7 | 8 | 9 | 10 Always present |
| Not important | 1 | 2 | 3 | 4 | 5 | 6 | 7 | 8 | 9 | 10 Extremely important |

13. Order and discipline established through consensus and consistent application.

| Not present | 1 | 2 | 3 | 4 | 5 | 6 | 7 | 8 | 9 | 10 Always present |
| Not important | 1 | 2 | 3 | 4 | 5 | 6 | 7 | 8 | 9 | 10 Extremely important |

Please use the space below to make any additional comments about the items on this survey.

_____

_____

_____

Source: Christopher Wagner (Wagner and Masden-Copas, 2002). Reprinted with permission of the authors and the National Staff Development Council. All rights reserved.

TIPS FOR LEADERS #7.2

Impact of Circadian Rhythms on Schools

The adolescent cognitive rhythm is about an hour later than in pre- and postadolescents. Here are five implications for secondary schools to consider (Sousa, 2001a):

- *School Start Times.* Teenagers are sleepier in the morning and stay up later at night. They come to school sleep deprived and often with an inadequate breakfast (i.e., lacking glucose). District leaders should consider realigning opening times and course schedules more closely with the biological rhythms of students to increase the chances of successful learning.

- *Morning Exercise.* Even if changing to a later start time is not possible, suggest to teachers that they use learning activities that require students to move around the room, especially during the morning classes. Physical exercise oxygenates the blood and reduces fatigue.

- *Classroom Lighting.* Sleep-deprived adolescents have a high amount of melatonin (the hormone that induces sleep) in their bodies when they awake. One of the best ways to reduce melatonin levels is with bright light. Keep classroom lights on, open blinds, lift shades, and look for ways to get the students into outdoor light, especially in the morning (Kripke, Youngstedt, and Elliot,1997).

- *Testing.* School districts usually give standardized tests to all grade levels in the morning. However, high school students tend to perform better in problem-solving and memory tasks later in the day rather than earlier. Testing later in the morning and early afternoon could improve their test performance and scores.

- *Classroom Climate.* The teacher sets the learning climate of the classroom. Problems arise in high schools if the teacher is in the post-noon trough when the students are at their pre-trough peak (Figure 7.1). The teacher is likely to be irritable, and minor discipline annoyances can easily escalate into major confrontations. Many high school administrators report that student referrals for discipline increase significantly in the early afternoon.

TIPS FOR LEADERS #7.3

Key Points to Consider About Year-Round Schools

If your school district (or school) is considering implementing a year-round schedule, some important questions need to be answered. Review each question below and write down any comments that you believe address the issues raised. If you cannot respond to any question, find out who does know the answer so that district and school leaders are fully prepared to welcome the supporters and calm the critics.

● *What are the real reasons for implementing a year-round schedule?* _____

_____

_____

_____

● *Do you have sufficient and reliable data to support your rationale for this move?*_____

_____

_____

● *Is the single-track or multi-track format better suited to your needs? Why?*

_____

_____

_____

● *What schedule format (e.g., 45/10, 45/15, 60/15) is best suited to your needs?* _____

_____

_____

● *Have teachers been part of this discussion, and how do they feel about year-round schools?* _____

_____

_____

- *Have parents been part of this discussion and how do they feel about year-round schools?* _____

_____

_____

- *What impact will the implementation have on the school budget?*

_____

_____

_____

- *What kinds of instructional opportunities will be offered to students during intersessions?* _____

_____

_____

- *Will teachers in the year-round school have problems participating in professional development opportunities outside the district (or school)? If so, what can be done?* _____

_____

_____

- *What scheduling accommodations can be made for students who rely on summer jobs or who participate in extracurricular activities?* _____

_____

_____

- *Are the schools air-conditioned for the summer months?* _____

_____

_____

- *Are you convinced that implementing a year-round schedule will result in an improvement in teaching and learning? Can you convince others?*

_____

_____

_____

TIPS FOR LEADERS #7.4

Strategies for Forming Effective Teams

Here are some suggestions school leaders should consider when forming school teams.

- Include team members who have the expertise to contribute positively to the mission. Because cohesiveness is so crucial to success, including a member who refuses to reach consensus, or who attacks others personally, can undermine or hamper the team members' work.

- The mission should be very clear. Every member should be able to answer the question "Why am I here?"

- Team members should understand their roles and responsibilities. It is wise to have a facilitator (or team leader), a recorder, and one who observes and gives feedback on group processing.

- The team should establish ground rules for its operation, such as a specific agenda, starting and ending times, and serious efforts to eliminate interruptions while meeting.

- The team should adopt a mechanism for resolving differences of opinion, such as finding a middle-road solution, imposing majority rule, or tabling the issue for later discussion.

- The team should formulate a strategy for dealing with personal conflicts that arise during the team's meeting, such as one person dominating the discussion or blocking decision making.

- The team should adopt measures that periodically monitor the progress of the team toward reaching its goals.

- Ensure that outcomes and deadlines are clearly explained.

- Consider hiring a professional consultant to train members in how teams should work. Part of the culture of a team includes discussing the structure of their process and work. This training can enhance communication skills as well as show the team how to reach consensus, respect the opinions of others, and advocate their decisions to other constituencies.

Avoiding Failure

Teams are likely to fail if they

- Do not clearly understand the team's mission.

- Include members who are divisive, unwilling to cooperate, or fail to buy into the team's purpose or goals.

- Do not understand or carry out their roles and responsibilities.

- Do not understand the processes needed to work as a team, such as building consensus, listening, and accepting the opinions of those they disagree with.

- Do not measure periodically their progress toward achieving specific goals.

TIPS FOR LEADERS #7.5

Steps for Problem Solving at Interdisciplinary Team Meetings

As teachers face the challenge of providing instruction to increasingly diverse groups of students, interdisciplinary teams need an efficient process for solving problems at their meetings. Gable and Manning (1999) suggest the following ten steps:

1. At the start, the team leader (or facilitator) introduces any non-team members, records the names of participants, and explains the purpose of the meeting.

2. The team leader assigns roles (e.g., recorder, timekeeper) and reviews the responsibilities associated with each role, and the guidelines for team discussions.

3. The team leader outlines the procedures that the team will use to address the problem at hand.

4. The discussion shifts to exploring the instructional strategies that the team will use and to identify students who may have difficulty with the standard method of instruction.
   [Steps 1 to 4 should take approximately 5 minutes.]

5. The team leader aims the discussion to reach consensus among the participants regarding any special accommodations that will need to be made for certain students, including content changes and methods of instruction. Team members resolve any uncertainties regarding student needs across content areas. The team leader encourages all members to participate in the discussion and may pose questions to ensure that the team has a clear understanding of all aspects of the discussion.
   [Step 5 should take approximately 5 minutes.]

6. The team leader introduces the brainstorming phase to generate a list of possible solutions. Team members give their suggestions with no

elaboration or prejudgment.
[Step 6 should take approximately 3 to 5 minutes.]

7. The team leader shifts the discussion to decide about a plan for instruction. The team weighs factors such as (a) practicality and time demands of the possible solutions; (b) applicability to other students; (c) congruence with existing curriculum and instructional routine; (d) the complexity and intrusiveness of the various proposals; and (e) ease with which the proposed plan can be evaluated. After reviewing these factors, an initial plan is selected.
[Step 7 should take approximately 3 to 5 minutes.]

8. The team discusses procedures for implementing the plan and ways to evaluate its effect on student performance. Evaluation generally consists of monitoring the faithfulness of implementation and assessing the impact on learner achievement.
[Step 8 should take approximately 3 to 5 minutes.]

9. The team establishes follow-up procedures to ensure that the plan is carried out as agreed. One or more team members are assigned the responsibility of troubleshooting any unanticipated difficulties during implementation.
[Step 9 should take approximately 2 minutes.]

10. The team leader conducts an evaluation to determine how satisfied the members were with the process and outcome of the problem-solving meeting, and whether any adjustments are warranted in the future.
[Step 10 should take approximately 3 minutes.]

Teachers have a finite amount of time and energy, so the problem-solving meeting should last no longer than 25 to 30 minutes. The meetings can occur daily, weekly, or biweekly, depending on the common planning time available and the needs of the students.

Evaluating the Meeting

Team leaders can evaluate the meeting in several ways. One method is to devise a short checklist that team members use to rate anonymously each part of the meeting. A Likert-type scale (1=strongly disagree, 2=agree, 3=strongly agree) could be used to reply to questions such as:

The meeting

- ▸ Was well managed
- ▸ Began and ended on time
- ▸ Followed the problem-solving format
- ▸ Accomplished the stated goal
- ▸ Allowed for satisfactory participation by all members

Another evaluation possibility is to ask team members to use a simple narrative to describe the most effective and least effective aspects of the meeting.

Maintaining Records

Teams should consider keeping records of their meetings, including the cumulative data of positive student outcomes resulting from each intervention. These records serve as a valuable resource of past deliberations and interventions that the team can review while providing the documentation to support further actions and referrals that may be needed for struggling students.

TIPS FOR LEADERS #7.6

Attributes of Staff Development Programs at High-Achieving Schools

The extensive study of the relationship between staff development and school culture conducted by the Georgia Council for School Performance (GCSP, 1998) revealed a number of attributes that were common to staff development programs in higher achieving schools. The attributes are categorized into five guidelines. School leaders can use the following survey to assess the extent to which these attributes are present in their own staff development programs.

Guidelines for Effective Staff Development

Guideline 1: Is leadership for staff development provided in the school?	Rarely Sometimes Frequently 1 ------ 2 ------ 3 ------ 4 ------ 5
School improvement plans and goals provide direction for staff development.	1 ------ 2 ------ 3 ------ 4 ------ 5
School administrators provide strong support for staff development	1 ------ 2 ------ 3 ------ 4 ------ 5
Part or full-time school staff members have multiple staff development responsibilities.	1 ------ 2 ------ 3 ------ 4 ------ 5
Sufficient resources, including time and funding, support staff development.	1 ------ 2 ------ 3 ------ 4 ------ 5
Staff development activities are integral to school operations and expectations.	1 ------ 2 ------ 3 ------ 4 ------ 5
Guideline 2: Is the faculty collectively involved in staff development decisions and implementation?	Rarely Sometimes Frequently 1 ------ 2 ------ 3 ------ 4 ------ 5
Teams have staff development responsibilities for planning decisions, delivery, and implementation.	1 ------ 2 ------ 3 ------ 4 ------ 5
Training in adult collaborative skills occurs regularly for teachers in the school.	1 ------ 2 ------ 3 ------ 4 ------ 5

The school uses a collaborative process for staff development decisions.	1 ------ 2 ------ 3 ------ 4 ------ 5
The decision process emphasizes results measured by student and teacher changes.	1 ------ 2 ------ 3 ------ 4 ------ 5
Teachers see staff development participation as essential to being professional.	1 ------ 2 ------ 3 ------ 4 ------ 5
Guideline 3: Is staff development focused on improving student performance?	**Rarely Sometimes Frequently** **1 ------ 2 ------ 3 ------ 4 ------ 5**
Desire to improve student performance drives selection of staff development.	1 ------ 2 ------ 3 ------ 4 ------ 5
Teachers participate in staff development in order to have an impact on students.	1 ------ 2 ------ 3 ------ 4 ------ 5
Data on student performance are used in planning staff development activities.	1 ------ 2 ------ 3 ------ 4 ------ 5
Results of staff development are monitored by changes in student performance.	1 ------ 2 ------ 3 ------ 4 ------ 5
Guideline 4: Is staff development focused on the classroom?	**Rarely Sometimes Frequently** **1 ------ 2 ------ 3 ------ 4 ------ 5**
The desire to improve curriculum and instruction drives staff development selection.	1 ------ 2 ------ 3 ------ 4 ------ 5
The desire to incorporate technology in instruction influences staff development selection.	1 ------ 2 ------ 3 ------ 4 ------ 5
Classroom observations, lesson plan review, and skill acquisition assess staff development results.	1 ------ 2 ------ 3 ------ 4 ------ 5
Guideline 5: Are training strategies that promote positive outcomes used in staff development activities?	**Rarely Sometimes Frequently** **1 ------ 2 ------ 3 ------ 4 ------ 5**
The format for staff development is organized in an ongoing series of workshops.	1 ------ 2 ------ 3 ------ 4 ------ 5
The rationale and principles behind the new skills are explained.	1 ------ 2 ------ 3 ------ 4 ------ 5
New skills are demonstrated live or through videotape.	1 ------ 2 ------ 3 ------ 4 ------ 5

Sufficient guided practice is provided in the training.	1 ------ 2 ------ 3 ------ 4 ------ 5
Peer coaching/observation is part of the training.	1 ------ 2 ------ 3 ------ 4 ------ 5
Peer study groups are part of the training.	1 ------ 2 ------ 3 ------ 4 ------ 5
Sufficient follow-up and support for implementing new skills are provided.	1 ------ 2 ------ 3 ------ 4 ------ 5
The change process is studied and used to guide innovations in the school.	1 ------ 2 ------ 3 ------ 4 ------ 5

Source: Georgia Council for School Performance. Reprinted with permission.

Analysis

What areas are particularly strong? _____

_____

_____

What areas are weak? _____

_____

_____

What actions will you take as a result of this survey? _____

_____

_____

_____

_____

Putting It All Together

Managing a school or district today is a tough job; leading one is even tougher. Leaders need to be creative, ethical, inspiring, and respectful as well as knowledgeable about curriculum, methods of instruction, and school culture. They have to articulate a clear vision to the school community. They should know how to identify and support areas that enhance the mission of the school and modify those areas that impede it. As the needs of students change, leaders must work to bring about those small or major adjustments necessary for the school organization to successfully address those needs. If leaders are made and not born, how can an individual acquire the skills needed to be a leader and not just a manager? How will one use these skills to implement change?

A WHOLE-BRAINED APPROACH TO LEADERSHIP

The Cerebral Forces at Work

Cognitive processes, emotional relationships, and learning preferences will all influence an individual's thoughts and actions. Identifying specific components and how they interact can be helpful in examining and explaining leadership style. There are many ways to categorize the cognitive and emotional functions of the brain. Researchers generally choose the model that will best fit their purposes. Based on what neuroscience knows so far, I suggest that people in positions of true leadership, those who see themselves primarily as change agents, are subject to the following five major cerebral forces influencing their thinking and behavior:

- *Creativity (more right-hemisphere situated).* The tendency to seek out alternatives for solving problems and taking action that contribute to survival, quality of life, and excellent performance. This force helps one explore options, think outside the box, support change, and clarify the vision of where to go next and in the future.

- *Stability (more left-hemisphere situated).* The tendency to retain and protect activities that bring stability, certainty, order, and logic to daily situations. This force helps one keep control over those resources that maintain balance and allow for a calm existence. The fact that most humans do not take well to change may attest to the power of this force.

- *Relationships (likely centered in the limbic area).* The tendency to seek out linkages and connections to others and to avoid taking actions that undermine those relationships. This force influences one to rely on the loyalty and commitment of others to support initiatives.

- *Results (frontal lobe and limbic).* The tendency to get things done and to feel the satisfaction of accomplishment. This force enhances the positive feelings that come with closure.

- *Purpose (whole brain).* The tendency to justify any and all actions as being consistent with a life purpose, vision, and mission. This force tends to integrate all the other forces to help one arrive at a final decision.

These forces are independent but complementary parts of a whole-brain processing system, and vary in intensity. They can act together in various combinations depending on the specific situation. How each force influences a given situation will often determine what skills and information a leader will use to solve a problem or handle conflict (Figure 8.1).

For example, faced with the deteriorating effectiveness of a teacher who is also a personal friend, a principal might avoid discussing poor job performance for fear of damaging a long-standing friendship. In this case, the relationship force, based primarily in the emotional area of the brain, wields greater influence than the results and stability forces that seek to maintain good teaching. If the classroom performance worsens, the principal might use creativity to design strategies that support the teacher in positive ways, thus lessening the chance that such action would adversely affect their personal relationship.

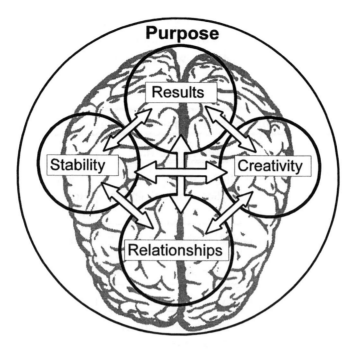

Figure 8.1 The four cerebral forces of creativity (right hemisphere), results (frontal lobe), relationships (limbic area), and stability (left hemisphere) interact in varying degrees, depending on the situation. Purpose (whole brain) integrates their influences to help the individual arrive at a final decision.

Personal Habits of Mind

The brain directs and controls the many different functions that affect how we think, decide, and act. Thus, our thinking style, learning preferences, varying intelligences, and personality traits enhance or hinder the influence of the cerebral forces. People who are gregarious and strong in interpersonal intelligence, for instance, are likely to be more influenced by the relationship force. Those who are stronger in logic may be influenced more by stability. Table 8.1 lists some of the personal habits of mind that guide us through these cognitive and emotional processes, and the range of variations that exist in individuals.

Take the concept of hemispheric preference as an example. Chapter 2 includes an instrument for helping individuals assess their hemispheric preference as being more left-brain, right-brain, or balanced. Remember that these distinctions are more behavioral than physiological because not all functions associated with the left hemisphere are located on the left side and not all functions associated with the right hemisphere are on the right side. Nonetheless, the descriptions of hemispheric preferences are useful in that they describe radically different ways of thinking. As described in Chapter 2, the left-hemisphere preferred person has a logical, sequential, and analytical approach to thinking that is substantially different from the right-hemisphere preferred person, who has a holistic, intuitive, values-based approach.

Table 8.1 Habits of Mind That Affect Decision Making		
Characteristic	**Varies From...**	**To**
Hemispheric Preference	(Left-Preferred) Analytical, logical, linear	(Right-Preferred) Holistic, intuitive, values-based
Working in a Group	Collaborative (High interpersonal intelligence)	Independent (High intrapersonal intelligence)
Evaluating Evidence	Analysis and logic	Emotions and values
Experiences	Abstract information as books, videos, and conversations	Interacting directly with people and things
Speed of Decision Making	Speedy, no matter the issue	Deliberate, well-thought-out process, no matter the urgency
Perspective	Focus on detail and data (High logical-mathematical intelligence)	Look at relationships that form the big picture (High visual-spatial intelligence)

Other important thinking style differences also exist. When gathering information or solving problems, some people prefer to collaborate while others prefer to gather information and process it alone. Some people evaluate evidence based on logic and analysis. Others rely more on emotions and values to guide their decisions. How we experience the world also differs among us. Some people prefer an abstract approach, collecting experiences through books, videos, and discussions. Others want to interact directly with their environment and get first-hand experiences. In other words, the former prefers to watch the vacation videos produced by the latter. Furthermore, how quickly people make decisions and their perspectives on data are also variables that influence cognitive processes.

Whenever leaders (or anyone else, for that matter) make decisions, all these cerebral forces are at hand, subconsciously directing which skills are brought into play and influencing what information is used or ignored in the decision-making process. By being aware of these forces and the role each one plays as well as their own thinking preferences, leaders are more apt to make decisions that are ethical and supportive of the school's mission.

Leonard and Strauss (1997) suggest that leaders consider assessing the thinking styles of the people they are responsible for by using an established diagnostic instrument. Using a well-tested tool is far more reliable and thorough than the subjective impressions of even the most observant of leaders. Many of these tools are commercially available and offer the leadership team a valuable opportunity to discuss their thinking preferences. It is important to remember, however, that:

- ▸ Preferences are neither good nor bad, but are assets or liabilities, depending on the situation.
- ▸ Distinctive preferences emerge early in life and tend to remain stable through the years.
- ▸ We can expand our repertoire of preferences so that we can act outside our preferred style, but it is difficult.
- ▸ Understanding the mind preferences of others makes communication and collaboration easier.

From Thought to Action

When individuals identify their thinking styles, they gain insight into how their preferences unconsciously guide how they behave, lead, and communicate with others. Their actions may encourage or stifle desirable behaviors in others. When working in a group, for instance, a left-brain thinking leader who reveals a step-by-step suggestion for solving a problem will probably suppress the flow of creative ideas from right-brain thinkers. On the other hand, a right-brain leader whose meetings lack structure in order to encourage openness and creative thought may unsettle those left-brain thinkers who need time to process ideas and search for logical solutions. In both cases, the leaders are inadvertently stifling the very creativity they seek in others. It is equally important for the creative leader to recognize the contributions of the logical thinkers as it is for the left-brain leader to acknowledge the ideas of the visionaries.

Embracing Different Thinkers

Once leaders have gained an understanding into their personal thinking and leadership styles, they need to hire and interact regularly with people whose thinking styles are very different from their own. This is no easy task because we generally prefer to be around those who think and act as we do, thereby raising our comfort level. When we discuss a problem with people who think like us, they are apt to just agree with our position and not offer any out-of-the-box idea that radically differs from that view. Although our ego is stroked by this validation, there are no new ideas for consideration.

Suppose, on the other hand, we discuss the problem with someone whose thought patterns are very different from our own. It may be difficult at first to get past the differences in perspectives. But the feedback is likely to suggest new options that will improve the quality of our decision making. These individuals often offer ideas that complement our weaknesses and exploit our strengths. Leaders make better decisions when they are forced to look at all sides of an issue and entertain potential solutions that their thinking style might have rejected.

When trying to talk others into action, we should tailor our mode of delivery to that of the listener. Some people respond better to graphic presentations while others prefer stories and anecdotes. Still others get their information by digesting statistics and facts. The point here is to use the preferred learning modality of the recipient to ensure meaningful and accurate communication.

Create Whole-Brained Teams

Chapter 7 discussed the important contributions that teams can make in transforming school culture and for implementing change. When creating teams, care should be taken to avoid homogeneity of thought. Although homogeneous teams will function efficiently, the number of proposed solutions or creative opportunities will be limited. Most problem solving requires looking at the situation both analytically and holistically, not just one way or the other.

Leaders should strive to include on a team individuals representing a broad range of thinking styles, thereby encouraging a whole-brained approach to the problem. In this environment, people cross-fertilize the ideas of others, thereby providing a range of potential and innovative solutions. However, this may not come easily to the team because members do not naturally understand one another. Thus, when the team is deliberating, the leader has to manage the creative process by getting members to acknowledge their differences and, if needed, devise guidelines for working together before they tackle the problem at hand.

Establishing rules about how to work together may seem silly to an adult group whose members have had years of experience in dealing with people. But Leonard and Strauss (1997) argue that work teams often stagnate because most people tend to value politeness over truth, avoid emotional topics, and opt out of discussions if their proposals are not appreciated.

Conflict may arise because people who do not understand the cognitive perspectives of others can get irritated. Disagreements may become personal. In this situation, the leader should depersonalize the conflict and defuse the anger by noting that differences of opinion do not indicate stubbornness but merely represent another perspective. No one thinking style is inherently better than any other. Rather, each style brings a uniquely valuable perspective to the discussion, allowing all team members to assess a variety of options and solutions.

Building a Community of Leaders and Learners

As schools adjust to the rapid demographic and technological changes in our society, educational leaders will soon realize that they can no longer lead from on high. Leadership in schools will need to be less controlling and focus on more learning so that all members of the school organization are sharing new knowledge. In the future, the principal will be only one of the leaders in the organization and leadership will be distributed among diverse individuals and teams who share responsibility for accomplishing the organization's goals.

Expanding the Leadership Team

Leaders, then, will need to build a community of other leaders within the school organization. This means developing three types of in-house leaders (Senge, 1997):

- *Teacher leaders*, who have responsibility for introducing and implementing new ideas about such areas as classroom management, extracurricular activities, and curricular changes.
- *Unit leaders*, such as department heads, who mentor the teacher leaders, guide cultural changes through shifts in their own behavior, and provide staff with new learning opportunities.
- *Internal networkers*, such as parents, resource personnel, and consultants, who have no formal authority but who move within the school fostering and spreading commitment to new ideas and practices.

These three types of leaders will need to work with the building principal and rely on one another to create an environment where the spread of knowledge and continual innovation are ensured.

Expanding Knowledge

The spread of knowledge among the leaders and staff in a school organization is fostered through

▶ *Action research*, the disciplined pursuit of discovery and understanding within a classroom setting, and the sharing of the results with colleagues.

▶ *Professional development*, a carefully planned program to enhance the knowledge and capabilities of teachers that is consistent with their own aspirations and the mission of the school.

▶ *Practice*, the opportunity for people to work together to build their skills as educational practitioners.

Building a community of leaders and learners helps to overcome the disadvantages of the fragmentation in schools where highly specialized and disconnected activities are occurring with few opportunities for research, integration, personal development, and practice. In a sense, we are returning to the older notion of society where people worked together and were appreciated for their own skills, where elders were respected for their wisdom, and where leaders empowered groups to learn.

The Dangers of Success

Conscientious leaders want to be successful. But success can also spoil a leader. People can get so wrapped up in their past successes that they begin to stall and can no longer sustain the innovative thinking and creative energy they once had. More often than not, these leaders do not recognize that this is happening to them. On the contrary, in their minds they are doing as well as ever. They fail to realize that they are slowly becoming supporters of the status quo. How does this happen? Mainly because

▶ *Leaders interpret and evaluate the modern-day events in terms of their past successes.* When people focus too much on their past successes, these memories dominate the working memory area of the brain thereby limiting the amount of memory available to concentrate on the present. Because memories of the past are more comforting than the problems of the present, all new events are colored by the past. Although it is normal for the brain to interpret new situations in light of past experiences, those who concentrate on past successes fail to see new trends and patterns that may be emerging in the present. As they cling more to the past, some leaders begin to interpret innovations as a threat. Those who rest on their laurels are wearing them at the wrong end.

▸ *Thought processes of leaders become hardwired in their brain to form a network that acts as a filter of new information.* The successful thinking and problem-solving routines that leaders have used in the past eventually get hardwired in the brain and become almost automatic. This automatic response may seem desirable, but it can also be a drawback because leaders miss many opportunities to detect new patterns. They get caught within their own stereotypic thinking paradigm and avoid challenging their previously held beliefs.

▸ *Leaders lose their sense of naïveté and humility, become egotistical, and begin to value only their own opinions.* Leaders who have had a string of successes with no failures in between are particularly vulnerable to becoming egotistical. They believe they know and do their job well and may close their minds to new ideas. If they stay in one organization too long, they get comfortable and complacent and less willing to disturb their environment with innovation.

Leaders should watch for signs that they may be falling into any of these three routes to failure. **When they talk too much about past successes, rely too heavily on instinctive problem-solving strategies, and feel very comfortable in their position, it is time for them to stretch into unfamiliar domains.**

Modern Leaders in Modern Schools

One of the paradoxes of modern times is that social and technical change are occurring at such a rapid pace, yet the cognitive and emotional processes of the human brain have hardly changed at all. Surely, *what* the brain processes today is very different from a thousand years ago. But *how* it processes the information has not really changed much since recorded history. This explains why Socrates, Aristotle, Democritus, Michelangelo, da Vinci, Galileo, and Newton, for example, could explain highly complex concepts, from philosophy to astronomy, in thought patterns that we can still understand today. How these great minds explained their ideas was based largely on their thinking styles. Socrates was an early constructivist. Aristotle and Democritus were abstract thinkers who explained scientific phenomena through reasoning rather than through experimentation.

Michelangelo and da Vinci used graphic media to express their ideas. Galileo and Newton were concrete thinkers who used observations and experiments to support their theories.

If people have always had cerebral preferences when interacting with their environment, why are we just now recognizing the importance of different thinking styles? **My own feeling is that the strong tradition of egalitarianism that has permeated public schooling for decades has slowly and unnoticeably morphed the notion of *equal educational opportunity* into *equal educational treatment*. As a result, educators over time inadvertently encouraged students to emulate patterns of thinking that were alike at the expense of pursuing and honoring those who thought differently.** Solving the contemporary problems of a complex world requires individuals to develop quickly the ability to work together. Ironically, our schools are becoming more heterogeneous in many ways, offering educators unique opportunities to direct the output of different thought processes into constructive, meaningful, and innovative learning experiences.

DEVELOPING AND RETAINING EDUCATIONAL LEADERS

Public school administrators at all levels are leaving the profession in staggering numbers. School districts everywhere from rural to urban and suburban areas are reporting shortages of qualified candidates to fill administrative positions. By some estimates, nearly 40 percent of our 93,000 principals and about 50 percent of the 15,000 superintendents are nearing retirement age. As states ponder what to do about the problem, it is clear that steps need to be taken to develop and train new educational leaders while finding ways to retain the ones we have.

Developing Leaders

Too many of the educational administration training programs at colleges and universities still focus on traditional course work developed during the 1960s and 1970s. Surely, some of this material is still appropriate for leading and managing contemporary schools. But too little emphasis is placed on the skills that educational leaders really need to be successful and happy in their jobs during the 21st century. Few courses include areas such as

- ▸ how to work collegially and share power,
- ▸ how to establish and nourish work teams,

> ▶ how to foster ethical and spiritual behavior,
> ▶ how to understand and modify school cultures,
> ▶ how to support action research,
> ▶ how to develop brain-compatible curriculum and support brain-compatible instruction, and
> ▶ how to manage stress and stay mentally and physically healthy.

I have already discussed some of these areas in the previous chapters. One area that bears additional discussion is the common recognition of building principals as instructional leaders. Although principals have always accepted that the quality of classroom instruction was a part of their responsibilities, the recent explosion in standards-based accountability systems has thrust instruction into a major role. Explicit standards, high-stakes testing, and the demands for tangible evidence of student success have all reaffirmed the significance of instructional leadership. Yet, despite the importance of instructional leadership, few principals and superintendents have had formal, in-depth training in fulfilling that role, particularly in the standards-based environment of today.

What Is Instructional Leadership?

Instructional leadership is a lot more than just visiting classes and evaluating teacher performance. If we are to think of contemporary schools as learning communities, then instructional leadership embraces a much broader range of responsibilities. The National Association of Elementary School Principals suggests that instructional leaders have the following six roles to play (NAESP, 2001):

> ▶ Making student and adult learning the priority
> ▶ Setting high expectations for performance
> ▶ Gearing content and instruction to standards
> ▶ Creating a culture of continuous learning for adults
> ▶ Using multiple sources of data to assess learning
> ▶ Activating the community's support for school success

These roles reflect best practices. It is unclear, however, to what extent principals actually attend to these responsibilities on a daily basis. Too often, the principal is handling minutiae, moving from one small task to another, many of which have no direct connection to instruction. What can principals do to provide instructional leadership amidst a seemingly unending demand for their attention?

When examining schools where principals had a positive effect on student learning, Blase and Blase (2000) found certain common behaviors that centered around open communication and professional development, while respecting the knowledge base and autonomy of the staff. Specifically, teachers reported that their principals gave feedback, made suggestions, modeled effective instruction, solicited opinions, supported collaboration, provided meaningful professional development opportunities, and praised effective teaching.

Developing Instructional Leaders

The national movement toward standards-based accountability in schools and the requirements of the "No Child Left Behind" Act have changed the traditional role of the building principal in the following ways (Lashway, 2002):

- Instead of monitoring and encouraging teacher performance in the classroom, principals must now lead teachers to produce tangible results in student performance on ambitious academic standards.
- Principals, then, must be able to recognize whether lessons and student assessments are aligned with the standards, and to evaluate whether student performance meets those standards.
- Principals must have the knowledge base to coach teachers through demonstration lessons using practical examples.
- Principals should model the same behaviors they expect in teachers, including willingness to be driven by results, openness to new ideas, persistence, and collaboration.

Given these new responsibilities, administrative training programs can develop instructional leaders by helping them to

- Design a comprehensive professional development plan to address the skills they need
- Develop a vision of the school's goals
- Understand and apply best practices to student learning
- Work in cohort programs to develop collaborative skills with peers
- Participate in internships where they get extensive experience in the field
- Use case studies and problem-based learning that provide simulations of complex instructional issues.

At the same time, school districts can develop instructional leadership by

- Expecting all employees to be teachers and learners
- Conducting periodic meetings of leaders to discuss instructional issues

▸ Giving principals opportunities to attend conferences that focus on instructional issues and practices

▸ Establishing mentoring programs for new principals and encouraging mentees to discuss instructional problems as they encounter them

▸ Encouraging principals to visit other buildings to observe and discuss specific practices with their colleagues

In addition to these activities, principals develop into instructional leaders when they are closely involved with all aspects of instruction. Visiting classes, talking with teachers and students, and providing teachers with resources and support, are all ways in which principals can monitor instructional progress and gain insights into the practices that lead to successful learning.

Retaining Educational Leaders

Educational administration is not the attractive job it once was. Society is placing such high demands on schools that educators are beginning to wonder if they can meet these demands successfully. In the age of accountability, school and district administrators, especially principals and superintendents, become the focus of the pleasure or displeasure that a community expresses over student performance. As a result, principals and superintendents are leaving the profession at an alarming rate.

Beside retirement, the major reason administrators leave their jobs is stress. Working long hours, supporting a heavy workload, supervising endless evening activities, getting less pay differential, completing mountains of paperwork, feeling overwhelmed with very high expectations, and dealing with complex societal problems are just some of the factors that make their jobs so stressful. In the past few years, the standards-based accountability movement and the requirements of the "No Child Left Behind" Act of 2001 have added even more responsibilities to the school and district leaders' roles.

The human body and brain can handle stress adequately, provided it occurs in short doses. But when an individual is constantly under stress, some unpleasant things happen. Cortisol, a steroid intended to alert the body to danger and to be in the bloodstream for just a few minutes, is continually present. Over time, the cortisol affects memory, increases irritability, degrades motor coordination, and erodes the ability to solve problems and resolve conflicts with logic. Work performance and job satisfaction begin to deteriorate, and those who recognize what is happening to them decide to quit. As these experienced leaders depart, the pool of candidates applying to replace them is shrinking. This shortage of qualified candidates makes retaining current leaders a high priority. What can be done to retain successful educational leaders? How can we encourage educators to apply for leadership positions?

Reinventing the Principalship

Because stress is the major reason principals quit, some school districts are looking at ways of redefining the role of the principal to reduce the work burden and relieve stress. One format is through job sharing that divides the responsibilities of the principal among two people who possess skills in different areas (Muffs and Schmitz, 1999). For example, one may handle managerial tasks while the other deals with curriculum and instruction. They also split school-related evening assignments to give them more time with their families.

Following a common British model, some districts are handing over budgeting and building management functions to an in-house business manager. This school-based person oversees the budget, payroll, transportation, data and facility management, supervision of noninstructional personnel, and regulatory compliance. In some cases, the business manager is hired in lieu of an assistant principal.

Another possibility is to provide carefully tailored professional development opportunities that enhance the skills of those already on the job. Principals admit that poor interpersonal skills and poor decision making are high on the list of skills needing further development. Principals also need to be able to network with other principals on a regular basis to exchange ideas, evaluate the demands of their jobs, and talk about ways to implement change. These networking meetings should be followed up with suggestions of how to translate these ideas into practice.

Yerkes and Guaglianone (1998) suggest that school boards can also help by educating the community about the changing role of the principal to garner support for principals and to lessen the demands on their time. Specifically, they advise school boards to take the following steps:

- ▸ Offer financial support for sabbaticals to give burnt-out principals a reprieve
- ▸ Create a family-friendly environment to accommodate principals' personal lives
- ▸ Review the salary schedule and find ways to reward principals
- ▸ Determine flexible attendance requirements and expectations at school functions
- ▸ Redesign the organizational structure of the job

There is no magic solution for retaining good principals in the job role now demanded by society. But perhaps by reexamining that role and parsing out some of its responsibilities, principals can have the time to do the most important parts of their job successfully.

District Superintendents

District superintendents are faced with trying to do a nearly impossible job amid changing demographics, growing diversity, decentralization of power, increased accountability, and unrealistic expectations. To compound the problem, job security is at an all-time low because superintendent-school board relations can easily sour, more often over a political than an educational issue. When I was a superintendent in New Jersey, the average tenure for that job in the state was about 2.5 years; the national average is less than five years.

The "No Child Left Behind" Act of 2001 affects the role of the superintendent in at least three ways: (1) It will add another layer of responsibilities by mandating annual testing to measure progress toward goals, and schools that fail will face a variety of consequences. Although the act puts superintendents in the spotlight for keeping districts on track, it does nothing to enhance their authority. (2) On the other hand, the law does heighten their role as instructional leaders by holding principals and teachers accountable for implementing effective teaching practices. (3) The annual yearly progress standard required by the act is a highly visible report that the school board is likely to use as a major component in the evaluation of the superintendent.

Trying to lead a district in this climate is a daunting challenge and a growing number of superintendents have decided to leave. To retain superintendents, some of the issues mentioned above have to be addressed. Some possible solutions are the following:

- ▸ School boards need to make clear to superintendents their expectations for performance and their criteria for evaluation. Superintendents who are concerned about their board support are unlikely to take the bold steps needed to change schools.
- ▸ Superintendents need to make instruction their number one priority. Although the political and managerial components of the job will not disappear, focus should be on continuous improvement in instruction.
- ▸ Universities should ensure that their training programs for administrators include the knowledge and skills they will need to lead and transform schools as learning organizations.

No one expects the strong push for standards-based accountability to lessen any time soon, especially now that the federal government is so heavily involved. Consequently, the superintendency will continue to be a stressful and turbulent job. Perhaps with a few modifications, it can become a rewarding one as well.

Developing In-District Leaders

One surprising revelation amidst the growing shortage of educational leaders is that few school districts are taking any overt steps to develop a replacement system for departing administrators. Some districts have mentoring programs for aspiring administrators, while others have established leadership academies or are collaborating with local universities to address the shortage.

Quinn (2002) suggests that a more aggressive policy, such as succession planning, is needed. The purpose of succession planning is to create a cadre of candidates with strong knowledge, skills, and attitudes who can be trained for future leadership positions. The plan nurtures and develops the talent pool that exists in every district and grooms that pool to be competent leaders. Among other things, the succession plan

- ▶ Provides a specific method for identifying potential leaders
- ▶ Retains upwardly mobile employees in the district
- ▶ Ensures a ready supply of in-house replacements for leadership positions
- ▶ Offers challenging and rewarding career possibilities through meaningful professional development
- ▶ Reduces lost productivity that occurs when an outside replacement is on the time-consuming learning curve

Quinn (2002) further explains how to design a screening process for candidates, how to assess the skills of the candidates, and how to provide ongoing support for potential leaders. Succession plans can help resolve critical supervisory staffing needs at all levels.

CONCLUSION

The job role of an educational leader today is extremely difficult, but possible. This book tries to help the leader to work a little easier by suggesting a few ideas, many supported by cognitive neuroscience, that can get a school community closer to fulfilling the important mission of educating its youth to their fullest potential. No magic exists to make this happen easily. On the contrary, studies suggest an almost interminable list of qualities that leaders must have to be successful. Perhaps one way this book can be of service is to offer the shortest list of leadership qualities that I have seen. It comes from Tornabeni (2001), who suggests that among all the qualities that leaders need, the three most important are

- ▸ *Purpose*. A sense of purpose helps to establish a goal, articulate it, make it tangible, and work toward it every day. Keep asking yourself, " What can I do to take me one step closer to realizing my goal?"
- ▸ *Perspiration*. Leadership takes hard work. Only by walking the walk will you inspire others. When your colleagues see how hard you work, they are more likely to work harder, too.
- ▸ *Passion*. Passion is sincerely believing in what you are doing and it keeps you going when things get tough. Education can make profound differences in our lives. That is what drew you into the profession and what continues to fuel your ambitions as an educational leader.

True leadership is a matter of influence, not position. Influence results from being liked and respected. A new definition of leadership expects that leaders will share responsibilities that they once thought were exclusively theirs. Increasing pressures from within and outside the school are collapsing traditional bureaucratic structures and reshaping the school community. As teachers grow professionally, so will leaders who can become more accommodating and responsive instead of fixed and bureaucratic. Collaborative strategies are what get people to follow. And when people follow because they want to, rather than have to, everybody wins.

MAJOR POINTS IN CHAPTER 8

❏ A whole-brained approach to leadership recognizes the contributions of creativity, results, stability, relationships, and purpose to decision making. These forces can act in various combinations depending on the situation and context.

❏ Our thinking and learning styles are continually influencing how we process and act in a given situation. Thinking styles vary greatly among individuals, and people of opposite styles are often uncomfortable with each other.

❏ By working with people whose thinking styles are very different from their own, leaders are likely to get a broader range of potential solutions to a problem.

❏ Leaders should be aware that continued success can lead to overemphasis on past successes, overconfidence in their thinking style, and an egotistical view that their own way of doing things is the best.

❏ School districts need to develop strategies and programs for developing and retaining educational leaders as well as identifying potential leaders in their schools.

Glossary

Amygdala. The almond-shaped structure in the limbic area of the brain that encodes emotional messages to long-term storage.

Angular gyrus. A structure in the brain thought to separate words into their individual phonemes for decoding.

Apoptosis. The genetically programmed process in which unneeded or unhealthy brain cells are destroyed.

Axon. The long and unbranched fiber of a neuron that carries impulses away from the cell to the next neuron.

Bloom's Taxonomy of the Cognitive Domain. A model developed by Benjamin Bloom in the 1950s for classifying the complexity of human thought into six levels.

Brain stem. The part of the brain that receives sensory input and monitors vital functions such as heartbeat, body temperature, and digestion.

Cerebellum. One of the major parts of the brain, it coordinates muscle movement.

Cerebrum. The largest of the major parts of the brain, it controls sensory interpretation, thinking, and memory.

Circadian rhythm. The daily cycle of numerous body functions, such as breathing and body temperature.

Closure. The teaching strategy that allows learners quiet time in class to mentally reprocess what they have learned during a lesson.

Constructivism. The concept that the brain constructs its own meaning during the learning process and that these constructs are more likely to occur when the learner is actively involved in choosing the content, context, and sequence of the learning opportunities.

Corpus callosum. The bridge of nerve fibers that connects the left and right cerebral hemispheres and allows communication between them.

Cortex. The thin but tough layer of cells covering the cerebrum that contains all the neurons used for cognitive and motor processing.

Critical attributes. Characteristics that make one idea unique from all others.

Dendrite. The branched extension from the cell body of a neuron that receives impulses from nearby neurons through synaptic contacts.

Frontal lobe. The front part of the brain that monitors higher-order thinking, directs problem solving, and regulates the excesses of the emotional (limbic) system.

Glial cells. Special cells in the brain that surround each neuron and provide support, protection, and nourishment.

Hippocampus. A brain structure that encodes information from working (temporary) memory to long-term storage.

Limbic system. The structures at the base of the cerebrum that control emotions.

Mentoring. A process whereby experienced teachers (called *mentors*) share their professional expertise with less-experienced colleagues (called protégés or *mentees*).

Motor cortex. The narrow band across the top of the brain from ear to ear that controls movement.

Multiple Intelligences Theory. A theory proposed by Howard Gardner that intelligence is not a unitary concept, that humans possess at least seven intelligences, and that an individual is predisposed to develop each of the intelligences to a different level of competence.

Myelin. A fatty substance that surrounds and insulates the axon of a neuron.

Neuron. The basic cell making up the brain and nervous system, consisting of a globular cell body, a long fiber called an axon which transmits impulses, and many shorter fibers called dendrites which receive them.

Neurotransmitter. One of nearly 100 chemicals stored in axon sacs that transmit impulses from neuron to neuron across the synaptic gap.

Phonological awareness. The recognition that oral language can be divided into smaller components, such as sentences into words, and words into syllables and, ultimately, into individual phonemes.

Primacy-recency effect. The phenomenon whereby one tends to remember best that which comes first in a learning episode and second best that which comes last.

Prime-time. The time in a learning episode when information or a skill is more likely to be remembered.

Prosody. The rhythm, cadence, accent patterns, and pitch of a language.

Rehearsal. The reprocessing of information in working memory.

Retention. The preservation of a learning in long-term storage in such a way that it can be identified and recalled quickly and accurately.

Reticular activating system (RAS). The dense formation of neurons in the brain stem that controls major body functions and maintains the brain's alertness.

Somatosensory cortex. An area of the cerebrum that responds to touch or pressure, temperature, pain, and limb movement and placement.

Systemic change. The belief that true reform can come only by fundamentally changing the hierarchy and basic systems of an organization.

Thalamus. A part of the limbic system that receives all incoming sensory information, except smell, and shunts it to other areas of the cortex for additional processing.

Transformational leadership. A leadership style that motivates followers through charisma to emotionally identify with the vision of the leader and to sacrifice their self-interest for that of the organization.

Windows of opportunity. Important periods in which the young brain responds to certain types of input to create or consolidate neural networks.

Working memory. The temporary memory wherein information is processed consciously.

References

Acebo, C., Wolfson, A., and Carskadon, M. (1997). Relations among self-reported sleep patterns, health, and injuries in adolescents. *Sleep Research, 27,* 149.

Amabile, T. M. (1998). How to kill creativity. *Harvard Business Review, 76,* 77-88.

Archer, J. (1998, February 18). Students' fortune rest with assigned teacher. *Education Week,* p. 9.

Asp, E. (2000). Assessment in education: Where have we been? Where are we headed? In *Education in a new era,* R. Brandt (Ed.). Alexandria, VA: Association for Supervision and Curriculum Development.

Bass, B. M. (1985). *Leadership and performance beyond expectations.* New York: Free Press.

Beatty, J. (2001). *The human brain: Essentials of behavioral neuroscience.* Thousand Oaks, CA: Sage Publications.

Blase, J., and Blase, J. (2000). Effective instructional leadership: Teachers' perspectives on how principals promote teaching and learning in schools. *Journal of Educational Administration, 38,* 130-141.

Blase, J., and Blase, J. (2003). *Breaking the silence: Overcoming the problem of principal mistreatment of teachers.* Thousand Oaks, CA: Corwin Press.

Bloom, B. S. (1956). *Taxonomy of educational objectives (cognitive domain).* New York: Longman.

Bol, L., Stephenson, P. L., and O'Connell, A. A. (1998). Influence of experience, grade level, and subject area on teachers' assessment practices. *Journal of Educational Research, 91,* 323-330.

Burke, K. (1997). *Designing professional portfolios for change.* Arlington Heights, IL: IRI Skylight Publishing.

Buzan, T. (1989). *Use both sides of your brain* (3rd ed.). New York: Penguin Books.

Carskadon, M. A., Acebo, C., Wolfson, A. R., Tzischinsky, O., and Darley, C. (1997). REM sleep on MSLTS in high school students is related to circadian phase. *Sleep Research, 26,* 705.

Carter, R. (1998). *Mapping the mind.* Los Angeles: University of California Press.

Chapman, C., and King, R. (2000). *Test success in the brain compatible classroom.* Tucson, AZ: Zephyr.

Character Counts! (2002). *The South Dakota Study, 1998-2000.* Available online at http://charactercounts.org/doing/ SD2000report.htm.

Chase, B. (1997, October 22). Teacher vs. teacher? Nonsense. *Education Week,* pp. 26, 29.

Clark, D. C., and Clark, S. N. (2000). Appropriate assessment strategies for young adolescents in an era of standards-based reform. *The Clearing House, 73,* 201-204.

Clement, N. I. (2002). Strengthen school culture using a customer service audit. *School Administrator, 59,* 39.

Cogan, M. (1973). *Clinical supervision.* Boston: Houghton Mifflin.

Covey, S. R. (1989). *The seven habits of highly effective people: Restoring the character ethic.* New York: Simon and Schuster.

Covrig, D. M. (2000). The organizational context of moral dilemmas: The role of moral leadership in administration in making and breaking dilemmas. *Journal of Leadership Studies, 7,* 40-59.

Damasio, A. (1994). *Decartes' error.* New York: G. P. Putnam.

Danielson, C., and McGreal, T. L. (2000). *Teacher evaluation to enhance professional practice.* Alexandria, VA: Association for Supervision and Curriculum Development.

Davis School District. (2002). *Student and Parent Surveys.* Farmington, UT: Author.

Deal, T. E., and Peterson, K. D. (1999). *Shaping school culture: The heart of leadership.* San Francisco: Jossey-Bass.

Denig, S. J., and Quinn, T. (2001). Ethical dilemmas for school administrators. *The High School Journal, 84,* 43-49.

DePree, M. (1992). *Leadership jazz.* New York: Dell Publishing.

Diamond, M., and Hopson, J. (1998). *Magic trees of the mind: How to nurture your child's intelligence, creativity, and healthy emotions from birth through adolescence.* New York: Dutton.

Dickmann, M. H., and Stanford-Blair, N. (2002). *Connecting leadership to the brain.* Thousand Oaks, CA: Corwin Press.

Doolittle, P. (1994). *Teacher portfolio assessment* (ED 385 608). Washington, DC: ERIC Clearinghouse on Assessment and Evaluation.

Droz, M., and Ellis, L. (1996). *Laughing while learning: Using humor in the classroom.* Longmont, CO: Sopris West.

Drucker, P. F. (1999). *Management challenges for the 21st century.* New York: Harper Business.

Drucker, P. F., Dyson, E., Handy, C., Saffo, P., and Senge, P. M. (1997). Looking ahead: Implications of the present. *Harvard Business Review, 75*, 18-21.

Duffy, F. M. (1997). Supervising schooling, not teachers. *Educational Leadership, 54,* 78-83.

Duffy, F. M. (2003). *Courage, passion, and vision: A guide to leading systemic school improvement.* Lanham, MD: Scarecrow Education.

Ediger, M. (1999). Who should select objectives? *Journal of Instructional Psychology, 26*, 149-150.

Evans, R. (1999, February 3). The great accountability wars. *Education Week,* p. 32.

Ford, A., Davern, L., and Schnorr, R. (2001). Learners with significant disabilities: Curricular relevance in an era of standards-based reform. *Remedial and Special Education, 22*, 214-222.

Fullan, M. (2002, September). Moral purpose writ large. *The School Administrator* (Web Edition). Available online at http://www.aasa.org/publications/sa/2002_09/fullan.htm.

Gable, R. A., and Manning, M. L. (1999). Interdisciplinary teaming: Solution to instructing heterogeneous groups of students. *The Clearing House, 72*, 182-185.

Gardner, H. (1983). *Frames of mind: The theory of multiple intelligences.* New York: Basic Books.

Gardner, H. (1993). *Multiple intelligences: The theory in practice.* New York: Basic Books.

Gardner, H. (2000). *Intelligence reframed: Multiple intelligences for the 21st century.* New York: Basic Books.

Georgia Council for School Performance (GCSP). (1998). *Staff development and student achievement: Making the connection in Georgia schools.* Atlanta: Georgia State University Applied Research Center. Available online at www.arc.gsu.edu/csp.

Glatthorn, A. A., and Jailall, J. (2000). Curriculum for the new millennium. In *Education in a new era*, R. Brandt (Ed.). Alexandria, VA: Association for Supervision and Curriculum Development.

Glickman, C. D. (2002). *Leadership for learning: How to help teachers succeed.* Alexandria, VA: Association for Supervision and Curriculum Development.

Goertz, J. (2000). Creativity: An essential component for effective leadership in today's schools. *Roeper Review, 22,* 158-162.

Goldberg, E. (2001). *The executive brain: Frontal lobes and the civilized mind.* New York: Oxford University Press.

Goldhammer, R. (1969). *Clinical supervision: Special methods for the supervision of teachers.* New York: Holt, Rinehart, and Winston.

Gregory, G. H., and Chapman, C. (2002). *Differentiated instructional strategies.* Thousand Oaks, CA: Corwin Press.

Grissmer, D., and Flanagan, A. (1998). *Exploring rapid achievement gains in North Carolina and Texas.* Washington, DC: National Goals Panel.

Gundry, L. K., Kickul, J. R., and Prather, C. W. (1994). Building the creative organization. *Organizational Dynamics, 22,* 22-36.

Halford, J. M. (1999). Longing for the sacred in schools: A conversation with Nel Noddings. *Educational Leadership, 56,* 28-32.

Hargreaves, A. (1994). *Changing teachers, changing times.* New York: Teachers College Press.

Hargreaves, A., and Fullan, M. (1998). *What's worth fighting for out there.* New York: Teachers College Press.

Hoyle, J. R. (2002, September). The highest form of leadership. *The School Administrator* (Web Edition). Available online at http://www.aasa.org/publications/sa/2002_09/hoyle.htm.

Huling, L., and Resta, V. (2001). *Teacher mentoring as professional development* (ED 460 125). Washington, DC: ERIC Clearinghouse on Teaching and Teacher Education.

Hyerle, D. (1996). *Visual tools for constructing knowledge.* Alexandria, VA: Association for Supervision and Curriculum Development.

Interstate New Teacher Assessment and Support Consortium (INTASC). (1992). *Model standards for beginning teacher licensing and development.* Washington, DC: Council of Chief State School Officers. Available online at www.ccsso.org/intascst.html.

Ishai, A., and Sagi, D. (1997). Visual imagery: Effects of short- and long-term memory. *Journal of Cognitive Neuroscience, 9,* 734-742.

Johnson, A. M., Vernon, P. A., McCarthy, J. M., Molson, M., Harris, J. A., and Jang, K. L. (1998). Nature vs nurture: Are leaders born or made? A behavior genetic investigation of leadership style. *Twin Research, 1,* 216-223.

Jones, T. M. (1991). Ethical decision making by individuals in organizations: An issue-contingent model. *Academy of Management Review, 16,* 366-395.

Josephson Institute of Ethics. (2002). *2002 Report card on the ethics of American youth.* Marina del Rey, CA: Author.

Kaiser, L. R. (2002). *Extended impact of spirituality*. Available online at http://www.spiritualleadershipinst.org/media/articles/leland/.

Kessler, R. (2000). *The soul of education: Helping students find connection, compassion, and character at school*. Alexandria, VA: Association for Supervision and Curriculum Development.

Kessler, R. (2002, September). Nurturing deep connections. *The School Administrator* (Web Edition). Available online at http://aasa.org/ publications/ sa/2002_09/kessler.htm.

Kidder, R. M., and Born, P. L. (2002, February). Moral courage in a world of dilemmas. *The School Administrator* (Web Edition). Available online at http://aasa.org/publications/sa/ 2002_09/kidder.htm.

Kim, K., Relkin, N., Lee, K., and Hirsch, J. (1997). Distinct cortical areas associated with native and second languages. Letter to *Nature, 388*, 171-174.

Kneese, C. (2000). *Teaching in year-round schools* (ED 449 123). New York: ERIC Clearinghouse on Teaching and Teacher Education.

Kohlberg, L. (1983). *Essays on moral development. Vol. II: The psychology of moral development*. New York: Harper and Row.

Kripke, D. F., Youngstedt, S. D., and Elliot, J. A. (1997). Light brightness effects on melatonin duration. *Sleep Research, 26*, 726.

Langer, E. (1997). *The power of mindful learning*. New York: Addison-Wesley.

Lashway, L. (2002). (ED 160). *Developing instructional leaders*. Washington, DC: U.S. Department of Education.

Leonard, D., and Strauss, S. (1997). Putting your company's whole brain to work. *Harvard Business Review, 75*, 111-120.

Liontos, L. B. (1992). *Transformational leadership* (ED 347 636). Eugene, OR: ERIC Clearinghouse on Educational Management.

Livingston, K. R. (1999, Fall). Teaching Albert honesty: Help from brain research. *Cerebrum, 1*, 79-89.

Malone, R. J. (2001). *Principal mentoring* (ED 457 535). Eugene, OR: ERIC Clearinghouse on Educational Management.

Marzano, R. J. (2001). *Designing a new taxonomy of educational objectives*. Thousand Oaks, CA: Corwin Press.

McFadzean, E., and Nelson, T. (1998). Facilitating problem-solving groups: A conceptual model. *Leadership and Organizational Development Journal, 19*, 6-13.

Mellett, E., Tzourio-Mazoyer, N., Bricogne, S., Mazoyer, B., Kosslyn, S. M., and Denis, M. (2000). Functional anatomy of high-resolution visual mental imagery. *Journal of Cognitive Neuroscience, 12*, 98-109.

MetLife Insurance Company (MetLife). (2002). *The MetLife survey of the American teacher, 2002*. New York: Author.

Mettetal, G., Jordan, C., and Harper, S. (1997). Attitudes toward a multiple intelligences curriculum. *Journal of Educational Research, 91*, 115-123.

Middleton, F. A., and Strick, P. L. (1998). Cerebellar output: Motor and cognitive channels. *Trends in Cognitive Sciences, 2*, 348-354.

Minority Student Achievement Network (MSAN). (2002). *What doesn't meet the eye: Understanding and addressing racial disparities in high-achieving urban schools.* Available online at http://www.ncrel. org/gap/ferg/.

Moats, L. C. (2000). *Whole language lives on: The illusion of "balanced" reading instruction.* Washington, DC: Thomas B. Fordham Foundation.

Muffs, M. I., and Schmitz, L. A. (1999). Job sharing for administrators: A consideration for public schools. *NASSP Bulletin, 83*, 70-73.

National Association for Year-Round Education (NAYRE). (2002). *Growth of ublic year-round education in the United States over a 15-year period.* Available online at www.nayre.org.

National Association of Elementary School Principals (NAESP). (2001). *Leading learning communities: Standards for what principals should know and be able to do.* Alexandria, VA: Author.

National Board of Professional Teaching Standards (NBPTS). (2002). *What teachers should know and be able to do: Five core propositions.* Available online at www.nbpts.org/about/coreprops.cfm.

National Center for Education Statistics (NCES). (2002). *Homeschooling in the United States, 1999.* Available online at http://nces.ed.gov/pubs2002/quarterly/fall/q3-2.asp.

Norris, C. (1990). Developing visionary leaders for tomorrow's schools. *NASSP Bulletin, 74*, 6-10.

North Carolina Department of Public Instruction (NCDPI). (2000, February). Year-round schools and achievement in North Carolina. *Evaluation Brief, 2*, 1-4.

Odell, S. J., and Huling, L. (2000). *Quality mentoring for novice teachers.* Washington, DC: Association of Teacher Educators.

Palmer, E. A., and Bemis, A. E. (1996). *Year-Round education.* Minneapolis, MN: University of Minnesota, Center for Applied Research and Educational Improvement. Available online at http://education.umn.edu/CAREI/Reports/calendar.

Peterson, K. D. (2000). *Teacher evaluation: A comprehensive guide to new directions and practices.* Thousand Oaks, CA: Corwin Press.

Piaget, J. (1965). *The moral judgment of the child.* New York: The Free Press.

Pisha, B., and Coyne, P. (2001). Smart from the start. *Remedial and Special Education, 22*, 197-203.

Pugach, M. C., and Warger, C. L. (2001). Curriculum matters: Raising expectations for students with disabilities. *Remedial and Special Education, 22,* 194-196, 213.

Quinn, T. (2002, October). Succession planning: Start today. *Principal Leadership, 3.* Available online at http://www.principals.org/ news/pl_succplan_1002.html.

Rahn, M. L., Stecher, B. M., Goodman, H., and Alt, M. N. (1997). Making decisions on assessment methods: Weighing the tradeoffs. *Preventing School Failure, 41,* 85-90.

Royal, M. A., and Rossi, R. J. (1996). Individual-level correlates of sense of community: Findings from workplace and school. *Journal of Community Psychology, 24,* 395-416.

Sagor, R. (1992). *How to conduct collaborative action research.* Alexandria, VA: Association for Supervision and Curriculum Development.

Sanders, W., Saxton, A., and Horn, S. (1997). The Tennessee value-added assessment system: A quantitative, outcomes-based approach to educational assessment. In J. Millman (Ed.), *Grading teachers, grading schools: Is student achievement a valid evaluation measure?* Thousand Oaks, CA: Corwin Press.

Scholey, A. B., Moss, M. C., Neave, N., and Wesnes, K. (1999). Cognitive performance, hyperoxia, and heart rate following oxygen administration in healthy young adults. *Physiological Behavior, 67,* 783-789.

Schwager, M. T., and Carlson, J. S. (1994). Building assessment cultures: Teacher perceptions and school environments. *Education and Urban Society, 26,* 390-403.

Senge, P. M. (1997). Communities of leaders and learners. *Harvard Business Review, 75,* 25-26.

Shaywitz, S. E. (1996, November). Dyslexia. *Scientific American,* pp. 98-104.

Simonton, D. K. (1984). *Genius, creativity, and leadership: Historimetric inquiries.* Cambridge: Harvard University Press.

Solomon, J., and Hunter, J. (2002, September). A psychological view of spirituality and leadership. *The School Administrator* (Web Edition). Available online at http://www.aasa.org/publications/sa/2002_09/solomon.htm.

Sousa, D. A. (1997). *Sensory preferences of New Jersey students, grades 3 to 12.* Unpublished data collected by graduate students at Seton Hall University, 1994-1997.

Sousa, D. A. (2001a). *How the brain learns,* (2nd ed.). Thousand Oaks, CA: Corwin Press.

Sousa, D. A. (2001b). *How the special needs brain learns.* Thousand Oaks, CA: Corwin Press.

Sousa, D. A. (2003). *How the gifted brain learns.* Thousand Oaks, CA: Corwin Press.

Sowell, E. R., Thompson, P. M., Holmes, C. J., Jernigan, T. L., and Toga, A. W. (1999). In-vivo evidence for post-adolescent brain maturation in frontal and striatal regions. *Nature: Neuroscience, 2,* 859–861.

Sternberg, R. J. (1985). *Beyond IQ: A triarchic theory of human intelligence.* New York: Cambridge University Press.

Swanson, L. J. (1995). *Learning styles: A review of the literature* (ED 387 067). Syracuse, NY: ERIC Clearinghouse on Information and Technology.

Sweeny, B. (1994). *A new teacher mentoring knowledge base of best practices.* Available online at http://teachermentors.com.

Thompson, J. (1994). *Systemic education reform* (ED 370 178). Eugene, OR: ERIC Clearinghouse on Educational Management.

Tomlinson, C. A. (1999). *The differentiated classroom: Responding to the needs of all learners.* Alexandria, VA: Association for Supervision and Curriculum Development.

Tornabeni, J. (2001). My own take on what it really takes to lead. *Nursing Administration Quarterly, 25,* 1-8.

United States Census Bureau (USCB). (2001). *Reasons by parents for choosing home schooling.* Available online at http://www.census.gov/population/documentation/twps0053.

Velthouse, B. A. (1990). Creativity and empowerment: A complimentary relationship. *Review of Business, 12,* 13-18.

Viadero, D. (2001, September 5). Study finds benefits from starting school later in the day. *Education Week, 21,* 11.

Wagner, C., and Masden-Copas, P. (2002). An audit of the culture starts with two handy tools. *Journal of Staff Development, 23,* 42-53.

Weisman, D. H., and Banich, M. T. (2000). The cerebral hemispheres cooperate to perform complex but not simple tasks. *Neuropsychology, 14,* 41–59.

Wheatley, M. J. (2002, September). Spirituality in turbulent times. *The School Administrator* (Web Edition). Available online at http://www.aasa.org/publications/sa/2002_09/wheatley.htm.

Wolf, K., Lichtenstein, G., and Stevenson, C. (1997). Portfolios in teacher evaluation. In J. H. Stronge (Ed.), *Evaluating teaching: A guide to current thinking and best practice.* Thousand Oaks, CA: Corwin Press.

Wolfson, A., and Carskadon, M. (1998). Sleep schedules and daytime functioning in adolescents. *Child Development, 69,* 875–887.

Wynn, K. (1995). Origins of numerical knowledge. *Mathematical Cognition, 1,* 54-63.

Yerkes, D. M., and Guaglianone, C. L. (1998). Where have all the high school administrators gone? *Thrust for Educational Leadership, 28,* 10-14.

Resources

Note: All internet sites were active at time of publication.

Curriculum

Center for Applied Special Technology (CAST)
www.cast.org

Ethical and Spiritual Leadership

The Character Education Partnership
www.character.org

The Giraffe Project (Character Education)
E-mail: office@giraffe.org

Indiana Department of Education
Partners for Good Citizenship: Parents, School, Communities
http://ideanet.doe.state.in.us/charactered/instruction.html

Josephson Institute of Ethics
www.josephsoninstitute.org
(Since 1992, the institute has conducted periodic surveys on the ethics of
American youth, providing a historical perspective on how ethical behavior has
changed over time.)

Leadership/Change

Accelerated Schools Project
http://www-leland.stanford.edu/group/ASP/index.html
(The Accelerated Schools Project began at Stanford University in 1986 as a comprehensive approach to school change, designed to improve schooling for children in at-risk situations.)

AASA Total Quality Network
http://www.aasa-tqn.org
(The AASA Total Quality Network is a subscription service that provides information on how to translate quality management principles to systemic improvement of schools.)

Annenberg Institute for School Reform
http://www.aisr.brown.edu/aisr/
(The Annenberg Institute for School Reform at Brown University seeks to nurture, promote, and sustain a comprehensive, nationwide school reform movement.)

Association for Effective Schools
http://www.mes.org
(The Association for Effective Schools offers professional development activities as well as providing supportive products, resources, and services.)

Center for Leadership in School Reform
http://www.win.net/ ~clsr
(The Center is a nonprofit corporation that provides strategic consultation, training, and technical assistance to schools and school districts committed to improving the quality of the experiences of students in school.)

Coalition of Essential Schools
http://www.ces.brown.edu/ces
(The Coalition is a school reform organization started by Ted Sizer and based at Brown University in Providence, Rhode Island.)

National Education Association: "KEYS to Excellence"
http://www.nea.org/resource/keys.html
(After five years of surveying teachers and school staff at high-achieving schools, NEA researchers identified 11 "keys" to school quality.)

National Science Foundation: Statewide, Urban, and Rural Systemic Initiatives
http://www.ehr.nsf.gov/EHR/ESR/index.htm#6Drivers
(The systemic approach of the NSF holds school systems accountable for sustainable system-wide or systemic outcomes rather than for outcomes of isolated projects.)

North Central Regional Laboratory: Pathways to School Improvement
http://www.ncrel.org/ncrel/
(Pathways to School Improvement Internet Server offers easy-to-find, concise, research-based information on school improvement.)

Quality Education for Minorities Network
http://qemnetwork.qem.org
(The QEM is a nonprofit organization based in Washington, D.C., dedicated to improving the education of African Americans, Alaska Natives, American Indians, Mexican Americans, and Puerto Ricans.)

Smart Schools
http://www.projectzero.harvard.edu/HPZpages/SmartSch.html
(The Smart Schools principles for good education, developed by David Perkins and colleagues at Harvard Project Zero.)

The School Development Program
http://info.med.yale.edu/comer
(The School Development Program is committed to the total development of all children by creating learning environments that support the physical, cognitive, psychological, language, social, and ethical development of children.)

Southwest Education Lab Leadership for Change Project
http://www.sedl.org/change/
(The goal of the Leadership for Change Project is to promote leadership and facilitate change among educational professionals in order to foster systems and schools that improve learning for all students, especially those at risk.)

School Culture

The Center for Improving School Culture
http://www.schoolculture.net

National Association for Year-Round Education (NAYRE)
www.nayre.org

Teacher Evaluation

Action Research Collaborative of Greater St. Louis
http://info.csd.org

Consortium for Research on Educational Accountability and Teacher Evaluation (CREATE)
http://www.wmich.edu/evalctr/create

Interstate New Teacher Assessment and Support Consortium (INTASC)
www.ccsso.org/intascst.html

National Board of Professional Teaching Standards (NBPTS)
www.nbpts.org

Teacher Mentoring
http://teachermentors.com

Index